Which Way?

One woman's traumatic journey
and her daughter's explanation of
how to turn pain into power.

JANN AND SHARI SIMMONS, LCSW

DEDICATION

~~Jann Simmons~~

My portion of this book is dedicated to the precious people in my life who never gave up on me. They saw my heart and believed in me. They stood by me when everyone else walked away.

My daughters, Shari and RaeLynn, who gave my life purpose and who showed me what it feels like to be loved unconditionally.

My three precious grandchildren, who brought a bright light into my darkness and continue to fill my soul with joy.

My daddy, who held me close to his heart, but left my life far too soon.

"Gregory", who heard the judgments, but never judged and took the time to really know me.

To each of you, I love you unconditionally ~ Mom, Nana, Jann-a-Baby

~~Shari Simmons~~

My portion of this book is dedicated to my son, Dakota, who melted my heart from the beginning and who continues to make me proud and honored to be his mother.

My mother, Jann Simmons, who changed this family's legacy and proved that one can rewrite their story; that strength can be born from tragedy and that the ultimate treasure lies at the end of the path each of us was designed to walk.

My clients throughout the years, who suffered at the hands of others but triumphed, showed the world their brilliance and allowed me to enter their stories.

To each of you, I'm better because of you.

Introduction

This book is both a memoir and an instructional/self-help manual. I, Shari, am a mental health therapist. I've specialized in trauma for the last 28 years. My interest in the topic has been two-fold. Having grown up as a child of a trauma survivor, I witnessed firsthand what post-traumatic stress disorder (PTSD) looks like and how emotional woundedness plays out when it is not addressed.

I've often wondered why some people choose to do the work required to heal from pain in their lives and why others choose to remain stuck, unhappy, and unhealthy. Over time, I've learned the one thing that can't be taken from us is our free will. With it, we have the power to create happiness, change our attitude, role model love, and heal from tragedy.

When I began my career as a caseworker, my main task was to remove young children from abusive homes. I was intrigued with how quickly the minds of little ones developed coping mechanisms to survive their losses. I then became a family therapist, and my fascination with trauma and its aftereffects deepened. Working with children who'd been severely mistreated further exposed me to the tragedy of trauma as well as its equally powerful counterpart, resiliency. Those brave little warriors taught me just how strong the brain is in overcoming tragedy.

As a clinical director, I developed treatment centers for adolescents and taught other clinicians how to provide services that recognized and celebrated the mind's ability to compensate for tragic events. In today's world, people who are odd, aggressive, detached, depressed and anxious are often misunderstood and judged. This book celebrates the uniqueness and the sameness we share as human beings when we try to shield ourselves from pain.

Today, I am a consultant for treatment facilities and a professor committed to teaching two things. First, I teach that our brains work overtime to shield us from the hurt in our lives. Secondly, I stress that the strategies our brains construct are there for our protection. Do our coping skills work for or against us?

My sections in this book document the defining moments with my mother that ultimately solidified who I would become. I also draw on my years of clinical work with clients who created methods, healthy *and* unhealthy, to cope with their pasts and my years of trauma/resiliency research.

Everyone has different perspectives about the events and relationships in their lives, depending on the filter with which they view the world. This "filter" comes from our unique experiences, values, beliefs, and DNA. *Which Way?* contains OUR perception of what occurred in OUR lives. While some readers may have a different perspective, this story is told to the accuracy with which we remember it.

Victorian poet Mary Anne Evans, known by her pen name George Eliot, once said, "The strongest principle of growth lies in the human choice." (Eliot, n.d.) This book addresses the choices we all need to make regarding what we want for ourselves and the generations who will follow.

Forward

~~Dakota~~ Shari's son and Jann's grandson

I hated all of them. Every morning, I looked each one of them straight in the eye. I'm not one who avoids eye contact. From my perch, I see their pity, their disdain, their insolence. To me, they are pompous and self-righteous, driving by in their freshly washed cars, sipping mocha lattes. Some adjust their radios, pretend to fix their lipstick in the mirror or busy themselves on their phones, just to avoid eye contact with me. Others throw me a few dollars and remind me that "Jesus loves me." They drive away smiling, convincing themselves that they did their part.

I try to make a living this way, not because I enjoy their half-hearted handouts, but because the only thing holding me back from the surge of heaven that I'll pump into my veins later tonight is the $50 more I need to score the ounce of pure white powder that will take me away from the hellhole that is my life.

In all fairness, I haven't known any different. I did what she taught me...and I hate her for it. The images of her being dragged by her hair, wadded in the fists of her latest fling after they both snorted their breakfast have long since left my mind.

Her yelling is what time hasn't diminished. I can still hear her voice, the second I close my eyes each night. "Why did I even have you? All you have done is make my life miserable. I could have been something!" There were days when she was too out of her mind to even remember my name. That never bothered me, but the yelling, always the yelling...

She came by the drinking and the verbal abuse honestly. My grandmother was no gem either. I met her one morning when I was four. She showed up at our apartment with a black eye and a bottle of Jack. She mumbled a few words to my mother before she stumbled to the couch, where she stayed, blacked out for the rest of the day.

I woke up that night to the sound of glass breaking as she and my mom hurled insults and dishes at each other. She reminded my mother of what a "worthless piece of shit" she is, slammed the door and walked down the street with nothing but her purse and her near-empty bottle.

That's how my life should have gone...that's how addiction and abuse often go when one generation passes down its legacy to the next. My family had been plagued by alcoholism and anguish for generations...and because of that, my life should have followed the same path...**but it didn't...**

"You own everything that happened to you. Tell your stories. If people wanted you to write warmly about them, they should have behaved better."

~ Anne Lamott

~~*Shari*~~

The three of us had always been close. We shared a bond that went beyond three generations. This bond was cemented in our belief that a loving, honest relationship would be the only path to our freedom. While the outside world saw grandmother, mother and teenage son, we felt something much deeper. Yes, we were three generations, but we were kindred spirits.

Our relationship felt deeply emotional and grounded in something bigger than ourselves. I often wonder if God sent my son to save my mother. In a lot of ways, that is exactly what happened.

And, now, we were traveling together for the first time, bound for Maui. My son, Dakota, and I bubbled over with excitement as we flew over the ocean, while my mother tried desperately to find solace in a situation that absolutely terrified her. She'd always been scared of flying, scared of water, and scared of just about everything. Flying over the Pacific was the worst combination of danger for her.

His head resting on a balled-up sweatshirt, my son listened to music on his headphones as we flew. Halfway through the flight, he fell sound asleep on the snack tray. The serene look on his face contradicted my mom's petrified expression.

Her entire body was tense, her skin blotchy, her breathing shallow and strained. Eyes squeezed shut, she mouthed silent prayers over and over. Every few minutes, she'd clutch my hand and stare out the window, a look of sheer terror on her face.

"Breathe, Mom," I reminded her, as I'd done so many times throughout my childhood, my sorry attempt to bring her some relief.

In the whole scheme of things, this was not that strange a scene. Several people were obviously nervous about flying. But for Mom, so much more was happening beneath the surface. I doubted that anyone who noticed the beautiful, classy-looking woman clutching her daughter's hand would truly understand just how deep her fear ran.

Four days into our adventure-filled trip to Maui, the three of us were playing in the pool outside our hotel that overlooked the ocean. Surrounded by palm trees and exotic flowers in hues not found where we live, our view was incredible. We'd been having a great time when our discussion about what seafood to order for dinner was interrupted by an eerie siren sound.

We hadn't heard such a noise before, but we quickly dismissed it as an intrusion into our important conversation. I noticed that people were climbing out of the pool rather quickly, but again, I was preoccupied with whether to have swordfish or tuna for dinner. Not until a woman yelled, "Get out of the pool! Can't you hear the siren?" did we jump out and grab our towels, although we didn't understand why.

"What does the siren mean?" my son asked. The woman yelled, "Tsunami!" We exchanged terrified looks and began running to the hotel room. Mom tripped on the wet cement and as I helped her stand up again, I noticed for the first time, how dark and threatening the sky looked. As we made our way to the elevator, people were clamoring to get in and nervously chattering about getting to their rooms, so they could listen to the news. To save time and because the elevator was already over-crowded, we decided to take the stairs.

Safely sheltered in our tenth-floor room, we turned on the TV and learned a tsunami was projected to hit Maui in the next two hours. Island residents and visitors were advised to make their way to higher ground immediately. We stared at the television in disbelief.

But while my son and I sat on the couch with our eyes glued to the TV, my mother sat on a chair in the corner. She rocked back and forth, her body folded into itself and trembled uncontrollably. Her tear-filled eyes were huge. She was having trouble breathing.

"What do we do, Shari?" she asked over and over. "What do we do? What do we do?" Despite my best effort to console, her trance could not be broken. "What do we do? What do we do?"

My heart broke for her. She looked so tiny, so afraid, like a frightened animal with wild eyes and hair standing on end. I swore I could hear her heart pounding.

"Mom," I said, "we are going to be okay. We are on the tenth floor. Let's watch TV a bit longer. If the hotel instructs us to leave, we'll drive to higher ground," I spoke in the calmest, most emotionally regulated voice I could muster.

"What do we do? What do we do?" She wasn't hearing me. My son and I exchanged knowing glances. We'd both become accustomed to my Mom's panic attacks. In these moments, she was out of her mind with fear. We were all scared by the tsunami warning. But something more was going on with Mom that those who didn't know her well, wouldn't understand. She was haunted, frightened by things unseen.

When the tsunami passed a few hours later, it was time to retire to bed. My son and I made a snack because we realized we hadn't eaten dinner in the chaos of the evening. My Mom couldn't eat or even lie down. After I persuaded her to go to bed, she sat up in bed all night, staring out the window. Days later, she finally caught her breath again, stopped shaking, and allowed herself to relax enough to unfurrow her brow and smile.

She was engulfed by demons from her past that mocked her, terrorized her and threatened her safety. Not until we returned home did they retreat. Only then was she able to regain a sense of safety.

Safety.

Her panic attacks were always about safety. To understand why you'd have to start from the beginning.

~~*Jann* ~~

Every family has a legacy, this is where mine begins, at least what I know of it. I know nothing about how my parents met, how long they dated, when they married or how long before they started their family, which makes me sad. Their first child was a girl who died at birth, followed by a boy and, finally, me. I am told, I was the apple of my daddy's eye. I was the little girl he could dote on…and dote he did. He took me almost everywhere.

I was the product of very successful parents. But, I am getting ahead of myself. My mother's dad was an alcoholic and died young, but not before he fathered nine children. Her mother was an angry, religious bigot. The family struggled to make ends meet, often having to flee their home in the middle of the night because they couldn't pay rent.

My mother was an exceptionally bright student. So bright she was allowed to skip two grades in high school, even while waitressing in a local restaurant. She was a skilled seamstress who made all the drapes for our windows and impeccably decorated our homes. She had a flare for complimentary colors and a wonderful taste in furniture and art. Her style was Victorian.

My grandfather left the family when daddy was only five-years-old. He didn't have contact with him again until he was fifteen-years-old.

Daddy finished school and took a job as a taxi driver to help his mother. One evening, he picked up two men who said they wanted to go to a tavern about five miles away. Moments later, one of them leaned forward from the backseat, put a gun to the back of dad's head and told him to take the next left on a deserted county road.

Near a large tree, they demanded that he stop and get out of the car. The second fellow began rummaging in the front seat to locate the cab money my dad had collected for the evening, while the man with the gun told him to lie on the ground and put his hands behind his back.

Dad did as he was instructed, not knowing what the two men were planning next. After tying his hands and ankles, they left him lying in the dirt.

He calmly looked up at one of the men and asked, "If you're planning to leave me here, will you give me a cigarette?"

I have a yellowed, tattered newspaper article with a picture of my young father lying by the edge of a road with a cigarette in his mouth. After his rescue, he reenacted the scene for the newspaper. The police never caught the thieves or recovered the money, but his life was spared.

My parents owned three homes, all of which were decorated in similar Victorian fashion. They were elaborate, including large wingback chairs, upholstered in heavy brocades and ornate, deeply etched, dark-wood tables. The paintings on our walls depicted women and men dressed in eighteenth-century clothing.

Daddy was a well-established manager for a large car dealership and we traveled between these three locations for his work. As was typical for that era, my mother was a homemaker. Because of my Dad's position in his company, my parents threw large dinner parties in our homes, hosting business representatives and their wives.

He was handsome and the light in any room, funny and charismatic. He loved people and they loved him. My mother was beautiful and very outgoing with a winning smile. They made a striking couple.

Unfortunately, my mother had a temper and when it flared, she'd throw the nearest thing within her reach. My mother's oldest sister told me she saw my mother throw a plate at my dad's head during a dinner party or hit him with her purse on the way to the theatre. My aunt said Dad never retaliated. I still wonder where my mother's rage first grew roots.

My parents accumulated friends, wealth and an extensive travel portfolio before they started their family. Life seemed to be going great. However, my parents would soon discover that my mother was not well.

It's hard to tell if the death of her first child played a role in her dark spiral downward or not. She drank too much and smoked even more, and she did both throughout her pregnancies. Shortly before she was due to deliver me, she was diagnosed with tuberculosis. Although she was ill, she carried me to term. Immediately upon delivery,

I was quarantined and, my mother was sent to a separate facility for treatment.

I didn't see my mother for the first six-months of my life. Instead, I was isolated to protect others from possible exposure to tuberculosis. Eventually, I was labeled a tuberculosis carrier, although I was immune to the disease, and released to go home.

My mother remained in the hospital until her status was changed to 'inactive'. No one in her family of origin remembers how long she was hospitalized or who cared for me while Dad worked.

While I only remember pieces of this time in my life, I do recall my dad's term of endearment for me--'Jann-a-baby'. The only other beautiful memory I have is of flying from one home to another, seated on his lap beside the window. The dark frightened me, so he made the nighttime magical. He talked to me about the stars and told me told me that the crescent moon was his toenail. I laughed as he said it, because I knew it wasn't really his toenail.

I still cling to that memory, and I'm grateful for it because the only other memory I have is of him lying in a casket shortly after that plane trip. Without warning, he died of a brain aneurysm at the age of 36. I was only three-and-a half-years-old. My daughters grew up hearing me tell them the crescent moon was their grandfather's 'toenail'.

My brother and I must have wondered where our dad was. Did we inundate our mother with questions? "Why did he leave us?" "Where did he go?" "When will he be coming home?" "Did he leave because we were bad?" I have a feeling we never asked our temperamental mother any of those questions. I'm also quite sure we never got any answers.

In those days, children were seen and not heard. The vulnerable, confused little spirits of children were not considered in such traumatic events. At least, they weren't acknowledged in our family. I was not allowed to process my grief, the grief I didn't understand. All I could fathom was that my daddy was no longer in my life and I missed him terribly. But I could never express my sorrow to anyone.

Our mother was overwhelmed by grief. I remember she spent entire days in bed, in a darkened room either in a deep depression or a drunken stupor. My brother and I were left to fend for ourselves. We passed the time playing in our backyard and fixing our own meals and probably being very mischievous, as children who are left to their own devices will be. At night we slept in the same room, in individual beds and, silently wondered why our lives were going so terribly wrong.

One day not long after my father died, my paternal grandmother came to visit. As she was leaving, she gathered some of my brother's clothes and I was told he was going to live with her. Silently, I exclaimed, "Wait! Where are you taking my brother? I don't want him to go, he looks after me." I didn't know what I would do without him.

I'm quite sure I was too young to verbalize my questions, even if I'd had someone in my life to explain what was happening. I watched my brother climb into the car and our grandmother place a small bag of clothes in the seat behind him. She started the engine and drove away without even a glance in my direction. I stood on the curb in front of our house, watching my brother disappear from sight. My heart was aching. I wanted to cry. I turned to walk toward my mother, but she had already gone inside the house. I slowly sat down on the front yard and wept.

Soon after that, my mother began binge drinking daily. I spent long days alone outside, occasionally forcing myself to play with neighborhood children.

I was not allowed to invite friends into our house because my mother tried to keep her drinking a secret from the world. I had no problem obeying that rule because I didn't want anyone to see what she did when she was drunk. I pretended to be happy, but inside I was terrified, ashamed and alone.

In addition to the binge-drinking, my mother began to fill her loneliness with men. The constant stream of strange men into our home compounded my sense of fear and loss. I missed my father. I missed my brother. I also missed not having a real mother. I had no idea then that the fear from my abuses and the loss would create the path I would walk for the next 35 years of my life.

I took care of myself as best I could. I roamed the streets without supervision and spent many hours alone. To pass the time, I sat on the front porch and watched families in our neighborhood come and go. I wanted my family back!

I'd close my eyes and pretend I was riding in a car with my mommy and daddy in the front seat and my brother beside me in the back. We'd go on a picnic in the park and we'd play ball or hide-and-seek together. My brother and I would perform for mom and dad, basking in their love and laughter.

Afterward, we'd sit on a blanket under a tree and eat our lunch. But, each time I opened my eyes, the idyllic scene would vanish like the dream that it was, and the ache rushed in. If only I didn't open my eyes.

One morning, I was at a friend's house, watching her mother braid her hair and tie pretty yellow ribbons at the end of each braid. I thought she was the luckiest little girl in the world to have her mommy brush her hair.

My friend said they were dressing to go to Sunday school. I asked, "What's that?" She looked surprised by my question. "I hear stories about Jesus there!" Then she said the most amazing thing. She told me that Jesus loved little children. An adult who loved children? I wished I could meet him!

I ran home to tell my mom about this man named Jesus who loved children. But, when I walked through the door, I saw her bent over the sink in the kitchen, violently coughing. I stood there, wondering how to help her. When she finally straightened and turned in my direction, I saw the red stain down the front of her cream sweater.

Silently, she walked toward her bedroom. I crept over to the sink's edge and jumped backward when I saw it spattered with blood.

She had had a tuberculosis relapse and was soon hospitalized once again. I have no idea who cared for me during her hospital stay. Later, when I asked my mother's family if they recalled who cared for me, none of them knew.

My mother married fairly quickly after her hospitalization. This would be one of many marriages. During her hospital stay, she'd met the man who would become my first stepfather. He, too, was in the facility for tuberculosis.

That man never tried to attach to me, but I wanted his attention. One morning when I saw him and my mother drinking coffee at the kitchen table, I called him "daddy" as if I'd done it all my life. The word came natural and easy to me because I so badly wanted to be loved and to belong to someone.

He looked up from the newspaper he was reading, barely revealing the rims of his glasses over the paper. Without a hint of emotion in his voice, he told me to never call him "dad" again. I learned at a very young age that I was on my own. I couldn't help but wonder why I was so unlovable.

~~*Shari*~~

I remember that summer afternoon like it was yesterday, probably my first memory. I must have been about three-years-old. I was supposed to be taking a nap, but I was wide awake. While some details are foggy, I distinctly remember hearing the ice cream truck's familiar jingle. I immediately jumped up to look out the window. I could see children racing out of their houses and mothers running behind with their wallets. I remember wanting to be one of them more than my little heart had ever wanted anything.

At that moment, my mom dashed into the room. For a split second, I thought I was in trouble. I rarely got in trouble, so why this was my first thought, I don't know. I jumped back onto the bed, pulled the covers up and pretended to be asleep.

Rather than scold me, my mother scooped me into her arms. "How about we skip naptime and go get some ice cream?" That was the happiest day of my three-year-old life and a memory that still warms my heart today.

I had no idea at the time that this little gift from my mother was something so foreign to her. This act of empathy and understanding of how a three-year old's mind works came out of her own longing rather than from any context of what should happen. I had no idea her childhood had been so vastly different from mine. I had no idea that while my life was filled with love, tenderness, and safety, hers was filled with the tragedy of a childhood gone horribly wrong.

~~*Jann* ~~

The drunken days and nights that endlessly filled my life always climaxed with fighting and with someone injured and bleeding, sometimes my mother, sometimes me. My mother became argumentative and violent when she drank, and the men she brought into her life and ultimately, mine, always had the last word, which was spoken with a fist against her face. I found refuge under my bed, terrified at the sound of the blows that pummeled my mother.

One night toward the end of one of her six marriages, the violence escalated. I heard my mother screaming and water running and I ran into the bathroom, where her husband was holding her face under the bathtub faucet. Seeing the tub filling with water and my mother's face completely submerged shocked me. I lunged toward his back, begging him to put me under the water and let my mommy go.

He loosened his grip and my mother was

able to rise up from the water gasping for air. She steadied herself on the tub's edge as she climbed out, her hair and unclothed body dripping water on the bathroom floor. She said not a word, nor did she look at me. I stepped aside for her to pass by. I was left standing in front of him, tears streaming down my face. He looked at me for a moment with rage in his eyes, stood up and came toward me. He picked me up by my arms, I closed my eyes and waited for him to put me under the water. My face was so close to his I could smell the alcohol on his breath. He continued to hold me in the air for a while, but I was too scared to open my eyes. Without saying anything, he lowered me to the floor and staggered into the kitchen.

At that moment, the realization I had to protect my mother was seared into me. The abuse continued for a while, and I intervened every time, then one day he just never came home. I was so happy. I thought now my mommy and I could be safe. I would take care of her and she would take care of me. I would no longer be alone.

Maybe she'd play dolls with me or maybe she'd brush my hair or maybe we'd bake cookies together. Or maybe, just maybe, she would take me to Sunday school, so I could hear more about the man who loved little children. I wondered if he could love me. But that was impossible. He didn't even know me.

One of my frequent pastimes was to make up new images in my mind, anything to escort me from the realities of my existence. With my eyes tightly closed, shutting out the hopelessness of my life, vibrant colors would fill my vision. The joy and peace that played out in my dreams were a welcome relief from the horror of my home.

The saddest thing about my dreams was that I could never stay there. They always vanished, and the beautiful colors turned black. Peacefulness was replaced with the sound of fighting and yelling.

Not long after that husband left, my mother began leaving me home alone, sometimes all weekend, while she went out drinking and hunting for another man to fill her emptiness. But then, when she "captured" a man, she'd provoke him, and he would beat her, then she'd beat me. My life was a vicious cycle that played itself out night after night.

Although I was only six-years-old, I recognized the cycle of terror. Yet, I had no idea how to escape the loop we were in. My mother couldn't possibly have enjoyed the violence, but I think now she must have felt she deserved it. I kept hoping that the last beating she suffered would BE the last one.

I loved to watch her dress to go out, while simultaneously dreading what her return meant for me at the end of the night. As she combed her long black hair and meticulously applied her makeup, I saw her transform into a princess.

Her face softened in the mirror's reflection and her eyes sparkled, a stark contrast to the rage I saw when she was drunk or the emptiness that was there when she didn't know I was looking.

I wondered if I would be as pretty as she was when I grew up, and I longed to ask her questions. *Mommy, are you going to make your lips bright red? Are you going to wear your blue high-heeled shoes tonight? Which dress are you going to choose? Can I go get it for you?* But, I didn't dare talk to her, I might make her angry, and I knew what would happen if I did.

One time I asked too many questions as she was getting ready to go out, she sent me to my bedroom with instructions to lie on the bed. I don't know how long I was there before she entered the room and started hitting me with her high-heeled shoe. I rolled over, trying to somehow escape the blows and I cried.

She yelled at me to shut up, or she would give me something to cry about. In that moment, the shoe landed on the right side of my lower back. Searing pain burned into my flesh like a hot poker and went deep inside. I didn't understand it then, but she'd hit my kidney. When the pain subsided enough for me to move again, the sun had set, and she was gone.

Most children anxiously await their parent's return from work, or shopping, or running errands. I was not one of those children. I would listen for the sound of my mother's car in the driveway. That was my cue to hide in the closet or under my bed, too scared to breathe, terrified of being found, and I'd wait for the yelling to start.

My mother never looked for me or called for me when she arrived home. But out of all the men she brought home, there were two who knew she had a little girl. These two men always found me and dragged me from my hiding place after my mother passed out, and they hurt me.

I felt like all my mother's sadness, all her drinking was because of me. When she beat me, the reason for the beating was my fault, never hers. If I could just be a better child, the nightmare would stop. I tried desperately to become invisible, be unnoticed. When my mother was sober I was, indeed, invisible to her. But when she was drunk, I was her target.

Neighbors started reporting my weekends spent alone without supervision. I had inadvertently alerted them when I went to their houses to ask for food or just to be near a family in a house where I wasn't alone. Grocery shopping was not something my mother did often. Her meals were the liquid variety, so she didn't need food.

Perhaps the men she met took her to dinner when they saw how pretty she looked. Of course, that was before they started drinking and she became ugly. No one is pretty when they're drunk.

When drinking, my mother and her friend's smelled bad, their clothes got sloppy and sometimes, they even came home without all of their clothes. I remember a morning when I heard the door open and looked up from where I was coloring at the kitchen table. My mother stood before me in nothing but her blouse and one shoe.

The stench of booze and vomit filled my nostrils. Her hair was a matted mess. Her lipstick was smeared onto her right cheek and her mascara had run halfway down her face. Blood seeped from a small cut by her eye.

I knew better than to say a word, but I swore to myself that I would never allow something like that to happen to me. At the tender age of six, I wasn't sure how I would avoid her lifestyle, but I KNEW that I would!

A few weeks later, my mother came home with yet another man. When I heard the car and the sudden loud voices, I climbed out of my bed and scurried to the darkest corner of the closet, I waited and listened. I could hear the pounding of my own heart above their escalating argument. They must have settled down enough that I was able to fall asleep because when I awakened the next morning,

I was still in a ball on the floor of my closet.

I sat up, listening for the loud man's voice. The house was quiet and still, so I cautiously crawled from the closet and walked out of my room. My mother's bedroom door was open. She was asleep and she was alone.

I quietly approached her bed, where an enormous amount of blood soaked the pillow, the sheet, and her face. I resisted the urge to climb onto the bed and somehow help her, not knowing what she'd do to me if I did.

I wanted to scream, but nothing came out of my mouth. Finally, I whispered, "Mama", "Mama?"

She didn't respond, she didn't move. I stood there for the longest time, willing her to open her eyes, but she didn't. I grabbed hold of the large brown post at the foot of the bed and hoisted myself up. I crawled over to her, smelling blood mixed with alcohol.

My eyes couldn't fathom this terrifying scene. I put my head close to her chest and could hear her breathing. When I lifted my head, the side of my face was covered with her blood.

Her long black hair was wet with the dark red liquid, except for a few long strands that trailed down her pillow. Those were dry and matted and stuck to the pillowcase. I carefully examined her scalp by separating her thick hair section by section.

I had to swallow a scream when I looked into the gaping gash on the right side of her head. I jumped off the bed and ran to the kitchen to get a towel that always hung on the oven handle. I couldn't reach the shelf in the linen closet in the hallway, and the bathroom towels were in the washer, so the kitchen towel was my only option.

Broken bottles littered the kitchen floor and glasses tossed into the sink were shattered. The cloth I was going to get for my mother's head was crumpled on the floor and stiff with someone's dried blood. I ran back to her room, pulled off my yellow-flowered gown and gently pressed it around her head so that I wouldn't awaken her.

She didn't even stir. I sat on the side of her bed for what felt like hours, crying, and wondering if she was ever going to wake up. If she didn't, what would happen to me? The house was silent and peaceful, unlike the violence that must have taken place the night before. I wondered why the noise didn't roust me from sleep. I was helpless, sitting there by my wounded mother. I screamed, silently, for someone to rescue us. Suddenly, I felt her move.

I quickly slid down from her side because she would not have approved of me being on her bed. She blinked a few times and raised her hand to her head. As she felt the gown, she asked in a weak voice, "Did you do this?" My reply was barely audible, "Yes, you were bleeding." She closed her eyes without saying anything more.

I went to the kitchen to clean up the mess. As I wiped the blood and swept the broken glass, I quietly wept. I wanted my brother. I wanted my daddy. I wanted a mother!

The next day, when mama tried to wash the blood from her hair, I could see all the gashes in her scalp. How did she survive such an attack? How did I manage to sleep through it?

~~*Shari*~~

To truly understand my mother's story, one must first understand how the brain works and what happens when it's been exposed to trauma. Trauma can be triggered in different ways. It can result from our experiences, an incident we witness, a story someone tells us, or even a show or newscast we view on television.

Our society is traumatized over and over by something as simple as opening Facebook and seeing images of the latest tragedy in the world. Our brains cannot tell the difference between trauma we experience, trauma we see or trauma we hear about. To the brain, trauma is trauma.

In simple terms, the brain can be described as having three major components, the limbic system, the cerebrum and the prefrontal lobe. The limbic brain, often called the "survival" brain, is completely developed when we're born and is located toward the base of the brain. It oversees our most primal needs--food, shelter, safety--and constantly assesses whether or not we're in physical or emotional danger.

When the limbic brain perceives danger, it sends blood to our extremities so that we can defend ourselves or run away. The ONLY thing our limbic brain cares about is your survival, which includes our safety. It sends signals for us to fight, flight, freeze, faint, fornicate or feed in order to feel safe and "okay" again.

When in our limbic brains, we act rather than think, as a young child or adolescent might do. We cannot access the part of our brain that controls our thoughts and language because the action part of our brain is activated. When we sense danger, we regress to our limbic brain, where our survival mechanisms live, so that we can protect ourselves. These responses to danger manifest in one of the following ways.

Fight – Instead of taking a calming breath and keeping our emotions regulated in a stressful situation, sometimes we pick a fight, get defensive and/or attack. We've all experienced this in the midst of a difficult conversation that collapses into one or both individuals becoming defensive, yelling and/or hurling insults. On the outside, we see an angry, rageful or vindictive person, but on the inside, fear reigns. For some of us, a tense conversation can cause us to fear rejection. This fear results in feeling unsafe.

A simple illustrative equation might go something like this: "She looks upset at me." + "I think I am being rejected by her." + "I'm scared of losing her." + "I need to push her away before she pushes me away, so I can feel safe again." = Angry words and hurtful attacks.

My mother witnessed this pattern again and again when her mother fought with the men she brought home. My assumption is that my grandmother had feelings of fear based on her own childhood abuse and the loss of her one safety net, her first husband. She most likely lived in a constant state of fear. Remember, when someone is scared, they go to their limbic brain.

My grandmother responded to the men in her life and her own daughter by attacking, hurling insults, hurling objects and inflicting pain. A paradox of human behavior is that scared people sometimes try to find safety by making other people scared. When they sense impending rejection or abandonment, they attempt to find safety by fighting.

I've seen this response over and over throughout my career as a therapist. I once worked with a 16-year-old client in a residential facility where I was the clinical director. Every time she spoke to her mother on the phone, she was promised a visit, and every time visiting hours rolled around, her mother was a no-show. With this sad realization came a rageful storm that I and my staff came to dread.

After waiting all evening, she would call her mother, leave an angry message and throw the phone, aiming for one of our faces. She'd run screaming to her room and spend the next three-to-four hours destroying it. She'd rip apart her mattress, tear up her artwork, yank down her curtains and throw everything out into the hallway.

She yelled obscenities at the staff members who tried desperately to offer her comfort. If she saw me walk by to check on her, she'd screech at the top of her lungs that I was a horrible director and mother and she hoped my son would commit suicide (she had seen his picture on my desk).

She'd damn him, me and anyone who happened to be working that day to hell. Despite her long black hair, caked-on makeup, sharp black nails, swastika tattoo and hardened demeanor, she was a lost little girl who desperately wanted her mommy. When she felt rejected or abandoned by her mother, she would **fight**.

Flight – For some of us, instead of staying grounded in the present moment when stressed, our limbic brains kick into action and we make plans to disappear. This disappearing act can take on the form of sabotaging a relationship or running away physically or metaphorically from someone or something. It can also take on the form of denying ourselves the things we need to survive, such as food.

The equation may look like this: "He is angry with me and I'm scared he's going to leave me." + "I can't live without him." + "If I leave the room, I won't have to deal with this right now." = "I'm outta here."

Flight can be defined as people literally leaving the room or leaving a relationship. It can also mean they starve themselves. People who are anorexic and are dwindling away to nothing are attempting to "flee" from their lives.

One of my favorite radio shows has a segment called "Second Date Update." In this show, men and women call in to say they went on a date that "was wonderful" with promises to see each other again. These callers go on to paint a sad picture of how, despite several attempts to call or email, they never hear from the other person again.

The radio host then locates and calls the person who's been silent and asks the 50-million-dollar question; "Why haven't you responded?"

The answer is the same every time. They "got scared" and didn't know any other way to respond than to simply--leave.

Not only did my grandmother fight when she was scared, she ran away for days at a time, leaving her daughter to fend for herself and scavenge for food. Feeling scared was a way of life for my grandmother. She was desperate to escape her life and attempted to do so by fleeing her home.

I once counseled a 10-year-old who'd found her father's guns in an unlocked safe in the basement and decided to play cops and robbers with her best friend. She selected a black pistol for herself and gave her friend a rifle. As they chased each other around the house, they made gun noises and threatened to lock each other up.

My client cornered her friend. Feeling triumphant that she'd captured the "enemy," she pulled the trigger on her gun, not realizing it was loaded and killed her friend. Two days after, her distraught, traumatized little 10-year-old self couldn't handle the enormity of what had happened. She found her older brother's gun, loaded it and shot herself in the head.

Fortunately, the bullet skimmed the surface of her brain and exited the back of her skull. Much to the astonishment of the ER surgeons, she survived the suicide attempt with no brain damage. She was however, court-ordered into treatment with me as her therapist.

Her first words to me were, "I hate myself and just want to leave my life. I can't even kill myself right." She was a devastated little girl. Over the course of the next year, whenever she was struck by the sadness and awfulness of her situation, she'd attempt to kill herself, run away or disappear under her bed. She was desperately trying to escape her life through, **flight**.

<u>Freeze</u> – For some of us, rather than removing ourselves from a stressful situation, our bodies shut down and we can't move. We literally freeze. We've all seen this with animals that sense an attacker and freeze in place, but it can happen with humans, too.

When frightened and fearful for our safety, our brain tells our body to stop functioning. The equation looks like this: "I am terrified for my safety." + "I don't see a way out." + I will blend into the environment by being still." = Frozen body posture with little cognizance of the situation that may be unfolding around them.

My mother would hide in her closet, slow her breathing and become still as a statue in an attempt to avoid the horrors playing out in the other room. The fact that mom "didn't hear what happened" the night her mother had a screaming, knock-down, drag-out fight that resulted in her being beat into unconsciousness was because Mom--froze. Crouched in her closet, trying not to make a sound, she literally shut down and became numb to what was occurring in her environment.

This response became an ingrained behavior for my mother, one she continues to exhibit today whenever she's frightened. When another person looks or sounds even the slightest bit annoyed with her, she completely shuts down. This coping strategy began years ago, while she was hiding in her closet, a young child desperately trying to escape the terror that unfolded in her home each night. She responded the only way she knew how, by "paralyzing" herself.

I conducted therapy sessions with a 12-year-old boy who'd been raised by cruel parents, who were in a cult and committed horrendous crimes on others and their own son. He was a delightful little boy but one that many therapists had trouble connecting with. As a new graduate, I was assigned to work with him because no one knew how to reach him.

He and I immediately connected, and he used his therapy time to talk about all of his favorite things. We went on walks during our sessions. If he didn't have to sit face-to-face with me, he talked about his horrific past.

One day his father, whom he hadn't spoken to for years, called him at the facility and told him if he didn't keep the family secrets, he'd be punished. From that day on, the boy sat in group therapy, at the dinner table, in the schoolroom and in my office completely still, a position he'd maintain for hours. He stared off into space, completely unresponsive.

After another three months of therapy sessions, I finally gave up trying to make him talk and placed colored pencils and sheets of blank paper on the floor. Eventually, he picked up a pencil and started stabbing holes in the paper.

At the end of the session, he'd hand me the paper, without speaking a word, and walk out of my office. Another month went by before I realized that if I held his "picture" to the window, I could see the private messages he'd written to me. He was speaking, without speaking. I never heard his voice again, but he found a way to communicate. He was a terrified boy who responded the only way he knew how to protect himself, he **froze**.

Faint – When a person is stressed and can't find someone or someplace to provide safety, they'll faint or fall asleep. A farm I live close to has acres and acres of the cutest goats. These are unusual little creatures because they are called "fainting goats". When they hear a dog bark or someone sneaks up behind them and makes a loud noise, they stiffen and fall over.

The poor things look like they're dead, but they are just "playing dead". They faint out of fear. Several animals respond this way when frightened. The behavior is nature's way for prey to let a predator know they're already dead. The equation goes like this: "I feel scared." + "If my body shuts down, I won't have to deal with this." = I pass out.

I worked with an extremely angry 13-year-old who perceived almost every response as an attack. When he thought he was being verbally attacked, he responded like a Tasmanian devil and could destroy his room or the living room of the facility within minutes. He once sprang out of his chair, threw it across the room, leaped over a sofa and pinned me against the wall with his fist raised inches from my face.

I said in a firm voice, "Enough!" He lowered his fist, turned around and went to his room. Just as fast as he'd hovered over me, he fell asleep on his bed, something he did every time he became enraged. Within seconds, he'd fall into a deep slumber that lasted 15 hours. His tough exterior was menacing, but when frightened, he'd go to sleep or, **faint**.

Fornicate – Rather than implementing a healthy coping skill to help us calm down when stressed, some of us look for sex and/or pornography. I've counseled couples in marriage therapy who said they didn't know how to communicate effectively with one another. As a result, they didn't have a deep, emotional connection, which is ultimately what most couples, female *and* male, want from one another.

Oftentimes, one partner had become addicted to pornography or engaged in extramarital affairs. Other couples said they never resolved their conflicts. Rather than talking through the discomfort, they had meaningless or hostile sex with one another.

In any of those scenarios, the couples used sex to replace a deeper longing. Their equation often looked like this: "Emotional intimacy is too scary because if she discovers the real me, she won't stay." + "I can't take that risk." + "I'll watch porn to satisfy my sexual needs, where the people aren't *real* and I won't have to worry about being abandoned." = Habitual porn or sex addiction.

In the world we live in today, we're often given the erroneous message that we don't have to go through the tough emotional stuff in our relationships. We can feel full and valued and get ALL our needs met through sex, without engagement or commitment.

Yet another response my grandmother displayed when she wanted to feel safe was fornication, which took on many forms. She was promiscuous and had a string of partners, many of them one-night-stands. She dressed seductively and put herself in risky situations with men she didn't know.

We can't know if she was promiscuous to obtain alcohol or to please the men. Whatever the motive, her behavior became habitual. When sexualized behavior of any kind becomes chronic in order to replace emotional intimacy, we are, **fornicating**.

Feed – Another method of handling stress involves substituting the support of healthy people with feeding, whether on drugs, alcohol, food, exercise, self-harming behaviors or work. For a person who feeds when they are stressed, the equation looks like this: "My life feels unsafe or stressful." + "The only thing that makes me feel whole, funny, lovable or valuable is_____." = A feeding frenzy.

One of my most memorable clients was a precious green-eyed beauty with red hair and the face of an angel. She was gorgeous but looking at her from her chin down was difficult because every inch of her body was covered in horrendous, thick, ugly scars. She had cut every part of herself in a desperate attempt to numb the internal pain she carried. She had cut herself so much, for so long, that it had become an addiction. When there was nowhere left to cut, she started swallowing glass and batteries.

My grandmother drank her way to the bottom of any bottle of liquor she could get her hands on. What started as social drinking when she was married to my grandfather, turned into full-blown alcoholism after his death. She was a walking example of someone who lived in a heightened state of terror and she resorted to almost every reaction that lives in the limbic brain.

These reactions are not meant to be destructive. They are simply the limbic brain's means of survival. The limbic brain doesn't think, it reacts. When we can calm ourselves and regulate our emotions, we can get to our "thinking" brain and make healthier choices for ourselves.

Like my grandmother, many individuals never learn how to stop, take a cleansing breath and find safety through meditation, self-talk, walking, yoga, listening to music, or other calming mechanisms. I've sat with dozens of addicts who desperately needed something to make them feel whole again, whether it was one more cut, another line of coke, one last martini, or just three more hours of work added to their 14-hour workday. Watching them pace, sweat, wring their hands, turn red and scratch their skin in an attempt to stop the behavior that was killing them would make my heart break every time.

Hearing their stories of despair or self-loathing and why they chose to numb their feelings of pain and inadequacy with an addiction was gut-wrenching. On the outside, they were lawyers, doctors, homeless veterans, schoolteachers, and pastors. On the inside, they were hurting and the only thing that brought them an ounce of relief was, **feeding**.

~~*Jann* ~~

My mom rarely stayed home on weekends. In order to find something to eat, I had to get creative. I must have been about five or six-years-old, when I decided to put flour and sugar in a bowl, like I'd seen my friend's mom do. I mixed the two ingredients carefully and put them in a pan in the oven, just as she did.

I had no idea how long to bake my concoction, but when I took it out of the oven, it sure didn't look very good and, it tasted even worse. The crackers and mayonnaise I ate on a fairly regular basis weren't much better.

One night while I was alone, the police came to the house. They asked me where my mom was. I was too afraid to answer them. The lady officer helped me into their car and we drove away. She had a soft voice and told me not to be afraid. She said, "We are going to help you, you're safe sweetie." I couldn't tell her that nothing in my life felt safe, so I just sat quietly.

For other children, riding in a police car with the lights flashing might have been a fun adventure, but it was not fun for me. I didn't know what was going to happen to me or where were they taking me. But I knew one thing for sure, my mother was going to be very angry.

It occurred to me that a neighbor probably told the police I was at their house asking for food. The thought that I had done something that caused the police to appear at our door sent fear coursing through my body. I didn't mean to be bad. I was just hungry, but I knew that wouldn't matter to my mother. I was going to be in big trouble with her.

As we drove, I looked out the rear window and watched my house getting smaller and smaller. In only a couple minutes, it was out of sight. I slowly turned around and sat down in the seat, trembling. My fate was sealed, but I had no idea what my fate would be. I just knew I was on a journey to an unknown destination with scary officers.

My mother had taught me to fear the police. "They are not our friends," she told me more than once. I saw her act on her words the night she had me hunker down in the backseat of our car as she was leaving an all-day drinking binge at her friend's house. She was far too impaired to be behind the wheel, and we had not driven very far before a police car's lights were flashing behind us, summoning her to pull over.

The officer followed close behind us, but she didn't stop. Instead, she screamed profanities about the no-good cops trying to pull her over to give her ticket and hit the gas. I was slammed into the back of the seat by the force of acceleration. Frightened, I curled into a ball on the rear floorboard of the car.

I begged her to stop. I'd seen on TV that the police start shooting when people run from them, and I was scared they'd shoot my mother.

She told me to shut up, that she'd be taken to jail by the lousy cops if they caught us. "Is that what you want, for me to go to jail?" she yelled.

I started crying. "No, mama, no. I want you to stay with me. I don't want you to go to jail, ever."

After a long chase, she managed to elude the police, and we arrived home safely. Today, I look back on that night and cringe at the danger she put me in.

So, there I was, in a car with two policemen, perhaps the same policemen. When we stopped in front of the police station, I was sure they were going to put *me* in jail. The lady officer wasted no time reaching for the car door to the back seat. She offered her hand to me. I was trembling so badly my body couldn't move. She leaned in and whispered, "Are you hungry?" Her smile was so kind. I began to relax and took her hand.

Just inside the door, I stopped and looked around. A big policeman was taking a picture of a man in ragged clothing. I thought that was strange. Why did they want his picture? He looked awful. Another man was sleeping on the floor and a drunk lady was screaming for the cops to let her go. The room smelled bad. The odor of alcohol was familiar to me, but the stench of unwashed people was overpowering.

Someone said, "Uncuff her." But I didn't know what that meant. Scary people sat along the wall in a row of chairs, but I didn't see any children in the room, I was the only one.

A lady officer came over and took my hand. She had sparkling eyes and a look on her face that I'd never seen on a grown-up before, kindness. I thought she was very nice, but my mother's words that police officers were bad filled my head, so I didn't smile back at her.

I remember being lifted up onto one of the desks at the far right of the room. I was eating a cookie and drinking milk when my mother arrived at the station to get me. She came in with a look on her face that let me know I was in trouble.

She urged me to tell them that she was a good mother. And then, she told the officers I'd run away and she'd been out searching for me when they arrived at the house. "I have been worried sick," she said, furrowing her brows, and pacing back and forth. Fearful of what she'd do to me if I didn't cover for her, I told the officers she was right.

I loved my mother. She was all I had. I was afraid of losing her and obviously, this predicament we were in was my fault. I just needed to work harder at being a good little girl, one she could finally love. I was allowed to go home with her, but the tension was thick while in her presence.

My mother was determined not to let her parental responsibilities hamper her lifestyle. And she was not going to be without a man any more than she'd be without alcohol. Because she didn't want the police interfering in her life again, she came up with a strategy to avoid them. I would now go with her to every seedy dive bar and hotel, every weekend, all weekend long.

From that point on, I spent weekends in filthy hotels, trying hard to be unseen and unheard, crouched in the corner. I squeezed my eyes closed and covered my ears with both hands while she had sex right in front of me with the man of the night. Of course, as the nights wore on, the intimacy disintegrated and erupted into beatings, and I was witness to it all.

I would have gladly changed places with my mother. I could take the abuse, but what if they killed her, what would become of me? The pain was so great inside me as I watched, I'd feel like the beating was happening to me whether it actually was or not. Occasionally, the violence included me. If my mother happened to pass out, some of the men reached for me. They would offer me cigarettes and force me to drink their alcohol. The liquid burned all the way down my throat and I would choke. Sometimes, the coughing would make the man leave me alone. Other times it made the man angry and he would hit me.

One night my mother drove to her favorite bar with me in tow, as usual. But this time, she ushered me inside with her. The room was dark and noisy. The fans circling overhead did little to cool the stale air. I saw lots of people, some sitting, some standing. They seemed to all be talking and laughing at the same time.

My mother hurried me to a large, half-mooned shaped table in the corner that had a bench curved around it. She must have known the other people already seated, two men and a lady. My mother shoved me under the table where I crouched on the dirty floor for hours among her friends' feet without saying a word. Finally, the bar closed and my mother drove us home, too drunk to be driving, as always.

Another night, I was in the backseat as we headed to yet another bar. Smoke from my mother's cigarette filled the car. I rolled the window down and let the humid night air fill my nostrils. The fresh air was wonderful.

But then she put her hand out the window and flicked her cigarette to release the hot ash that had collected at the end. The ash hit my face and I instinctively blurted, "Your cigarette burned me!"

Immediately, she pulled the car over to the shoulder of the road and slammed on the brakes, throwing me into the armrest. I knew I was in trouble.

She flung open the door and jumped out of the car. "I'll show you what it means to be burned by a cigarette!" Before I could scramble from her reach, my mother pulled up my shirt and extinguished her cigarette on my abdomen.

Never again did I complain, no matter how many ashes found their way into my backseat.

I was only seven when the worst part of my abuse with my mother occurred. We parked outside a white frame house and walked a short walkway that led to the front door. A man opened the door and greeted my mother. I quickly found a place near the sofa in the living room.

After a while, I was taken into a bedroom and told to get on the bed. I was confused because I'd never been there before and I was filled with panic. The man balanced himself on his knees at my feet. I didn't understand what was happening, but I was filled with dread.

My mother removed my clothes from the waist down and positioned herself at my head. She grabbed my shoulders pinning me to the mattress. The man came at me and a sharp pain shot from between my legs and coursed through my entire body. I screamed, but no sound escaped my mouth. I looked up to see my mother's face hovering close to mine.

I searched her eyes for some sign of motherly protection but saw none. She held me down as the man inflicted the most excruciating pain on my small body. I closed my eyes so I could no longer see the vacant look in my mother's eyes.

We returned to that horrible white frame house on two more occasions. As we approached, I'd begin to tremble and softly cry. My mother would grab my hand and lead me through the door as if she were walking me into an ice cream parlor.

I wanted to beg her to not take me in there, I wanted to drag my feet, but I knew it would be futile. We both realized what was going to happen to me inside that house, but only one of us cared. Years later, I'd have to face the emotional and physical damage inflicted upon me during those encounters.

For a while, my mother had an affair with a man who owned a liquor store. He kept a bed at the back of the store. When customers weren't present, he and my mother would drink and have sex behind the curtain just beyond the counter where the cash register was located.

After several weeks, he decided he didn't want me in the backroom with them anymore. My mother's response was to lock me in the back-seat of the car, while she was with him. I was told to stay down on the floorboard, so no one could see me. I'd remain there for hours without food, water *or* a bathroom.

His store was located in a strip mall of sorts. In addition to the liquor store, the businesses included a hair salon, an ice cream/donut shop and a couple other stores, although I'm not sure what kind. As you can imagine, the parking lot was busy.

I could hear as cars pulled up and stopped and the doors opened and closed. Sometimes, I could hear people talking as they got out. I imagined a mother holding the hand of her child, then pulling her close. I'd smile when the dad laughed at something funny the mother said.

Their voices would grow fainter as they walked away. When they returned, I imagined they each held ice cream cones in their hands. The mother would bend down to gently wipe a dribble of melting ice cream from her child's chin before helping her into the car to head for home. I wished I was going home with them.

One bright, hot-and-humid summer morning, I was sitting on the front porch playing jacks, when my paternal grandmother drove into the driveway. I could see the top of my brother's head in the front seat. I jumped up and ran toward the car, barely containing my enthusiasm. My grandmother had brought my brother home.

I heard the screen door open and turned. Mama was standing there with a brown paper sack in her hand. I walked over to her but kept glancing back to see if my brother was still in the car. Mama handed the sack to me and said I was spending the night with my cousin who lived on my grandmother's property. I peeked inside the bag and saw my pajamas and play clothes for the next day.

My grandmother told my brother to stay in the car and she got out and walked the short distance to where my mother was standing. I stood off to the side not knowing what to do. I desperately wanted to run to my brother, but he didn't move, so neither did I. We just looked at each other like we were strangers.

I heard my grandmother ask Mama for Daddy's ring. I knew which one she was referring to, a beautiful lion's head, sculpted in gold. I'd noticed it on Daddy's hand in a picture Mama kept on her dresser. Its open mouth held a large diamond in place with four gold "fang" prongs. Grandma said she wanted to hold the ring in safe-keeping for my brother.

My mother told her I lost the ring. *What? I didn't lose my daddy's ring!* My grandmother glared at me and ordered me to get into the car.

To be blamed for my daddy's missing ring broke my heart. I had no idea what had happened to it, but I was certain it had nothing to do with me. I slipped into the back of the car without saying one word to my brother, whom I hadn't seen in a long time.

My grandmother joined him in the front seat, and she proceeded to tell him that because of ME he would not be getting HIS father's ring. She shamed me for my reckless behavior. I sat in silence.

We arrived at my grandmother's property and she parked in front of my cousin's house. I got out of the car without a word to either my grandmother or my brother. My cousin met me at the door. He was married and had an adorable little baby girl with the darkest eyes and the blackest hair. Sometimes, after the baby went to sleep, my cousin, his wife and I would watch TV, but on this night, I just wanted to go to bed. I thought if I could get to sleep, maybe he wouldn't bother me. He always wanted me to sit on his lap, and this visit was no different. I hated to leave my safe place on the couch next to his wife, who was now sleeping soundly with her head nestled into the huge flowered pillow at the end of the sofa.

But, I did as I was told. I slowly, and with such dread, walked over to him knowing full well what he had in mind. He grabbed me by my ribs, pressed me into his lap and started pushing me back and forth. His grip was so tight, I couldn't fill my lungs with air and could barely breathe.

Eyes closed, he grunted and breathed strangely. I could feel and smell his hot, stinky breath on my neck. The shoving and grunting lasted into the wee hours of the night.

I wanted his wife to wake up and make him stop. But she never did. I was helpless during those times and would escape in my mind. I was unable to take my thoughts to a place where I was loved and supported because no such place would be waiting for me at the end of this torment.

To keep my sanity, I created one. This night, I was a pink balloon just released from the tight fist of a child. I soared higher and higher in the sky until I finally disappeared into the clouds, floating far away from my abuser.

I loved playing with their baby when my cousin and his wife entertained their guests. She was a precious baby with chubby cheeks and a crooked little toothless grin that erupted across her tiny face when we played peek-a-boo. As much fun as I had with the baby, when I heard the adults laughing in the kitchen, I was afraid they were laughing at what I never wanted anyone to know.

In the middle of the night, my cousin would pick me up from the couch where I slept, take me to his bed and hurt me throughout the night. I was so ashamed, and the crazy thing is, I didn't hate him. I hated myself for what he did to me.

All the while his wife was beside us in the same bed. My mind questioned how she could sleep through all that was happening right next to her, but apparently, she did.

My cousin threatened me, saying if I told anyone about what went on in that bed, I would be in a whole lot of trouble.

I thought, *Who am I going to tell? No one cares about anything that happens to me.*

What he did to me hurt a lot, but he made me tell him it felt good. I didn't know how to make him stop. I wanted to cry out so that his wife would wake up. If she knew what was happening, she'd surely tell him to let me go back to the couch. But she never woke up, never helped me. I thought, *Maybe she doesn't care, either.*

I remember those nights all too vividly.

His sweaty body is on me. He's heavy. I can't breathe. I need him to move, to let me up. I feel trapped under his weight.

And then I feel a pain that causes me to draw in a huge gasp of air. I want to scream, but I have no voice. My mouth is open, yet nothing comes out.

I'm so scared. It's dark. He whispers words in my ear, words I'm too little to understand, and he reaches for my hand. He places it on him and moves it up and down. Then he gasps and pulls me close.

I hold my breath and the pain stops. I'm not a pink balloon this time. It's me, and I can fly. Here I go, ascending to the ceiling where I remain the rest of the night.

After that night, every night I was with my cousin, I floated to the ceiling.

I couldn't feel the pain when I was flying on

the ceiling. Nor could I feel the tears that collected in a pool in the back of my throat. Tears that I was too scared to release. My life had become so unbearable at that point, I no longer remained present while the abuses took place. I couldn't bear the fear, the kind of fear that paralyzes a child, or the pain, or the loneliness, or my growing hatred I had for myself.

Somewhere around this time, I must have started elementary school, because I remember wanting to become a Brownie like some of the girls in my class. My mom let me join, and I loved the little beige uniform with the dark-brown beanie we got to wear to school one day a week.

Finally, I felt like all the other little girls. I was doing something JUST LIKE THEM. I was so happy to belong to something, to be equal for the first time. But, my newfound social standing was not to remain intact for long.

The Troop meeting was at a neighbor's house just down the street from mine. I could walk over after school, which was the only means I had of getting there because my mother worked. I hadn't been a member long when it came time for snacks at one of our meetings. But, no one had brought the usual cookies and punch.

That's when all the other little girls looked at me in unison, declaring in words that sounded like they were blasting from a horn, "Jann, you were supposed to bring the snacks!"

Everyone took turns bringing snacks for the meetings, and it was my turn. But, I didn't *know* it was my turn. I DIDN'T KNOW, I silently screamed.

I was so ashamed that I wanted to run away from their glaring eyes. The leader asked me if the snacks were at my house. She said they would wait while I went home to get them.

I somehow managed to shake my head. No snacks were waiting at my house for me to go get. We didn't even have FOOD at my house. I ran out the door and to my own home as fast as my little legs could carry me, hot tears rolling down my cheeks.

When my mom got home from work, I told her today was my turn to bring snacks to the Brownie meeting. She walked over to me and ripped the uniform from my body, leaving me standing there in my underclothes. I begged her not to be mad as she gathered the clothing she'd tossed onto the floor. The dark brown beanie, the bright scarf and the beige dress that made up my uniform and made me feel so special were now balled in her fists.

Without a word, she marched out the front door, slamming it behind her. When she returned home only moments later, she no longer had my uniform in her hand and she didn't offer an explanation.

Instead, she opened her bottle of liquor for the night and I knew to never mention the Brownies again.

I hadn't seen my brother in a long time and I rarely thought of him. But one afternoon, I found his ball under a large flowering bush beside the house. My memories were transported to a happier time when we played ball and laughed and had fun together.

Those happy thoughts were interrupted when I heard my mom calling me to come inside. She rarely ever asked me to go in. I think she preferred for me to be out of her sight, so this seemed strange and put me on alert.

She was sitting on the gold brocade sofa when I walked in the front door. Her hair was tied back in a silk scarf at the nape of her neck. This was unusual as well. She most often wore her long hair loose, allowing it to cascade down her back.

Her eyes were fixed on me with their usual distant stare, but today I noticed a deeper, darker appearance to them that filled me with dread. What was she going to do to me?

I didn't have to wait long. She abruptly said, "Tomorrow morning, you'll go live in a new place called a "home".

A HOME? But I already have a home!

She said I would not be living with her anymore, but she would come to get me soon. Then she rose from the sofa, went to her bedroom and quietly closed the door.

As I sat there on that big green chair, my eyes welled with tears. With one blink, they spilled onto my cheeks, and I fell into despair. My life had been so chaotic, filled with such pain and loneliness, one would think I would have been relieved to know my circumstances were changing. But the opposite was true. My mother's pronouncement created enormous emotional conflict within me.

I didn't know how to make sense of what I'd just heard. I didn't understand, and I had no one to ask what her words meant. For a moment, I wondered if my mom was tired of taking me to the doctor when my back was hurting, or because I needed medicine, or because, sometimes small amounts of blood stained my panties. Mostly, I just thought she was sending me away because she didn't want me.

The only thing I knew for sure was that I couldn't bear to be separated from the only person I had left in the world. I'd learned to endure my life, horrible as it was, but I couldn't endure this. Separation was too much to ask of a small child.

Something horrible happens to a fragile soul when it isn't wanted. Mine exploded. And no one cared enough to pick up the pieces and put me back together again.

Panic. Fear. Dread. Run! But I had nowhere to run and no one to run to. I stared at the empty space my mother had occupied on the sofa just a few moments earlier and silently begged to not be sent away. I promised I would be good and that I'd never want anything, never ask for anything.

Unimaginable and profound sadness came over me, the likes of which I had not felt before. I don't know how long I sat there, staring at the sofa. Eventually, terror at the thought of being sent away mixed with copious amounts of adrenaline overwhelmed my mind and body.

I got up, walked outside and ran until my legs couldn't carry me any longer. Exhausted, I sat down on a street curb and sobbed. My life had finally become too great for me to bear. My little mind couldn't grasp what this change meant for me. My world, my life, my existence was crumbling around me, and I had no idea where to turn for help.

I felt so vulnerable and small. I was only eight-years-old and I was being sent away to a place I didn't understand. The weight of that news engulfed me and crushed me like a python crushes its prey.

I wondered if it was possible that my insignificant self could be reduced to ash and carried away with the evening breeze. My self-hatred escalated immeasurably that night.

I heard a mother calling her little boy in for dinner. I saw him drop his ball and mitt on the front porch before he opened the door and disappeared into the safety of his home. What a dissimilar meaning "home" held for me. The sun had gone down by the time I finally willed myself up from the curb.

When I reached my house, I saw that Mama's car was gone from the driveway. I walked inside. She hadn't left any lights on so, I assumed she must have left shortly after I did. I sat alone in the dark wishing I was dead like my daddy.

After a while, I went into my room and lowered myself to the floor. I was awakened by a ray of sunshine on my back as it pierced the gap in the curtains. I started to shiver, despite the sun's warmth.

I rubbed my eyes, and for a moment, I thought the nightmare of the night before was just that, a nightmare. But as I lay on the floor, I heard voices in the living room. My mother was saying something I couldn't make out because she was speaking softly.

Another voice, one I didn't recognize, responded. Caustic bile from my empty stomach rose up and burned my throat. But I didn't move.

I rolled over, peering beneath my bed, where I had so often tried to hide from danger. I saw a little doll with blonde curls that I must have left behind when someone dragged me out.

My closet door was ajar. No clothes hung from the rod. My shoes no longer cluttered the closet floor. The only objects in the closet were several empty hangers and a broken blue crayon lying in the corner forgotten…just like me.

This was the same closet that once sheltered me from the yelling and cursing, from the sounds of bodies being slammed to the kitchen floor during drunken fights. The same closet that had once been my refuge as I huddled behind my toy box in the darkness and held my breath as if doing so would somehow keep me safe.

My toy box that had stored my books, dolls and stuffed animals was empty. My dresser drawers gaped open. I crawled over and peeked inside. My pink gown with the satin bows on the sleeves was gone, along with all my underclothes, my pajamas, shorts, and tops. Where did everything go?

The unfamiliar voice came closer to me and startled me away from the inventory I'd been taking of my bedroom, the bedroom I once shared with my brother. I wanted to cover my ears with my hands as I usually did when I was trying to block out the fighting. Instead, I jumped up, suddenly frightened.

Standing in the hallway just outside my door was a lady in a dark suit and white glasses that made her eyes look much larger than they really were. Her hair was red and framed her face in short wispy curls. She beckoned me with her hand, but I froze right where I stood, unable to move.

A warm stream of urine puddled on the floor around my feet. She walked to me and said she would help me clean up. In her hand, she held my blue-and-white polka-dot dress with the yellow sash.

My mother was nowhere in sight. I wondered if she'd gone outside to smoke. The lady told me to raise my arms, so she could remove the striped shirt I still wore from the day before.

"I want my mommy!" I cried in a voice that could have been heard a block away. Using all my strength, I tried to squirm away from her, but she told me to calm down and overpowered me and continued to change my clothes.

I heard her tell someone in the other room that I felt hot. I didn't feel hot, I felt cold, very cold. She touched my forehead and said, "She has a fever."

Once I was dressed, she took my hand and led me into the living room, where I could finally see the person she'd been speaking to. A large man in a police uniform looked back at me. They continued to discuss things I didn't understand. Moments later, the man went into the kitchen to use our phone.

I pulled my hand away from the lady and sat down on the sofa. I felt I was going to be sick. The room smelled from my mother's stale cigarette butts and vodka. I reached to touch the scarf she'd left on the arm of the sofa. I pressed my face into the fabric and inhaled the faint aroma of perfume. My body began to tremble and hopelessness filled my soul.

In a tiny voice, I asked once again for my mommy, but the lady acted like she didn't hear me. When the call ended, the lady gently nudged me from the sofa. Together, the three of us walked out the front door without a word or a good-bye glance.

When I heard the door close behind me, I stopped and turned around, pulling my hand free. I wanted to run, but I had nowhere to run to. I looked at the brown door that was now tightly closed, barring me from returning to my home, a home I would never see again.

I turned to the driveway to see if Mama was

in her car. It was gone and so was she. Oil stains on the light grey cement were all that remained. The longing I felt went unnoticed by either adult.

Alone in the backseat of the car that was taking me away from my mother, my eyes stung, but I had no tears. And even though the sun was shining through the car window, I couldn't feel its warmth. I shivered like it was wintertime. My back was hurting so badly from sleeping on the floor.

I tried to dismiss the growing panic inside me, but my heart pounded like a drum inside my small chest. I heard nothing but the sound of the tires beneath me as they took me closer to my final destination.

Every time the car stopped at an intersection or red light, fright rose to my throat, threatening to choke me. When it started to move again, I knew we had not yet arrived at my new "home".

I couldn't bring myself to look out the windows of the car. I just kept my head down and traced the fabric pattern on the seat with my eyes. Grey, then black, then grey, then black connecting into small triangles, separated only where black piping was stitched into the fabric.

I had no desire to see this "home" I knew we were drawing closer and closer to. So I kept my eyes lowered, willing myself to fly away from the pain as I'd done so many other times. But today, I couldn't.

I tried to imagine how the new place could be my home. It wouldn't be a home without my mommy or my brother. I wondered if my brother would be waiting for me when I got there.

As we traveled in silence, my other senses took over what my eyes could not see. I heard traffic roaring and horn blasts. The hot, humid breeze that blew in my open window, burned like ice and made me shiver even more.

I could smell bread baking and knew it came from a local bakery. Seconds later, that pleasant aroma was overpowered by a putrid stench.

We'd reached the area of town where street people had sex in the back alleys and drank liquor from bottles that were hidden in brown paper sacks, and where drug addicts shared their needles, sweat, and vomit. I retched.

The car stopped, and this time it didn't start up again. As I was helped out of the back seat, I saw a tall building ahead of me surrounded by a perfectly manicured lawn. Beautiful red flowers framed the walkway, this was a hospital, not a home.

Wait, why are we stopping here? I don't understand.

A new fear overtook my body and my shaking intensified. The people in the car were replaced by nurses in white uniforms. They were calm and spoke in low rhythmic voices, but I was too scared to feel comforted by the gentleness.

The lights inside the hospital were bright. I could hear strange voices over loudspeakers. The floor was damp from being mopped. The walls had pictures of children hung on them, and some of the open areas had chairs with magazines on end tables.

I entered a small room that had a high table in the center. White paper covered it and there was a pillow on one end. The nurse helped me onto the table. Once she removed my polka-dot dress she helped me into a green hospital gown. The same nurse stayed with me until the doctor came into the room and examined me.

As soon as the exam was completed another

nurse came into the room and lifted me onto a bed with wheels. I was rolled into a room with big, scary machines that took pictures of the inside of my body.

Following the tests, I was taken to a children's ward. I could hear children talking as we neared double doors that had windows in them. The nurse helped me into a bed near the doors. A cold metal guardrail brushed my arm as she raised both rails into place, trapping me in the bed. I didn't care, I was too sick to try to escape.

The nurse poked me with a needle attached to a bag of clear fluid that hung above my head. The needle hurt, but I didn't even flinch. Once the nurses left I closed my eyes, too tired and too sick to move. I closed my eyes quickly, but it was a long time before I fell asleep.

Years later, I learned I was suffering from malnutrition, and the pain in my back was due to the kidney damage caused when my mother beat me. Eventually, the fever subsided, and my back didn't hurt anymore. I noticed several children in beds across from mine, but I didn't talk to them. If they looked at me, I looked away. I envied them when they received visitors, though. I longed for someone to visit me.

I don't know how long I'd been in the hospital when my lonely existence was interrupted. One night, as I was confined in my bed, alone and forgotten it seemed, I heard my mother's voice coming from down the hall. I came alive at that moment. My eyes blinked wide but thought I HAD to be dreaming.

But then, I heard her again. My mama was really here, in the hospital. She'd come to get me just like she had promised! I was so happy. She loved me after all!

My joy was almost instantly replaced with disappointment. She was drunk. I recognized the slurring of her words, the slow, determined whine in her voice, "That's my baaaaby!"

Before she could reach the children's ward, three orderlies in starched white uniforms rushed for the doors and blocked the entrance. I got up on my knees and leaned forward to see her through the windows in the double doors, a mere five feet away, the only thing between me and her waiting arms.

I was desperate to get to her. I no longer had an IV in my arm, so I climbed out of bed and ran toward the door, only to be captured by a nurse before I could reach it. I was placed back in bed and through the window of the closed doors, I sadly watched the police lead my mother away. Her hair cascaded down her back, like always, but her hands were caught behind her in handcuffs. I didn't know then that I wouldn't see her again for many years.

As I grew stronger, I was allowed to walk to the baby nursery and watch through a large glass window as nurses bathed and cared for the newborns. I loved this time so much. I felt like I was living in a warm, safe place where little babies grew. Their tiny eyes blinked against the intrusion of the bright lights above them. I loved to watch them squirm beneath their white blankets with the pink and blue stripes.

But, I was consumed with what might happen to them when they left the hospital. I worried about their safety. What if no one loved them? What if someone hurt them?

The nurses were nice to me, but all I wanted was to see my family. They didn't talk about where I would be going, so I thought I might be going back to my home soon. I planned for that day, I looked forward to it.

In fact, my dream of returning to my mother occupied my every thought and I held onto my growing hope. I didn't want to stay in the hospital one day longer. I was gaining weight and stamina and I heard the nurses say I would be leaving soon.

The tests and the treatments finally stopped. I had a sense that things were changing just by the way the nurses seemed more occupied with other sick children and no longer hovered over me. One day I heard one of them say, "She will be going to the orphanage soon." I asked a nurse what orphanage meant. She replied with the horrible word I feared most, "It's another word for "home"".

~~*Shari*~~

Dissociation is the mind's way of coping with extreme forms of abuse. It is a brilliant coping skill our brains develop to separate our physical bodies from feeling the enormity of the pain we're experiencing. My mother's mind taught her to leave her body and become a "pink balloon" or float to the ceiling or dream of something beautiful when the maltreatment began.

An innocent little child isn't wired to handle cruelty. In order to cope with the horrors my mother witnessed and experienced, a wonderful coping skill emerged that saved her from feeling the reality happening to and around her. Webster's Dictionary defines dissociation as "the disconnection or separation of something from something else." (Merriam-Webster's Collegiate Dictionary [11th ed.]). In this case, her mind separated from her body.

This coping skill is a double-edged sword. While it served as a way for Mom to deal with the tragedy of her childhood, in her adult life, it proved to be an annoyance. I grew up watching her literally leave her body, a skill she fine-tuned over the countless years of abuse or witnessing her mother's abuse.

As an adolescent, I'd be talking to her, and she'd suddenly just "go away". Her body was there, but her eyes were vacant. She couldn't respond to what I was saying because she didn't hear it.

I found this behavior baffling and scary. I didn't know what it meant, and in an attempt to bring her back, I'd shout, "Mom!"

She'd jump and return to the present moment, looking startled. She didn't know what I'd said and couldn't recall what we'd been talking about. In addition, she couldn't say "where" she went, only that she was sorry. My mother continues to have dissociative times, but they occur less frequently and she better understands what's happening to her.

I've seen dissociation frequently with clients. One minute they're sitting in my office, talking about their trauma. The next minute, they've left their bodies, and traveled to a place where they feel safe and untouchable by harm.

Our bodies hold memories. When we walk into a restaurant in the morning and smell bacon, we can be instantly transported back to a time we went camping and cooked bacon on a campfire. We're reminded of memories associated with that camping trip. Our bodies remember the smell.

Similarly, if someone who was bitten by a dog outside their house when they were young drives down the same street 40-years later, they can often feel the same pain, in the same spot, even though the wound has long since healed. Our bodies hold memories and sometimes, to escape painful memories, our brains signal a separation just like they do when we *actually* experience something awful.

Dissociation, not to be confused with amnesia, can happen during a traumatic event, at the memory of a traumatic event, or when something/someone reminds us of a traumatic event. Some people have described dissociation as a sensation that they're floating up to the ceiling. Other people can't describe where their minds go, only that they "blank out." Dissociation is a wonderful tool unless it inhibits our ability to function.

All of us can become upset by situations in our world. "Triggers" are often events or people who remind us of a past negative experience. Sometimes, a trigger occurs when what we see or hear is in direct conflict with our values.

For example, if you grew up in a peaceful home (experience), where your parents taught you to appreciate the differences of others (value), you might be triggered when someone bullies another person because of their race or religious preference.

When triggered, we all have reactions (physical cues) that occur in our bodies. Some people tense their shoulders, clench their jaws, ball their fists, or feel their hearts begin to race. Others turn red, tap their feet or experience shallow breathing.

To live a life that is responsive rather than reactive, we must understand what happens in us physically when we're triggered or upset. If identifying what occurs in you physically when you're triggered is difficult for you, ask your friends, co-workers or family members to observe your body and your breathing when you react and describe what they see to you.

Once you know the signals, watch for times when your muscles tense, you clench your fists, you feel the heat rising in your cheeks, etc. If you can't identify your physical cues, try to identify the things that upset you. Perhaps your boss walking into the office with a frown on her face makes you suddenly feel anxious. Maybe driving in rush hour traffic gets you upset. Hearing footsteps quickly approaching behind you could initiate a feeling of fear.

When you become aware of your triggers, pay attention to what "grounds" you or brings you back to the present moment. If you can't identify grounding techniques, name five things you see, then four items you could touch, three sounds you can hear, then two things you can smell, then one thing you taste (or any variation of this). This method often keeps people from dissociating.

You might want to place a picture in your wallet or on your phone that brings you a sense of peace when you look at it. Countless apps can be downloaded to your phone to help you center and ground yourself again in a matter of minutes. One of my favorites is https://youtu.be/wGFog-OuFDM.

With practice, you'll train your brain to calm itself. You'll move from the limbic brain--where only fight, flight, freeze, faint, fornicate or feed is possible--into the frontal lobe of your brain, where you can think clearly and respond rather than react.

Suggestions for therapists, counselors, life coaches, teachers or anyone who wants to help another person to regulate their emotions:

One of the tools I implement with clients who've experienced trauma is an anchoring or a grounding exercise. I want to understand what outward signs they display when they're triggered. While they're talking about something that disturbs them, I look for bodily reactions.

Do they turn red? Does breathing become shallow? Do their muscles tense or do they clench their fists?

I look for physical symptoms because those usually indicate the beginning phase of dissociation or of a panic attack or of the person becoming extremely overwhelmed. Before my clients are triggered, I help them identify something that could ground them to reality. This might be a memory of a time when they went to the beach, a picture of their child or a soothing song.

I ask them to tell me about the picture or describe what sounds they heard at the beach and how the sand felt on their toes, etc. If they have nothing that grounds them, I ask them to describe what they see in my office, what the chair they're sitting on feels like, what they hear going on outside on the street.

We practice grounding before they start to talk about their trauma or a painful memory so that they're prepared for me to stop them before they're triggered. When I see them entering a state of overwhelm, I help them become grounded in the present moment again. Doing so, often allows them to handle their emotions in smaller doses.

When a client starts to look visibly shaken, I ask if I can stop them for a minute. Then, I point out what I've observed about them and say,

"Susie, I notice that your face looks flushed and your breathing has become shallow. I'd like to interrupt and have you to tell me about that time you went to the beach.

"Can you explain what the sky looked like that day? What did the waves sound like?" Or I may ask Susie to pull out the picture of her loved one she showed me earlier and have her talk to me about the picture. I do this until she returns to the present moment and I see that her emotions are regulated, and her breathing is normal again.

This technique serves several purposes. Telling their stories in smaller chunks keeps my clients from entering a state of panic or dissociating. I want them to leave my office able to function in the outside world again. Grounding also teaches them how to regulate their emotions themselves when they're elsewhere and begin to feel triggered.

Helping clients become aware of what happens to their bodies physically (red face, shallow breathing, blank stare, tense muscles, etc.) in the safety of my office can teach them what to watch for in their daily lives. Knowing their physical cues can remind them to ground themselves. When we feel grounded in the present moment, we can think more clearly and better assess our needs.

~~*Jann*~~

I had been taken from the hell that I shared
with my mother and called "home" to the stark,
bright lights of the hospital, where I entered a dark
hole of complete hopelessness. A hole I didn't have
the will to climb out of. I had no idea how to
survive in the world or how to find hope in it.

The day came when I hugged my two nurses
good-bye and climbed into the back of a van in the
hospital parking lot without being instructed to do
so by either of the two men in the front seat. I
realized by then that fighting the system was futile.
As the van headed out of the parking lot, I
wondered if I'd ever see my nurses again, but I
didn't have the will to look back. They had both
been very kind to me. Their eyes were gentle and
their words were soft. I wanted to stay with them.

We had been driving since morning and now
the sun was low in the sky. I didn't know where we
were, nothing looked familiar to me anymore. We
entered a double gate that opened as the van

approached. The long driveway led to a three-story building. One-story buildings were scattered about the grounds where children of all ages ran around in the grass, played tag, threw balls back and forth and jumped rope.

Panic permeated all of my senses and a breath escaped me in such a violent release that I felt like I'd been hit in the stomach by a stray ball. But, that couldn't have happened because I was still in the van.

I wanted to open the car door and rush down the driveway before the iron gates closed and trapped me inside this fortress. I tried to swallow but I couldn't. My throat felt like a peach pit was stuck there.

My breathing was rapid and shallow. My hands trembled, my face felt red hot. I kept trying to swallow down the now baseball-sized lump.

The van slowed. Oh no! It stopped in front of the big house. No! No! Don't make me go in. I can't go in! Please don't make me go in!

The driver climbed out of the driver's seat, came around to the side, and reached for my door. I couldn't move, I wasn't sure my legs would hold me up.

The man reached his hand to help me out. The fear that he might become impatient with me gave me the ability to finally exit the van and enter the foyer of the big house.

But it didn't look like a house at all. The floors were covered in shiny wood and a large oak desk sat in one corner partially blocking the tallest window I'd ever seen. Three tall, open windows allowed a gentle breeze to lift the lace curtains, like billowing clouds.

A lady walked over to me from behind her

desk and said something I couldn't hear. My ears burned and my heartbeat pounded beneath my shirt. Her lips moved, but I couldn't hear her words. I had the odd sensation that my arms and legs were no longer attached to my body. They were just numb appendages.

I searched the room for someone to save me from the nightmare that played out before me. I was unable to accept the reality of where I had to live. The room was occupied by five ladies and not one of them tried to soothe my fears. Why couldn't anyone understand how much I wanted to go home, how much I wanted my family?

The driver unloaded all my things in the foyer. He'd barely dropped the last box on the floor when a teenage boy bounded up the steps and landed with one leap inside the room.

Without effort, he picked up a box and carried it through a door on the opposite side of the room. One of the women led me outside right behind him onto a sidewalk covered by a metal roof. We approached one of the long, low buildings. As we neared the open door I could hear the chatter of little girls coming from inside.

I was barely inside the long building when a young lady with shoulder-length brown hair approached me. She was not as tall as the teenage boy who stood beside her. She had a stern face and pursed lips formed into a straight line. The lady who walked with me from the main building told the new lady my name. The new lady informed me that I was to call her "Matron".

I soon learned my new home was called a dorm. It consisted of tiny little beds that lined two walls of a long room set on a concrete slab. A third wall was peppered with nails hammered into the wall that had clothes hanging on them. The entrance to the matron's private bedroom and bathroom was to the left of the clothes.

The biggest bathroom I'd ever seen was on the far right. Three open showers stood side by side on one wall, four toilets along another wall and four sinks on the third wall. The bathroom had no door, only a very wide entrance.

Frantically scanning this large new "home" of mine, I remembered my things. I needed my boxes, my belongings, my only connection with who I was in another life. They were the only means I had of remembering that I once had a real family and a real home, a lifeline helping me hold onto what little bit of identity I still had. I looked every direction but didn't see my things anywhere.

Then, the lady who walked over with me bent down to help a little girl buckle her shoe and I saw my boxes sitting just beyond her in the middle of the room. Finally, I could relax, at least a little. What remained of my life was arranged neatly in front of me in cardboard boxes.

Suddenly, all the chattering little girls converged on the boxes like starving animals desperate for food. They ripped them open, pulled out my clothes, including my favorite pink gown with the satin bows on the sleeves, my toys, and my stuffed animals that were my only comfort in life.

In a tiny voice barely audible to my ears, much less, the matron's, I cried. "They're taking all my things!"

Her response to my pathetic plea was loud, cold and pitiless, "Nothing here belongs to you. You must share!" That was the first and last time I attempted to speak out for myself during my years at the orphanage.

I slumped to the concrete floor in a heap as I cried my heart out. Faced with the terrifying reality that I was now completely alone in the world, I gave up. I felt profoundly broken. Many years would pass before the woundedness inside me would become manageable, and many more years would follow before the healing began.

When I came up off the floor that first day in the orphanage, the room was empty. I slowly sat up and looked around the room. At the far end of the room, I saw that my clothes were now hanging on nails along with other clothing.

My yellow-flowered dress with the white-satin trim and long flowing sash that tied in a large bow in the back hung beside my red-and-black plaid dress. My favorite pink dress was next to that. For some reason, my dresses seemed far, far away from me. Though the nails were easily within my reach, I felt like I would need a ladder to touch them.

From a distance, I studied my dresses one by one, as if to embed the details of each one into my memory. Suddenly, they looked ugly to me. I wanted to tear them off the nails on which they hung and throw them away. I hated them all.

While I lived in that dorm, I didn't once reach for my clothes. I just grabbed whatever was available on the nails each day. My toys were piled in a wooden box near the coat rack, but I never held them again. In fact, I never again held any toy as a child.

Nothing was ours to claim, not even our beds. Each night, we slept in a different bed. We rotated down a row and back up the next row. Neither the beds nor the thin blankets provided a barrier from the mice that nibbled at our toes

some nights when the room became dark and
quiet.

No one cared that I had a past, that I was
once a daughter or a sister, or a granddaughter or a
niece or a cousin. My dad, my mom, my brother,
my home, my family, my belongings, and my
former life were gone. And so was I. My losses
had mounted one on top of the other like layers of
an onion.

The orphanage is where I vanished and ceased
to exist. I lost my ability to fly to the ceiling to
escape from the pain that was with me every day of
my life. To survive the agony seared deeply into
every fiber of my being. I had to find a way to
forget.

The little human being who once had parents,
a home, and a brother I played with in the backyard
had been annihilated. For three years, I'd been
showered with hugs and kisses from a daddy who
adored me. I had my own bed, in my own bedroom.
I also had a mom and even though she wasn't good
to me, she was my mother.

This annihilation now defined me, the me who
could claim nothing as her own. I was so deeply
ashamed of being so unlovable and so unwanted.
The people who were supposed to protect me didn't
exist. The people who were supposed to love me
didn't exist. I was now imprisoned in a place where
I had no chance of ever being loved, and that
realization created a vast hole in my young soul that
I had no idea how to fill.

Sunday was visiting day. I had been in the
orphanage for four days, but the time seemed so
much longer. I got up early and put on a green
blouse I found hanging on the second row and
grabbed a tattered pair of orange shorts from one of

the dressers. Those dressers, which were in the center of the long room, separated the two rows of beds.

I couldn't find any shoes that fit me, and I had to hurry. I had to get outside and be ready when my mama or someone from my family came to see me. I gladly forfeited shoes for the greater cause, which was to hurry out the door and wait for my visitor. I didn't even take time to brush my tangled hair that hadn't seen a comb for days.

As all the other little girls headed to the cafeteria for breakfast, I raced for a position on the wall beside the gate. I wanted to locate the best vantage point for seeing each car as it drove in. The morning was warm so selecting the shorts and a sleeveless top had been a good choice.

I reached the wall and grimaced at how far away the top ledge was. How would I get up there? As I scanned the length of the wall futility began to fill my being.

But then I saw several random stones jutting out from the wall just ahead. They were probably decorative, but to me, they were obvious stepping stones. My feet were small enough that they easily fit on the "steps" and up I went, scaling that wall like a pro.

When I reached the top ledge, I stood up and I walked down a short distance so that I was closer to the iron gate which allowed more visibility to the street and the passing cars. I sat down to begin my wait, naively assuring myself I would not have long. I gazed down at my feet and wished I had found shoes to hide the dirt that covered them.

After a while, some of the other children joined me on the ledge, waiting for their own visitors. They chatted and laughed with each other, but I remained focused on each car that passed. Some of the cars slowed down, turned and entered the iron gate.

Inside the wall, I saw a boy stop playing ball, grin and run to one of the incoming cars as fast as his little legs would go, his gaze locked on the man and woman in the front seat. When the car parked the woman jumped out first, scooped him up and spun him around like a top. The boy giggled and giggled. I returned my focus to the street.

The bell that signaled time for all the children to stop playing and form a line in front of the cafeteria door for lunch rang. I remained on my perch. No way was I going to leave and miss my visitor. If I did, I'd have to wait a whole week for visitation day to come around again, and that sounded like a lifetime.

I was too anxious to see someone I knew, especially my mama. I dreamed of sitting beside her as she wrapped her arms around me and kissed the top of my head. Because I didn't want to miss that moment, I chose to not leave my post.

The sun reached high enough in the sky that the trees no longer provided shade, yet I refused to budge. I was thirsty and tired, but I still wouldn't climb down.

At some point in the afternoon, I heard a different bell ring out, I hadn't heard before. I learned that this was the signal for visitors to say their goodbyes, give their hugs and kisses and leave until next week. NO! I can't come down. My visitor hasn't come! NO! Stop! Don't lock the gate. Please--they aren't here yet!

Month after month I climbed that wall each Sunday waiting and longing to see a familiar face. I soon learned which children matched which car that came and went every week, as the children ran to greet their families. I'd try to imagine what it felt like to be held and loved, even if only for a few hours on a Sunday. Week after week, I climbed down off the wall and trudged back to my dorm to cry in the pillow of whatever bed I was assigned to that night. Finally, I accepted the futility of my vigil and stopped, never to return to the wall again.

My life in the orphanage consisted of profound feelings of abandonment. I had no interest in anything. I made no friends. I spoke only when spoken to by a teacher or staff member. When I did speak, the words didn't come out right. I stuttered and was ridiculed by the other children.

I already wet the bed every night, and now I stuttered. In the beginning, the matron had been patient with my wet sheets each morning, I suppose because she thought the problem would pass, once I settled in. Of course, it didn't, and she soon lost patience with my soiled bedding.

My punishment was to wash the linens each morning before school in the bathroom shower, wring them out as best I could, and hang them outside for all the other kids to see. We all knew what sheets hanging on the line outside the dorms meant. I wasn't the only child who wet the bed. How ludicrous for the staff to think shaming us would be the cure for a behavior we had no control over in the first place. What child *chooses* to wet the bed?

Late one night, I was tossing and turning, trying to fall asleep. Most of the other girls in the dorm had already fallen asleep. Hearing an unfamiliar sound, I slipped out of bed and noiselessly scurried to the far end of the dorm to crouch among the coats that hung on the wall.

I stilled my breathing and listened. Maybe I imagined the sound. When I heard boys whispering, I knew they must have entered the dorm when the matron shut her door to watch T.V.

I flattened myself against the wall and held my breath. But someone saw me, grabbed my arm and pulled me from my hiding place. I looked up to see the boy who'd helped carry my boxes the day I arrived.

He tried to kiss me. I turned my head away from him. I was frightened, but my legs wouldn't let me run. I stood motionless while he touched me in a way that had become all too familiar, by then.

I didn't hear anyone walk up, but, a teenage girl suddenly appeared in the gloom. She seized the boy by the shoulder and spun him around. Pushing him away from me, she told him he better never come to our dorm again or she'd report him. I scanned the darkened room, wondering if the other boys were still there. Though I saw no one, the sound of them running away brought instant relief.

For a split second, I thought the person who rescued me must not be real. She had appeared out of nowhere, like an angel. Maybe she WAS an angel.

The boy slunk away, and she pulled me into her arms. Her name was Helen, and as I felt her warmth, I knew she was real. For the first time since my father died seven or eight years earlier, I felt safe and melted into her comfort for several minutes. She tenderly stroked my hair, and we both cried.

Helen worked in the kitchen on weekends, which was the only time all the children dined together. From the kitchen serving window, she saw the older kids push me to the back of the line, which meant the food pans would be empty by the time I made it to them. Sometimes, a child from my dorm would offer me some of her food, other times, I just went outside with an empty tummy.

At the end of meal time, if I was still in the cafeteria, Helen would motion me to come around the building to the back door, where she'd give me a big glass of iced cold milk straight from the huge, stainless steel vats in the kitchen. Sneaking food to me was a big deal because we both knew rule-breakers got into trouble if caught.

I wasn't the only child she helped. Several of the other smaller girls were pushed back in the lines as well. The children who couldn't stand up to the older kids often had nothing to eat for that meal.

Helen also seemed to appear just in the nick of time to protect me from the bullies in the orphanage. She always seemed to know when I needed her, and I'm grateful she did. I don't remember the day, but suddenly she was gone, and I didn't get to say goodbye. She walked out of my life as quickly as she walked into it. I never saw her again, but I will never forget her.

We all had chores at the orphanage. Some worked in the kitchen with Helen. Some wiped down the dining hall tables and chairs. Some cleaned the bathrooms and some worked on the grounds.

My chore was to work in the laundry along with several other little girls. I put clothes in the washer, then the dryer, and then I folded them. When I grew older and bigger, I did the ironing, too.

The laundry room was in the basement of the big building I first entered upon my arrival at the orphanage. The room was filled with several huge washing machines and several even larger dryers. Four ironing boards were set up in a row, and two long tables for folding sat in front of the dryers.

Even though I was only nine or ten-years-old, I enjoyed doing the laundry. The work gave me purpose and helped keep my mind from wandering back to the family who'd abandoned me. To this day, I still find a small amount of internal purpose in ironing and folding clothes.

As time marched on, I longed more and more for a connection with someone, anyone who would love me, or at the very least "see" me. I had never forgotten my neighborhood playmate who told me she was going to church to learn about Jesus. Desperate for love, that night in the darkness, I decided to reach out to Him.

I told Him that everyone in my life had left me, and I wondered if He could love an ugly, unwanted child such as ME. The bed I was in on that particular night was not positioned near one of the many windows in the dorm, so I quietly walked to the closest window. I had seen a picture on the wall of the large house when I first arrived of a little girl and a little boy in their pajamas, kneeling by their beds with their heads bowed and hands clasped.

I assumed that same posture at the window and looked outside. The first thing I saw was the sparkle of the glistening moon on a small shovel. A forgotten book lay on a bench, most likely left by a child who'd taken it outside earlier that day. I thought about the punishment that child would receive if the book was found by a matron.

That thought brought me back to the reason I was at the window, to find the Man who loved little children. I looked up at the sky and said, "Jesus, can I come to Heaven to live with you?"

I knelt there for some time, trying to find words to say to Him. Of course, I now know He understood the innocent mutterings of a child who was lost, with no voice and no hope. I closed my simple prayer by asking, "Jesus, can you love me?"

A new feeling washed over me as I arose. For the first time in my short life, I felt peace. I couldn't understand it then, but when I crawled into my bed, I immediately fell into a restful sleep.

I wanted to experience that feeling again, so kneeling at a window became a nighttime habit I looked forward to every day. Jesus gifted me with a ritual that brought me comfort, and He was about to give me another one.

My trunk arrived shortly after I talked to Jesus that first night. Children don't really understand time, and I was no different. In fact, I was probably worse than most at comprehending the passing of time. My life was becoming more and more a blur to me. Living with the pain of being tossed away like I was nothing was difficult. Without my trunk, I doubt I would have noticed when day turned to night.

When all the other girls fell asleep, I'd get up to talk to Jesus and to open my trunk, which was too big and too heavy to lift. The matron must have moved it to the foot of the next bed for me each day because each night it was always right where it was supposed to be.

The outside of the trunk was smooth, made of dark-brown leather stretched over a thin layer of wood. Rows of gold buttons attached the leather to the wood. The handle was scalloped with narrow, alternating gold and silver bars. A heavy silver lock on the front prevented others from peeking inside while I was away. I was the only one who had the key.

Each time I opened the lid, the first thing I always noticed was how the contents sparkled in the moonlight. The interior sides and top were lined with a soft shiny fabric that was white with pink flowers.

The trunk was filled with the most beautiful jewelry, necklaces, rings, bracelets and more. I knew each piece by heart. I would painstakingly take the rings out one by one and gently line them on the floor.

Some rings had large stones. My biggest ring had a green stone. The gold leaves molded up the sides, formed prongs held the huge stone securely in place. Lights from outside coming in through the uncovered windows would flash off the facets, and the stones would sparkle in the dark. The effect was magical.

I would put the rings on my small fingers and admire their beauty. I'd also choose a different favorite each night and imagine which one my mom would choose for herself, then which ones my aunts would pick. I knew my grandma would select the blue one because it matched her eyes, which were blue, just like my daddy's and my brother's eyes.

The bracelets were next. I'd carefully put the rings back in their places inside the trunk and set the bracelets on the cement floor. One by one, I slipped them onto my wrist.

One bracelet had pearls strung on a gold chain. I liked the bracelets with sparkly stones that glistened in the moonlight the best. Sometimes, I arranged them on my arm all at once. They covered my forearm like a sleeve.

I wanted my mom to have the bracelet with the diamonds, which happened to be her birthstone. It looked just like the one Daddy gave to her and she'd lost after he died. She'd love that one the most, and she'd love me for replacing it for her.

My mom wore long dangly earrings. I loved to watch them sway back and forth when she turned her head. She had a lot of jewelry that I assume was given to her by my daddy. But, those pieces were either stolen by the men she brought home, or she pawned them to pay for her nights at the bar.

I hadn't seen my mother in so long that I almost forgot what she looked like. But when I gazed at the jewelry in my trunk, I could almost see her face again. It was serene and lovely, no longer filled with rage.

I imagined how she would enjoy my trunk full of jewelry when she finally came to see me. I couldn't wait to show her. I envisioned us sitting on the beige carpet of our living room floor, dumping out all the jewels and trying them on. I could see us experimenting with different combinations of necklaces, earrings, and bracelets and modeling them for each other. We would lie on the floor and laugh and laugh. And she would take me in her arms and hold me tight.

I was very protective of my trunk and its contents. I couldn't let anything happen to it. I was saving it for the day someone in my family came to visit, and I would give them the trunk full of precious jewels. When I handed them all these beautiful things, they would want me, and take me home with them. I would finally be loved.

After putting each piece back inside, I'd very quietly close the trunk and lock it securely. Then I'd climb into my bed for the night and think about the day someone from my family would wear the bracelet with the different-shaped charms hanging from it. Or the silver earrings that would sway when they walked. Or the pink-and-gold ring. I'd drift off to sleep, excited for that day to come.

~~*Shari*~~

Our minds are incredible, unique masterpieces capable of so much more than we can comprehend. They compensate for the pain, hurt and devastation we endure in life. Our hearts can crack wide open in response to the wreckage we see, hear about or experience firsthand. Yet, our minds are right there to put some form of protection in place to save us from succumbing to the devastation.

Such "protection" might come in the form of alcohol that numbs our souls, so we don't feel the crushing pain. Narcissism, a mental health disorder that keeps people so self-absorbed and locked in their own arrogance that they don't deal with their own pain or acknowledge anyone else's, is another protection approach. Another might be building a wildly successful career that requires 75-hour workweeks that "protect" a person from the challenges and obligations of emotionally close relationships.

Our minds develop coping strategies to keep

people at a distance, such as defensiveness, refusing to shower, putting on weight, and ambivalence in relationships. Our subconscious creates these coping strategies behind the scenes, without our awareness. It doesn't ask us for permission, it just scrambles to come up with ways to protect our hearts from feeling pain--pain from the past or pain we fear might be headed our way.

A 13-year-old client who stayed for over a year in a treatment facility where I worked had been abandoned as an infant and placed in a barbaric foster home. She suffered years of extreme abuse before she was finally adopted into a loving family. Yet, even though she was loved dearly by her new family, all the love in the world could not erase the abuse she endured in her preverbal years.

After being adopted, she soon became unmanageable and was sent to treatment, while her well-meaning adoptive family took classes to learn how to raise such a troubled little girl. As we worked with her, we discovered she'd woven together a beautifully elaborate fantasy about being born to a king who had arranged her marriage to a prince in a neighboring country. The arrangement was made when both my client and the young prince were very young and was to be executed when they turned 18.

This story was told with such intricate detail that it became difficult not to believe her. She said she'd fallen in love with this boy and reveled in her engagement to him, but then Social Services stepped in and tore her from him and her family. She additionally fabricated a story about why she was torn from her birth family and birth country.

The details of her story were so real and she talked with such conviction that the other youth in the facility soon believed her story. She described the color of the prince's eyes, the 350 green jewels hand sewn onto her wedding dress by her father's seamstress and the details of the home she and her betrothed would live happily ever after in. The tale she spun was so much a part of her everyday language that even some of the counselors started to believe it. She'd cry herself to sleep at night, lamenting her lost love.

In truth, some days when I listened to her, I'd think, "Who knows, maybe her father really is a king and the records we received from Social Services are wrong."

Of course, the records were correct. But her mind, in all its creative glory, developed such a convincing story to protect her from the painful reality of her past that we all wanted to believe it for her, too. Her imagined history was heartbreaking; yet, I marveled at the resourcefulness of her mind to create an amazing fantasy to mask the horror that lay lurking in the recesses of her memory.

In the case of my mother, her brilliant little eight-year-old mind jumped into action soon after she was placed in the orphanage. The frequent and persistent losses in her young life were too excruciating for a child to bear, even before she was abandoned. When she found herself "trapped" in an institutional setting, she didn't know how to deal with the unrelenting hopelessness of her childhood.

To deal with her heartbreak, her mind made up the jewel-filled treasure chest. She created this elaborate fantasy so she could still believe in and touch beauty in a world of dark despair. Her ability to create what was so lacking in her life crushes and astounds me at the same time.

I'm awed that a little girl who lost

everything and whose life had become so bleak could design such loveliness, even if only in her mind. When she prayed to Jesus, He answered by helping her desperate mind create "tangible" reminders that beauty still existed in the world, and she was an extension of that beauty.

I remember the night my mother's counselor helped her uncover the truth about her treasure chest. When Mom returned from therapy, her face was ashen and she was obviously upset. She walked over to her favorite chair in the living room, sat down, put her face in her hands and sobbed. Her tears lasted for days.

I didn't know why at the time, but later I learned that she'd just discovered her treasure chest had, in fact, been a creative coping strategy. My mom was lost for several days after learning that her trunk wasn't real. She walked around the house, able to function, but she was detached, void of any emotions. She always took care of my dad, my sister and me. She packed our lunches and cleaned the house. Like always, supper was on time, but she had a robotic look about her.

The treasure chest had been so closely tied to her identity and value. Coming to terms with the fact it wasn't real was devastating for Mom. She had to embrace the truth she'd been utterly alone, with no personal belongings or gifts to offer to anyone who might visit her. She truly had no one to love her and no belongings to call her own. The trunk symbolized her worth to the outside world and served as her last hope of leaving the orphanage.

When she learned as an adult that the trunk, her lifeline, had been a mere mirage, my mom felt adrift. She was sad and she was angry, unprepared to believe she had intrinsic value, even without her treasure chest. She hadn't yet learned she had significance, all by herself, with or without jewels. She couldn't fathom herself being worthy of love and adoration. Eventually, she stepped into the reality that she is lovable, but it was a long journey to get there.

Even today, she gets a little lost when she talks about the trunk. Her face lights up and she can still recount with clarity how the jewels felt, how they shined in the light, and which ones were her favorite.

Some may ask, "Why not allow her to keep the fantasy?" Total and complete healing comes when a person can look at the truth of his or her life, acknowledge it, own it--and move forward from it. Until this happens, we aren't whole, and we can't become our true selves.

Mom had to embrace the enormity of her loss, treasure chest and all, and grieve it. She HAD to mourn, and she HAD to become angry. When she was finally able to do so, she was able to own her story and celebrate her strength.

My mother's experience is an example of how crushing reality can be when a painful situation is truly understood. Our minds compensate for heart-wrenching events in our lives and create fantasies, lies and other mechanisms that help protect us. Part of healing is learning how our minds serve as our protectors. We must discover the elaborate schemes they create to guard us against truth so terrible we strive to forget it.

Healing comes when we acknowledge what we have devised to avoid the truth. Facing reality is hard to do, but our ever-fascinating minds are always at work, waiting for us to embrace who we really are. When we do the work of discerning our coping mechanisms, our minds are ready and waiting to create healthier strategies to replace the old ones.

I was 35-years-old and no longer a child but couldn't wait for Christmas. I was more excited for Christmas that year than any previous holiday. I had purchased several gifts for my mom, but the one I was most excited about was a ten-dollar little wooden treasure chest I'd found at a local department store.

Filled with Dollar Store fake pearls, diamonds, necklaces and rings, the chest was my way of saying, "I understand, Mom."

I recognized what the trunk of jewels she fabricated really stood for. I wanted her to know I was in awe of how her little mind created it as a way to survive unimaginable losses. By imagining the big, gold ring, she remembered and honored her earliest loss, her father. By envisioning the long earrings her mother used to wear, she could hold on to the image of what she looked like.

The original trunk was her mind's way of devising something beautiful and capturing hopefulness in the midst of deep darkness and despair. Filled with noble gifts, it held priceless offerings for her family members, who might finally show up to visit her.

The sparkle and loveliness found in that chest was her mind's way of enabling her survival. I'm so grateful for the hope it gave her to go on and to not give into her discouragement. The little trunk I gave her for Christmas now rests at the foot of her bed, reminding her each day how far she's come in realizing her worth.

Mom still loves jewelry. The jewelry she buys is not expensive, but she has accumulated quite a collection over the years. When I receive a tax return, I usually start planning a trip. When Mom gets a refund, she buys jewelry.

Sometimes when I visit her, I walk into her closet to look at her massive jewelry case. Each ring and necklace is on its own hook, all recently polished and displayed proudly, as if in a museum exhibit.

Each Christmas, Mom gives me and my sister stunning jewelry. After we unwrap the necklaces or rings or whatever she's chosen for us that year, she tells us all about the pieces. We learn the origins of the stones, the carat sizes, how the gems were first unearthed centuries ago, the metals used, and the proper way to care for the items. I cry a little inside because I see the bigger meaning. I have a deep admiration for my mom's mind, as well as those of my clients. For it was their minds that frantically created strategies, fantasies, and other ways to cope that ultimately provided them with a reason to live.

~~*Jann*~~

I dreaded going to school because of the bullying. Today, kids picking on other kids is called bullying, but back then it was just kids being kids. Whatever the behavior was called, it was cruel.

We orphans attended an elite public school, located in the middle of a wealthy neighborhood. One's imagination doesn't have to stretch far to understand the dynamics that occur when poor children are intermingled with affluent children. The contrast was sharp and vivid.

They wore perfectly matched clothes. We wore tattered hand-me-downs. Their curls were shiny and clean. Our hair was dirty and matted. They ate tasty, nutritious lunches. We ate government-issued meals that looked unappetizing and tasted bland.

Recess was the worst, not just for me, but for all the orphaned kids. We were mocked, teased, spit upon, and blamed for things we didn't do.

Being with children who got to go home to their families or who were involved in sports or some other activity after school was brutal for those of us who had none of those things.

I was a loner who stayed away from the kids on the playground as much as I could. I also ate lunch by myself. I didn't mind being alone, because no one could hurt me then. I hated the ridicule more than anything. The kids could be relentless. And my humiliation ran deep.

When I was asked where my parents were, I was too ashamed and too afraid of what they'd do with the truth. So, I told them my mother was on a trip for her work, and I was just staying at the orphanage until she could come get me. Even as I said it, I feared no one ever would. And deep down, I knew the least likely person to rescue me was my mother.

After school, we returned to the orphanage, usually to face punishment. If we'd gotten into any kind of trouble at school, the dorm matrons and masters heard about it from the teachers. Our punishment for doing bad things at school, even when we didn't actually do them, was to line up in front of the matron's bedroom and wait our turn to be hit with a wooden paddle.

That was one line I hurried to get to the front of. I just wanted to get the paddling over with. We weren't asked if we did the supposed offense or to explain our side of the situation. Instead, we were labeled and found guilty, and punishment was carried out without so much as a word being spoken. I didn't care about being hit. In fact, I didn't even feel the blows.

The need to guide and instruct us regarding right from wrong was not part of the orphanage curriculum. In the administration's eyes, we were ALL bad. None of us could be taught anything. We were disciplined with the paddle or a belt, but not for the purpose of correction. We were given what we supposedly deserved for being worthless.

From an early age, I had an overwhelming desire to be good. I *wanted* to know right from wrong. I wanted to learn how to become someone others would look up to rather than down upon. I made a conscious choice while still a young child, that I was not going to be a sloppy drunk like my mother or be mean like she was.

This choice brought with it a need in me to admonish myself as if unwarranted punishment from the adults was not enough. Nonetheless, if I said something unkind, I washed my own mouth out with soap until I gagged. If I did something I felt I shouldn't have done, I apologized to Jesus. If I did something really bad, like not sweeping under every single bed when I was told to, I wouldn't allow myself to open my trunk that night.

Although I had never attended church Jesus and I became very good friends. I wanted Him to be pleased with me. I sensed that a thirst for something greater in my life was developing and that made me very proud. I didn't know who I was, but I knew I wanted to be MORE.

I developed a strong moral compass, a sense of right from wrong, deep within my brokenness. I committed to myself and to Jesus to walk a path of decency and love. I knew I wanted to be able to hold my head high when I was an adult because I couldn't as a child. I was determined to absolve myself of the judgment, labels, and humiliation I lived with day in and day out as an orphan.

One of my teachers must have sensed the

emptiness and loneliness of the shy, little girl in the middle row. I never spoke a word to anyone and I rarely looked up to make eye contact. When the bell rang for recess one day, she dismissed the class but instructed me to remain behind.

The kids snickered as they passed by me to go play. I knew I was in trouble, but as usual, I had no idea what I'd done wrong. When all the children were gone, she asked me to come up to her desk.

Each step I took was painstakingly slow and deliberate. With my head down, I used the legs of the desks to guide my way to the front. When I reached her, she asked me to open her drawer and take out the package of candy that lay at the front. I did as she instructed and handed it to her.

She then told me the package had two pieces in it and that she couldn't possibly eat both. Would I help her out by eating the other one?

That was the first piece of candy I'd ever eaten. I ate it with such voracious enthusiasm that I almost choked on the creamy chocolate melting in my mouth. I stood by her, attentively listening as she spoke softly to me. I didn't know what she was saying. All I could take in was the kindness she showed to me at a miserable time and in a miserable place in my life.

My orphanage existence was the same every day. Nothing ever changed there. We had nothing to look forward to, no fun, no exciting experiences, no parks, no movies, no trips to Disneyland, no holidays. Neither Christmas nor birthdays were celebrated unless a child had the joy of spending them with his or her family before being returned to the "home".

I always wondered if it was worse to not celebrate at all or to leave and then be returned to the orphanage's lonely existence. Neither one seemed a good option. Both left a child feeling unwanted and unloved. I never wondered about the future, I never hoped or dreamed of a better life. I lived out each day as it came and accepted the fact that I had long since been forgotten.

When I was in the eighth grade, I was selected for a part in a play called "The Lottery." Cast as one of the townspeople, I had only a small part with one line. My character stood near the front, slightly to the right of center stage during the "stoning" scene.

We were more than halfway through the play when I heard a voice from my past coming from somewhere up the dark aisle. My heart lurched into my bone-dry throat. Years had passed since I'd heard that voice, yet I recognized it. My mother! I immediately turned to her, but the stage lights obscured my ability to see into the audience.

"That's my baaaaaby!" she cried.

At the sound of her slurred words, rising up louder than the speech being recited on stage--I became a little girl again. The searing humiliation was far greater than my desire to see my mother. In a panic, I abandoned the stage. I ran as fast as I could backstage to the stairway and to the bus that would take us to the orphanage once the play had ended.

I had to get away from that haunting voice. To this day, I have no idea how she knew I was in a play or that I was at the school that evening. Asking my teachers or the orphanage staff how she knew would have only made the humiliation real, so I didn't ask. I wanted to pretend it hadn't happened.

The next day, the drama teacher asked if the voice at the play was my mother or someone from my family. I was the one who ran off stage, so it was obvious the person knew me. I didn't answer her, but my downcast eyes spoke for me.

When I became a teenager, I moved from the dorm into the large house with the foyer and the shiny wood floors. The second floor had four bedrooms and each room accommodated two girls. Helen had lived in one of the rooms when she was a teen and worked in the kitchen. She had long since moved from the orphanage, but I could almost feel her presence.

Once in a while, I'd remember the night she saved me from the boy who grabbed me as I hunkered down behind the coats. I was so little then, and now I was a young lady. Unfortunately, I still felt as small and vulnerable as I did back then.

One day, I was sitting doing homework at my small desk in my new bedroom when I heard someone calling my name from the office below. She added, "Come downstairs, you have a visitor." Without responding, I jumped from the chair I was sitting in and ran down the winding staircase.

At sixteen, I'd never had a visitor, so I hurried as fast as I could. When I got to the main room I could see the back of a lady with short black hair. She was immaculately dressed in dark blue slacks and a cream silk blouse with a paisley print scarf around her shoulders. I could tell the woman wasn't my mother, but somehow, she looked familiar.

She turned to face me when she heard me enter the foyer and I immediately recognized her as one of my mother's sisters. Like my mother, she was a stunningly beautiful woman. She smiled and said she was taking me out of the orphanage to live with my grandmother.

My first thought was that I'd get to see my brother again.

She told me to run upstairs to grab my things. I did as I was told but realized when I reached the top landing that I had nothing that belonged to me. My trunk had gone missing. I thought about it often, but I didn't ask where it was. It was just another loss that I accepted but didn't question. After saying goodbye to the only girl I passed in the hallway, I bounded back down the stairs.

All the other girls were out, but I was certainly not going to take time to locate them. I was too afraid my aunt would change her mind. The girls wouldn't miss me anyway.

I hopped into her car with only the clothes on my back. It was a mild day, so I didn't bother to grab a sweater. I couldn't help but remember how different leaving felt than when I arrived with boxes of items I'd once called "mine". I quickly erased the horrible memory of losing everything.

My aunt set her purse on the empty backseat and situated herself behind the wheel. I held my breath, trying to calm my pounding heart. I was so ecstatic at the thought of seeing my brother again and tried to imagine what he must look like.

I was certain he must be six-feet tall by now, and handsome, with kind blue eyes. I pictured him running to me as I got out of the car. He would plant a big kiss on my cheek. I was sure of it.

I must have been daydreaming for some time because my aunt had apparently called my name three times before I heard her.

"Do you remember your grandmother's house?" she asked.

"No, I don't," I responded

She started describing it to me.

I stared at her in disbelief, my mind silently protesting. *Wait, that's not the grandmother who took my brother. I hardly know this one. I want to be with my brother! Please don't separate us again!*

We were headed to my maternal grandmother's house, where I would live for an undetermined amount of time. I would attend the same high school my mother attended, and I would start the next day. I could hear my aunt's words, but my head was spinning. Finally, she stopped talking and we rode in silence the rest of the way.

The first thing I noticed about my grandmother's tiny house was that it was surrounded by a large green lawn. A small lady of Native American descent, she had dark, piercing eyes, an olive complexion and, short black hair that framed her face. Her dark hair accentuated the deep wrinkles that trailed down the strong features of her face like miniature rivers. She had only a few strands of gray hair, which seemed odd for her age.

As I stepped out of the car, she studied me through silver-rimmed glasses, like a hawk examining its prey. She wasted no time informing me that the only reason she took me in was for the money the state would pay her. If I didn't follow her rules, she'd send me back to the orphanage. Oh, and she needed me to take care of her because she suffered from terminal cancer.

By now, I was used to hearing threats about what was going to happen to me if I didn't comply. However, I have to admit that the thought of being sent back to the orphanage sent cold chills surging up my spine. I do believe I actually shivered despite the warmth.

Her threat was still rolling around in my head when I paused and repeated her words silently to myself. Terminal cancer. Did she just say I'm supposed to take care of her? I don't even know her, and I sure don't know anything about caring for someone with terminal cancer.

Rage rose in my soul. No one could take the time to visit me while I was in the orphanage, alone and scared. But when the family needed someone to care for their dying mother, so their lives would remain unencumbered, they wasted no time in coming to get me.

My feelings confused me. I was furious because I had to care for my grandmother. I was also relieved to be out of the orphanage. I had no one to help me make sense of either feeling, so I stuffed them both. By this time in my life, I'd become quite adept at holding my emotions below the surface. The repercussions of displaying any feeling other than complacency were too great.

My grandmother lived in a one-bedroom house in a lower income neighborhood, where all the tiny houses nestled close to each other in rows. The kitchen and living room were one big room, and the dining table sat against the wall, halfway into the kitchen and halfway into the living room, with a chair at either end.

She was a woman of few words, which was fine with me. I was too lost to have any interest in talking with anyone, especially her. I quickly discovered she'd made enemies of all the surrounding neighbors. She was known as the "wicked witch lady," probably because she ran out of the house with a broom in her hands to chase children out of her yard. The children who'd already experienced my grandmother's wrath knew to stay off her lawn at all cost. Or she'd come flying out, screen door slamming behind her, waving a broom at them and yelling, "Move along! Don't dilly dally! Stay off my lawn!" They soon learned their boundaries.

Neighbors were accustomed to seeing all her blinds shut tightly, except for the slat she lifted just enough to keep her eye on neighborhood activities. They also kept a close eye on her, fearing her next outburst. I watched this ritual of hers play out day after day and wondered why my grandmother displayed such odd behavior.

One day a ball landed on the grass just beyond her mimosa tree. My grandmother ran out of her front door, snatched up the ball with her gnarled fingers and threw it into her garbage bin. While I lived with her, she amassed quite a collection of dolls, airplanes, a jump rope, numerous balls of assorted colors and sizes, and even a tricycle left at the edge of her curb. She kept the old garbage bin in a corner of her garage like some kind of trophy collection. The parents never confronted my grandmother or tried to retrieve the confiscated toys. I'm certain a few run-ins with her convinced them that replacing the toy was cheaper, in the long run.

Cats and dogs were chased off her property, as well. If she could have caught them, I cringe to think what she would have done to them. Whenever a BLACK cat crossed in front of her house, whether on the street or on her lawn, she'd pace back and forth inside the house, mumbling words I couldn't make out. She'd then refrain from going outside again until she convinced her tangled mind that the bad luck the oblivious black cat had somehow scattered in its wake had dissipated.

My grandmother surprised me one Saturday morning when she exclaimed, "Get dressed. We're going to see your mother!" Without a word, I threw on my clothes and hopped in her car. It had been a long time since I'd seen my mother and my emotions ranged from fear to excitement. We parked in front of a large run-down apartment complex. We walked up a flight of stairs and knocked. A huge man opened the door, and cigarette smoke billowed into my face from the apartment. Through the opened door I caught a glimpse of my mother sitting at the kitchen table. I stepped inside and silently stood just behind my grandmother. I began to tremble. I wasn't sure what was expected of me.

After a few seconds, my mother invited us into the kitchen where my grandmother immediately sat down. There wasn't a chair for me, so I quietly stood off to one side. I believe my mother spoke to me, but I was lost in my thoughts.

I wondered who the huge man was who'd opened the door, and I wondered why my mother's hands were shaking. I wondered if I should swat the cockroach crawling on the dirty plate in the sink, and about the swollen cut on my mother's cheek. I also wondered if she loved her mother who was sitting across from her, and what I could do to make her love me.

My grandmother was a very cold harsh woman. I tried to understand what made her so mean. Had she experienced a horrible life or was it just my presence that made her that way? She rarely spoke to me, never touched me, unless it was to slap me across the face for asking a question she didn't want to answer.

I wasn't allowed to bring friends from

school to my grandmother's house, not that anyone would WANT to be around her. I was not allowed to date, even though I was sixteen-years-old. I walked the halls of my mother's former high school and imagined her there. In a state of numbness, I attended my classes and hurried straight back to my grandmother's afterward.

My chores included hand-watering her massive front lawn and beautiful flower garden in the backyard every other evening, a chore I hate to this day. I'm satisfied to have silk flowers in my home. Every Saturday, I washed our clothes and linens on a washboard in a large tub and hung them to dry on the clothesline in the backyard. She didn't own a washer or a dryer and saw no need for such extravagances.

Twice a year, we loaded our blankets and bedspreads onto an old wagon, which probably once belonged to some unfortunate child who happened to leave it in front of her house. We marched in single file, my grandmother was ahead and I followed some distance behind her pulling the wagon loaded down with laundry. We traveled three blocks before arriving at the laundromat to use the machines.

Every Sunday, we went to church. Even though I had become close to Jesus during my time in the orphanage, I was not too fond of the God I learned about in this church. He was overbearing and threatening. No matter what we did for Him, we always fell short of what He expected of us.

We were moral failures and, being such, we were obligated to go before the congregation, name our transgression(s) and publicly ask for forgiveness. I had a difficult time reconciling what this God supposedly expected from us with the man named Jesus whose unconditional love felt so beautiful.

Hearing about hellfire and damnation every Sunday certainly gave me pause, but I held on to what I believed to be true about Jesus and His love for me because I had experienced it. I knew He loved me. I could feel Him in my heart. I also believed He loved women, which was in stark contrast to the teachings of that church.

Women were to be silent, other than to teach small children. We could not teach or preach to men, nor could a female say a prayer in the church. Why didn't God want us to pray? I wondered. Why was it wrong for women to speak up in class?

If we had a question, we were required to ask a man to present it to the teacher or the preacher. For women to be considered beneath men seemed ludicrous to me, but I kept my thoughts to myself. Many years passed before I learned that the God they presented wasn't who God really is. Men *and* women can embrace, honor, and worship Him, as the Bible says, "in spirit and in truth."

My grandmother never missed a church service, and she worked on her Bible lessons every night. She quoted scripture to me to back up her form of discipline. Her favorite Biblical quote was "spare the rod and spoil the child." My grandmother was too frail from her illness to beat me. If she was angry with me, she ignored me. She didn't speak to me, she didn't acknowledge my existence, and because of my desire to connect with someone, it tormented me. She never once spoke to me of God's unconditional love for us, only of His stern form of discipline which was to be cast into hell.

I began menstruating at a very young age.

In the orphanage, supplies were furnished. However, this was not the case at my grandmother's house. I was expected to use rags, wash them and reuse them.

When it was that time of the month at her house, I was not allowed to eat any meals with her, because I was "contaminated". I wasn't allowed to purchase products needed for such times because store employees would know I was now "bad". My grandmother clearly loathed being female and she loathed me because I was. I wished I could deny my gender, and often wondered why God created us if He hated us so much.

As my body developed, disguising my physique became more and more difficult. I didn't wear a bra, and I was afraid to ask for one. The girls in the locker room all wore bras. I was envious of them because they were covered by their underclothes.

My PE teacher finally sent a note to my grandmother. She felt I was not adequately covered in the locker room and suggested I be fitted for appropriate undergarments. My grandmother said that wearing a bra for all the boys to see beneath my outer clothing was advertising that I was a wanton slut. Needless to say, she did not purchase bras for me.

I always followed her rules without question, so while my fellow classmates carried themselves with confidence and seemed to embrace their budding femininity, I tried to hide mine. I attended school during the dresses-only era. The boys wore slacks, no jeans. I imagined my girlfriends as they dressed for school each morning, picking out their poodle skirts and matching sweaters, under which they wore their bra. I wore tee shirts beneath mine.

One night after my bath, I looked in the mirror at my unclothed, developing body and hated what I saw. My body was evil, and I felt such disgust and shame. From that day forward, I never looked at myself unless I was clothed. I never touched my skin when I was unclothed without a washcloth in my hand. I hated being female. I was born a girl, and that meant I was bad.

My grandmother suffered bouts of pain from her cancer. During those episodes, I'd sit on the edge of her bed and talk to her about the beautiful buds blooming in the backyard garden. To ease her nausea, I'd place a cool cloth on her forehead. I remained at her side until her pain subsided and she fell asleep.

I didn't form friendships at school, and I was unbearably lonely, as well as scared to death of this woman I didn't know. During my first year at my grandmother's house, I experienced the only Christmas I remember celebrating since Daddy died. We went out late on the afternoon of Christmas Eve to pick up a Christmas tree because we could get it free. I watched as she decorated the tree with one short string of lights and a few chipped ornaments.

Later that night, family members filled her small house. I was overwhelmed to see such a large family gathered in one place. Moms, dads, brothers, and sisters together for a party. The only missing relatives were my mother and my brother. I felt so awkward around those people, and I wondered if they knew about my abuses and my stay in the orphanage.

I decided I hated Christmas. Holidays were rooted in family, and I didn't have one. They were just another way to remind me I was unwanted and unloved.

One day after school, I came home to find my grandmother sitting in her favorite overstuffed chair in the living room. As I cautiously opened the door, never really knowing what mood I'd find her in, she jumped up and ran into the bathroom. I called after her, not understanding why she'd gotten up so abruptly, and asked if she was all right. But she didn't answer.

I tiptoed to the bathroom. The door was open. I could see in, but I kept my distance and continued calling her name "Grandma! Grandma!"

I peeked in, trying to see where she was and if she was okay. Then, out of the corner of my eye, I saw something odd. Through the gap between the opened door edge and the door frame, one large eye was staring back at me, a full halo of white surrounding her dark-brown iris.

I gasped and jumped backward so fast I bumped into a bench in the narrow hallway. I finally found my voice and asked why she ran from me. She didn't answer.

After a moment or two, I gave up and walked away. Some time passed before she finally came out. I never learned why she behaved so strangely that day.

Her odd behaviors became more and more commonplace. During the first thunderstorm, after I arrived, I was startled awake, not by a loud clap of thunder, but by her yanking the sleeve of my pajamas. She demanded that I get out of bed and follow her into the tiny hallway.

After closing the doors on each end of the hallway, she turned off the light and sat down on the bench, while I found my place on the floor. We stayed in the dark, stuffy hallway, hoping that we would not be struck by lightning. Storms in the deep south were commonplace. Sitting in that hallway and praying until the storm calmed became another hated ritual.

My grandmother bought a new hat for Easter. It was pink with little pink roses around the brim and matched the pink-and-white striped dress one of her daughters made for her. The cheery pastel colors she wore didn't make her look any less scary to me than her typical black dress and black hat. I wore a hand-me-down dress.

Like every other Sunday, we headed for church. I entered my Sunday school classroom and found a vacant chair next to my friend. I occasionally got together with her because she lived close to me. All of the girls in the class looked so pretty in their new outfits. Some wore gloves and two of them had on the cutest pillbox hats that matched their new spring dresses.

Then, I looked down at their feet. ALL of them wore stockings and heels. I wore the same loafers and socks I wore EVERY Sunday. This Easter Sunday was to be a coming-out party for all of us, the day we embraced our entrance into womanhood. We were young ladies now. They celebrated by putting away childish clothes for a more sophisticated look. I commemorated the occasion with shame.

I quickly sat down and tucked my feet as far under my chair as I could. I dreaded the ending of class when we would all file into the auditorium while proud parents looked on. My friends would appear before the congregation as the young ladies they'd become while I looked like I was trying to remain a little girl.

I loathed always being different. I longed to fit in with my friends. I longed to enjoy being a female like they did. But truth was, I wished I hadn't been born female. I actually wished I had not been born at all.

My grandmother eventually became bedridden. As cancer riddled her body, she lost control of her bodily functions. I made sure she was always clean and lying in a fresh bed. When she vomited blood, I held a container for her. I didn't love her, and I didn't feel loved BY her, but I did the best I knew how to make her final days as comfortable as possible.

About a week after my grandmother's confinement to bed, I was peering out the front door, watching a bird splash in the birdbath beneath a large tree, when a yellow taxi slowed down and stopped at the end of the sidewalk. The door opened and my mother stepped out.

I sucked in a breath. *Mama!* I hadn't seen her since going to her apartment about a year ago for a 30-minute visit. I opened the screen door to let her in. I was thrilled to see her, but I didn't know how to respond to this unexpected visit, so I just stood there holding the screen door open like a hotel doorman. She was sober, and a smile I'd rarely seen as a child, slowly spread across her face. We came together in an awkward embrace.

She stepped inside and sat a brown paper bag with handles beside the sofa. I could see it contained clothing and wondered if she was moving in. She went into my grandmother's bedroom and said, "I need a place to stay for the night." I decided her arrival at her mother's house probably had something to do with her very swollen black-and-purple face.

The awkwardness soon dissipated, and Mama and I were able to talk in a natural, easy way, like friends. We had a great time together, but I couldn't ignore the internal anxiety I was feeling at this odd reunion. I fought the unsettling emotions in favor of the joy of having her near me after so many years.

On a sunny day I shall never forget, after she'd been with us for three days, the two of us went to the grocery store, leaving my grandmother resting in her bed. We pulled out of the garage in Grandma's 1952 Chevrolet, cream with a green top and green stripe on each side. One block from her house, my mother asked me if I wanted to drive.

I had taken driver's education in school, but hadn't driven much, and had never been behind the wheel of my grandmother's car. I enthusiastically slid off the passenger seat and into the driver's seat in a matter of seconds and drove to the store with my mother giving me pointers. On our return trip, I pulled over in the same spot, where we'd earlier exchanged positions and did so again. Driving lessons from my mother was an unexpected moment of connection with her that remains safely tucked in my heart to this day.

Shortly after the driving lesson, I came home from school and told my mother I'd been asked on a date. My grandmother didn't allow me to date, so I knew I couldn't accept. But Mama felt differently about the situation. She told me to accept the invitation and she'd deal with her mother.

Well, the way she dealt with my date was to tell my grandmother I was going to my girlfriend's house. My grandmother let me go because it was my friend from church who lived up the street. I learned later that after an hour had passed, my grandmother told my mother to call me to come home. Mama kept making excuses, "I can't reach her. I'm getting a busy signal. We'll just have to wait until she comes home when we told her to." For the first time in my life, my mother had my back!

When I returned home that cold winter night, my grandmother was asleep in her bed. She turned off the living room heater at night to conserve utility charges. Because that was the only heater in her home, she had an electric blanket on her bed for warmth.

I slept on a roll-away bed in the corner of her bedroom. Before getting into bed on cold nights, I heated a brick on the gas stove in the kitchen, wrapped it in a towel and placed it at the foot of my bed. It provided warmth to me, but only until it cooled.

In the cold, dark living room, I could see my mother asleep on the couch. But she sat up when I closed the front door behind me and asked if I had fun. I told her all about the handsome boy with the bright blue eyes and the good time we'd had together.

When I told her his name was David Greenfield, she asked if he had a much older brother named Dan. When I said he did, she smirked and said she'd dated Dan at about the same age as I was now. I laughed with her, amazed that I'd formed the only bond I ever had with my mother. It was the greatest moment of my life! For once, someone was interested in knowing me and learning about my world. Even better, that person was my mother.

Two days later, I rushed home from school to tell her all about my day and about seeing David and what we talked about. But when I walked in, I immediately noticed her cigarettes weren't on the coffee table. I scanned the room, searching for her brown bag of clothes at the end of the sofa. It was gone.

I ran to the bathroom where she'd hung her bathrobe on the hook behind the door. Nothing. My grandmother's house contained no sign that my mother had ever even been there. She was gone from my life once more, leaving as quickly as she'd come.

I wouldn't see her again for years, but for a few special days, I had a mother, and I loved every minute with her. She was gone, but she took with her the secrets we'd shared and left me with a beautiful memory to hold forever in my heart. For a few short days, she stood between me and the harsh woman who was HER mother. For those few days, she was the mother I'd always wanted, and we were mother and daughter, enjoying life together.

Although I didn't encounter her again throughout my adolescence, I'd occasionally hear of her arrests due to drunken behavior and tavern brawls. I don't know how many nights she spent in jail over the years. Sadly, incarceration apparently did nothing to motivate her to change her way of life.

~~*Shari*~~

"It's a reason, not an excuse." I'm not sure how many times I've said those words in my counseling career. My mother's story is about how mental illness and addiction can manifest in people and be passed from one generation to the next. If my great-grandmother had been diagnosed, she would have been labeled with paranoid schizophrenia. As a therapist, I'd probably feel a great deal of empathy for her, if she hadn't been so mean to my mother.

Our genes hold information about our personalities, our physical traits, and our vulnerabilities. For example, a male relative from three-generations ago could have been diagnosed with bipolar disorder, a mental health condition where a person can experience extreme highs and lows. Let's say he then weds, and he and his wife have two children. His DNA passes on his genetic code and one of his two children is diagnosed with mild depression.

This child grows up, enlists in the military and witnesses the atrocities of war. He's already predisposed to depression, and now he suffers from PTSD. While this is a point of great controversy in the field of psychology, many theorists believe that the cells in his body that already have a slight trace of depression tendency are now altered to include the trauma he experienced.

Taking this story further, we could say after the war, he goes on to have three children of his own. One of them manifests signs of depression and another child is anxious. This child doesn't know why she's anxious. In her twenties, she seeks therapy.

She tells her therapist, "I don't know much about my grandparents but my dad was a war vet. My mom says he kept to himself when he returned from the war. He wasn't very involved in my life. I'm here because my anxiety is interfering with my relationships and my work. It's intensified to the point where I don't even like to leave the house."

Many people seek therapy because they're discontented, but they don't understand why. They may have experienced relatively normal childhoods, yet they can't seem to shake the feelings of depression or anxiety that disrupt their lives.

A good therapist will work with this client on her anxiety, provide her with tools and strategies to help reduce her symptoms of fear and isolation. A great therapist will retrieve as much information about her family history as possible. In the scenario above, rich data details the mental illness that's been passed on from generation to generation.

Her father's depression, along with his experience in the war and the PTSD he suffered was coded into his cellular makeup. When he married and had a child, his DNA was mixed with his wife's. Our client was born with traces of both of her parent's traits, including among other characteristics, eye color, skin tone, heart problems and...mental illness.

Genetic information from her parents' past experiences was also handed down. Many clinicians believe war, slavery, and traumatic experiences can change a person's cellular makeup, and that too is transferred to the next generation. Therapists who consider all of these factors can help their clients better understand who they are, why they respond a certain way, and how they can heal. Uncovering ways their ancestors were resilient or overcame challenges (or ways they didn't), can help a person carve out their own path to healing.

Below is an abbreviated lineage on my mother's side of the family.

Great-grandmother - schizophrenic (paranoid type).

Grandmother - bipolar disorder and alcoholic

Mother - anxiety and obsessive-compulsive disorder, predisposed to addiction (Because of her life circumstances, she also has PTSD and was at one time a workaholic)

Me - obsessive-compulsive disorder (in remission), mild depression. I too, am predisposed to addiction and must be very cautious of going overboard with work and exercise.

My son - mild anxiety. He is also predisposed to addiction and will need to be careful as he advances through life not to work too much, work out too much, or allow his affection for cigars to become a full-blown addiction.

Also hidden in this lineage, and in everyone's lineage, is information about strength. The women in my family had great fortitude. Had those who proceeded my mother chosen to live differently, their strength could have turned into something powerfully good rather than something intensely ugly.

I cannot stress enough that the choices we make can dictate an entire lineage. We hold a great deal of power when we look at the strengths and weaknesses, and physical and mental illnesses found in those who walked before us. We can evaluate what's been passed down, either through DNA or through the experiences of our parents and their parents and choose how to treat ourselves and our children. In doing so, we alter the course of the generations after us. WE get to decide how we want our bloodline to look long after we leave this earth.

"Which way?" We all have to answer this question at some point in our lives. What choice will we make when faced with how we want our lives to look? For some, this question can come early. I've had children as young as 10 in my office who proclaimed, "I will be different than my parents."

I've had teary-eyed clients in their 70s lament, "I wish I had not become my mother/father. I turned out just like her/him." My answer is always, "It is never too late to choose another path, Never."

However, choosing a path of happiness and love requires work. We must take a good, hard look at our lives, pick out the ugly parts, and acknowledge the dysfunction those parts have created. Change requires us to identify the pieces of ourselves that hurt us or others or both. Only then can we forgive ourselves, toss the old behaviors aside and learn new ways to deal with life.

My grandmother chose to live much like her mother--in fear and anger and by not getting the help she needed. My mother, on the other hand, chose to live with honesty and compassion for others. She sought and received the help she needed to become the best version of herself. She learned how to heal and in doing so, taught me. I was then able to teach my son how to help others heal.

He plans to become a pastor because he wants to influence multitudes of people to live with authenticity and purpose. I'm fully confident my grandchildren will be wonderful human beings who'll know without a doubt they're loved and adored. They'll understand how to communicate effectively, and they'll give to others because of the choices little Jann Simmons made years ago. With each generation that chooses healthiness, we move farther and farther from the dysfunction that may have bound our ancestors.

~~*Jann*~~

In the middle of my junior year in high school, my grandmother and I moved into a relative's home, where my grandmother died a couple days later. I was at her side as she struggled to breathe for several minutes. She sat up suddenly, then lowered herself back to her pillow and closed her eyes.

Her life was over. She was gone, and a burden was lifted from my shoulders. I was happy to be free of the intense care she required and equally happy to be free of her bizarre behaviors that kept me confused and frightened.

One evening before she died, in a rare display of consideration, I overheard her tell my aunt she wanted me to have her car. I was thrilled because it held such a sweet memory of the day my mother let me drive it. The gift of her car would serve as the only thank you I would receive from my grandmother or any of her family, for taking care of her. Unfortunately, the car was sold before I got to drive it again.

I remained living with my aunt and uncle, and shortly after my grandmother's funeral, my aunt told me she died believing I was pregnant. This revelation took me by surprise because I wasn't dating anyone. In fact, I had only been on the one date while my mother was with us.

I believe my aunt told me that crazy story because my family assumed I was destined to follow my mother's path. They had a pronounced ability to blame, shame, and pass judgment on everyone but themselves, so I bore the sins of my mother in their eyes. My mother made bad choices, so her daughter would make bad choices as well.

My mother's family rarely displayed love and affection, but they could certainly dish out criticism and shame as naturally as breathing. A couple of them ruled their children with one iron hand lifted in intimidation, while the other hypocritically rested on the Bible. Some of them controlled by guilt and threats and did it all in the name of God, just like their mother. They were fanatics operating under the protective umbrella of the church.

By now, I drifted through my days without emotion, without wanting, without needing and without feeling. I had long ago been mentally and emotionally stripped. No one cared if I was heard and I was terrified of being seen. No matter the situation, I tried to melt into the surroundings. I did exactly as I was told, and I did not ask questions.

I didn't wonder about life. I didn't have dreams or goals to reach for. I didn't have visions of grandeur. I didn't believe I had rights. But, occasionally, I pondered marriage and what it would be like to have a family of my own.

112

I had been so preyed upon by this time in my life that I had no identity left and, unfortunately, no one I knew could give me a clue as to how to acquire an identity. In those days, teachers didn't intervene, even if they suspected a child was in distress. I no longer stuttered, but even though I was no longer embarrassed to talk, I still didn't have any friends.

What good would it do me to make a friend? I'd just have to say goodbye to them at some point anyway. I never knew how long I'd be in a place before I'd have to move again.

My aunt enjoyed having me in her home and delighted in decorating the guest bedroom for me. I had my own bedroom for the first time.

My cousin was away at college, but we formed a close bond when he came home for summer break. I loved having him around, we often did things together and shared deep conversations. He meant the world to me.

My aunt and uncle seemed happy to have me fill their empty nest and I was happy to have a home. But theirs was a strict household and I scrambled to learn the rules quickly. We attended church three times a week, and with school, homework, and chores, little time was left for fun activities.

I was surprised when my aunt planned a swimming party and invited a few cousins, so I could get acquainted with them. No one had ever planned a party for me, and I was thrilled to see cousins I hadn't seen since Christmas at my grandmother's house.

The morning of the party, I innocently informed my aunt that I'd started my period and asked her for some rags.

Her face contorted into an angry grimace. "What?" she screamed. "You've just ruined the entire party! You cannot get into the pool with the others."

I dutifully did as she instructed. All day, through tear-filled eyes, I watched my new family play in the water. I'm not sure what they were told about why I was made to sit on the ground, but none of them came over to talk to me. Would I always be the girl standing on the outside looking in?

Due to my grandmother's death, and living across town with my aunt and uncle, I changed high school in the middle of my junior year. I excelled academically, but I had my work cut out trying to fit in with the student body at the high-school level. I was worried I'd once again be ostracized, or worse, that they'd find out I was an unlovable, unwanted orphan.

To face my new schoolmates, I transformed into someone who could be accepted by them. I forced myself to be outgoing and friendly, and soon I became very popular. I always smiled, I was always kind to everyone, always funny, always perfect in every way. My perfection covered the ugliness of my past, which I thought I needed to hide from everyone.

I was a shy, terrified girl on the inside and a well-adjusted, happy-go-lucky girl on the outside. I developed my people skills, most likely inherited from my outgoing dad. I showed others that I cared about them and that I was someone who'd listen to them if they needed to talk.

My hypersensitivity to the moods of others and their changing facial expression and body language served me well. Due to my years of adapting to my surroundings and the people in it, I had an innate ability to meet anyone I encountered right where they were in their lives. They usually responded to my caring concern with openness.

In those days, segregation was a way of life in the south, so integration in the schools was an adjustment for some and resulted in marches, riots, and racial unrest. The first day of my senior year, a typical warm, sunny, southern morning, I noticed several African American teens gathered near the flagpole. I recognized the wide-eyed look of apprehension on their faces from my time in the orphanage, when I was in the minority at the elementary school I attended. I knew full well the fear that beat inside their chests.

I walked straight over to the new students, introduced myself and welcomed them to their new school. I wanted them to know they were included. I knew what it felt like to not feel wanted.

Before long, my best friend, along with some of my casual friends from my junior year came over and introduced themselves. The strain on the faces of the new students started to ease and they seemed more relaxed. Helping them made me feel like I was doing something good for others and I was doing it on my terms. We all accepted each other. Unfortunately, that was not the case in other schools across the city.

I tried to get to know my family of origin, but they didn't seem at all eager to know anything about me. The circumstances that brought me to them mattered very little compared to what I brought to their lives, which was the accolades they received for taking in an orphan no one else wanted. I worried that they might decide I was too much trouble and send me back to the orphanage, so I followed all rules with strict internal discipline. I also worried that they would simply decide I was a major disappointment and want nothing to do with me. How could I remedy that? I was determined the answer was to do anything and everything I could to hide the darkness inside me.

Yet, I liked who I was becoming because I felt accepted. My aunt and uncle praised me for being such a wonderful young lady, so outgoing and loving to everyone. My teachers loved me, my classmates loved me, my aunt and uncle's friends loved me. And yet, I was filled with dread of making a wrong move.

How long could I keep up the facade? I knew I couldn't reveal my sadness or my loneliness. This sad, ugly, unwanted child who transformed herself into a presentable young lady was still an unwanted, ugly orphan beneath the mask I wore day in and day out. I didn't feel genuine. I didn't feel accepted for who I was.

I relished the joy I seemed to bring my aunt and uncle until I realized the pride they displayed was due to the pats on the back they received from their church friends. They made sure everyone knew that they'd taken in this pathetic child no one else wanted and turned her into a poised, charismatic young lady.

I was devastated by this. They had nothing whatsoever to do with who I had become. I made the changes all by myself. Why couldn't anyone see that?

I soon learned that they didn't think I was wonderful at all. They didn't trust me. They spied on me. They even checked my undergarments for telltale signs of sexual activity, in which I never engaged.

They kept me under their thumb at all times.

I was not allowed to go out with friends or boys unless they could keep tabs on me. They were afraid I would bring them shame. They enlisted the help of my friends' parents to report back to my aunt the details of my behavior.

One evening, I had just finished a shower and was headed into my bedroom near the family room when I overheard my aunt talking on the phone. I heard her say that it was only a matter of time before I became a promiscuous alcoholic, just like my mother. I'd barely digested her words, when she added, "Under NO circumstances will we keep her if she brings us shame."

The message was clear, I was hopeless. I was a product of my mother, without any redeeming qualities that set me apart from her.

The choices I made, despite my miserable life, to make myself a person of integrity were being credited to an aunt and uncle I'd only lived with for a few months. Even my friends were praised for keeping me on the straight and narrow when I was with them. How did my new caretakers, who scrutinized my every move, not see that I was the leader in my circle of friends? I was the one who didn't stray from the path, while it was my friends who challenged the boundaries laid down by their parents.

My senior year, I was voted Most Popular, Most Beautiful, Prom Queen, Football Sweetheart, Homecoming Queen, Chorus Sweetheart, and Rodeo Queen, and I consistently made the honor roll. My aunt and uncle's friends lavished them with kudos. They were so proud of--
THEMSELVES.

They took all credit for the person I'd fashioned for their world, and they made sure I daily expressed my gratitude. I was also expected to display complete reverence toward them. That reverence kept them in a place of lofty admiration among their friends while keeping me in a position of having the lowest possible view of my own importance.

I yearned for them to attempt to discover who I was on the inside. But no one took the time to notice that who I was to the outside world was not who I was inside. My appearance and demeanor, displayed to my aunt and uncle's friends, proved they had performed a miracle and that was all that mattered to them.

I once saw a book entitled, *I'm Dancing As Fast As I Can.* I remember thinking that title must be a description of me. I felt like I was doing everything I could to be what everyone wanted me to be. I was constantly trying to perfect "my dance".

I was secure, vivacious and happy in the presence of others, but behind my bedroom's closed door, I was alone and face to face with the person I hated most in life, ME! I often thought about ways to end my life. And then one day in biology class, I'd heard something that I interpreted as a means to accomplish this without causing any embarrassment to my family.

We were learning about cellular structure and how vital our cells are for keeping us alive. If every cell was damaged all at once, our bodies would perish. *That's it*, I thought, *that's how I will do it!* Now, that may not have been the actual teaching, but it's what my tormented mind understood. I couldn't wait to get home!

After school, I went directly to my bedroom, closed the door, plopped my books on my desk, and laid on the floor. I began to frantically roll around the carpet as fast I could in an effort to damage all of my cells at once. I attempted this ridiculous, futile ritual over and over, day after day, and lived through it each time. To my disappointment, I still didn't die.

Clearly, I had heard my teacher incorrectly, or I was doing it incorrectly. Prom Queen or not, honor roll or not, I wanted to die every day of my life. I despised who I was, and I desperately wanted to find a means of escape that wouldn't bring shame raining down on my family. Until I could figure out a way to accomplish that, I had no choice but to continue the facade I had created.

With the memories from my childhood fading from my mind, I was all too ready to let this new person emerge. While my family took credit, I quietly gave the glory for how I was conducting my life, my morals, and my conscience to Jesus. I would not speak of Him to anyone else for many more years to come. He was all I had, and I was afraid if others knew, they would take Him away from me just as they'd taken everything else. So, I kept Him safe inside my heart.

I continued to be the people pleaser everyone expected me to be. I was extremely outgoing, an introvert hiding in an extrovert's camouflage, a chameleon who turned into whatever I needed to be, depending upon who was around me at the moment.

Such behavior wasn't difficult for me. I learned at four years of age to read my surroundings as well as the people in my presence. My life depended on reading temperament and body language so I knew how to respond and avert impending danger. What normal people took for granted in their daily lives was never within my reach. I suppressed any wants or needs I had and accepted what I was given without question.

I wasn't accepted by anyone for who I really was, only for what I could give to them. I wasn't angry about the inequity in my life because a person must feel they deserve more before the realization of the injustice surfaces. No one believed in me, so neither did I.

Yet, I was laying the foundation of who I was to become with the personality choices I made. Under duress of abandonment and loneliness, I forced an acceptable personality to emerge. I later learned that my extrovert side was actually a part of who I was from birth. I just needed a chance to bring it out of insignificance.

Many years passed before I embraced the beauty of my own distinctiveness. The shift in how I later viewed myself came with the recognition that I am who I am for me, not for anyone else.

At age 18, I was still not in control of any part of my own life. I was once again reminded of this fact the day I decided to cut my long black hair. Not only did my long hair remind me of my mother, I wanted a change. I went to a salon within walking distance of my house. I picked up a style magazine lying on a table, found a style I liked, and the stylist picked up her shears.

When I got home, my uncle took one look at me and had a fit. He bordered on hysterics, which I thought was strange and a bit creepy. I couldn't understand why he invested so much emotion in MY hair. He was so enraged that he grounded me and refused to speak to me or acknowledge my presence for a week.

My relationship with my uncle became

increasingly strained. Although he didn't always forbid me, he got angry every time I had a date. He made it a big event each time I went out by sulking or making me feel guilty. I was expected to ask permission for everything I did, whether it was dating, going to the mall with my girlfriend or cutting my hair.

Parents from our church entrusted me with babysitting their children and I would soon graduate high school, but I was still being treated like a child in my aunt and uncle's home. I was only permitted to go out for fun one night a week. That meant I had to choose either a date or spending time with friends. And, I had a 9:30 P.M. curfew, at 18-years-old!

My uncle wanted me, not my aunt, to starch and iron his dress shirts. He wanted me, not my aunt, to prepare our dinners. He seemed far more invested in my life than he should have been, and that made me uncomfortable. My aunt seemed willing to let me take on her responsibilities. She didn't take a stance against my uncle even if she disagreed with him. The beliefs of our church, that the husband should be the head of the household was taken to the extreme. My uncle used the scripture to support his dominance and control over his household. My aunt and I were both submissive to him.

One night, as my date kissed me goodnight, the porch light suddenly came on. I quickly found my key and opened the door and my date hurriedly made his way to his car. When I walked in the foyer, my uncle was standing there in nothing but his undershorts.

I tried to walk past him, but he grabbed me and pulled me to him in an embrace that made me cringe. Not only did I not want to be that close to him, but his arousal was apparent. I pushed away from him, said I was sick and quickly escaped into the bathroom, where I closed the door behind me. I felt violated and had difficulty sleeping for a while after that. I closed my bedroom door, but there was no lock on it, so an unlocked door failed to provide me with much comfort.

He never did that again, but the damage was done. It was more than 50 years later that I spoke to him about the incident during a phone call. His only comment to me was, "You better get down on your knees and pray!"

I wanted so desperately to be in a home where I felt safe, but it would not be possible there. My uncle kept his distance; however, his eyes were always on me. I wondered if my aunt ever noticed his behavior.

She contacted me many years later by phone and apologized for the way I was treated while in her home. Of all the people who had hurt me, she was the only one to ask for forgiveness, and I readily gave it. We spoke often after that first call. We both cried each time she shared her personal struggles. I assured her I understood.

As I look back on that time in my life, I'm baffled by how robotic I'd become. I never considered my future to determine what path I wanted to take or what heights to reach. I wasn't encouraged to go to college. Although I was an A student, I didn't believe I was smart enough to enroll.

I took each day as it came to me, never taking charge of what I wanted to happen that day. Instead, I waited for someone to tell me my next move. I had no say over any part of myself as an individual. I was a young adult, yet I had no independent thoughts or actions. The fact that I was old enough to formulate my own direction never occurred to me.

When I was alone, I drew deeper and deeper inside myself. I should have been enjoying my youth and living life, forging my own journey and loving who I was. Instead, I was an empty shell. I kept a poem in my purse that I read often because it expressed my internal conflict.

> I look outside as birds fly free,
> I pick one out and pretend it's me.
> I leave all my struggles of the day before,
> spread my wings and begin to soar.
> Then I notice someone down below.
> She was shrinking behind a forgotten face
> slipping through life, afraid to leave a trace
> of the awful pain she feels inside,
> All the despair she hopes to hide.
> I quickly turn away and upward I go,
> but my hurried flight begins to slow.
> I'm trying to deny ME as others have done,
> I can't fly free until I'm completely one!
> The world is not real on the clouds I found
> and sorrow filled me as my feet touched the ground.
>
> ~Author Unknown

I didn't realize then that the numbing process that sheltered me from the agony of my life was also burying my past. I was becoming invisible, even to me, living a lie so that someone could love me.

I profoundly believed I was worthless and that I was nothing without my family telling me what to do or think. I couldn't trust my own heart or my own thoughts, so I had to rely on others to dictate them to me. No wonder I chose the man to marry that I did, a man who had no problem with dictation.

Jonathan was three years my senior, and he walked into my life with such bold assertion. He was handsome and strong with an air of confidence about him. I instantly fell head over heels for him.

Immaculate from his perfectly combed hair to his impeccably shined shoes, he looked like he'd walked straight out of a men's magazine. Our first meeting was casual, but he took my breath away. He was put-together and self-assured.

I, on the other hand, fumbled for my words, wringing my wet hands and twirling my keys around my fingers, hoping he wouldn't notice them trembling. The first time I met him, he asked me out on a date. I was on cloud nine. I'd never met anyone like him. He had dark-blonde hair, blue eyes, and insanely long eyelashes.

I wondered what he saw when he looked at me. I knew I appeared happy and vivacious, but what did he see when he looked into my empty eyes? I was a nervous wreck while getting ready for his 5:30 P.M. arrival. After I painstakingly applied makeup, I must have taken an hour to style my hair just right. I was spritzing perfume when the doorbell rang.

I barely recall the details of our date. However, I still remember how handsome he was and wondering why on earth he wanted to go out with me. I felt painfully inadequate from the start, completely inferior to him. He took command of the relationship immediately, and we fell into traditionally southern roles from the beginning. He was domineering. I was submissive. Because rejection was the blueprint of who I was, I knew I had to do whatever he asked, so he wouldn't reject me.

Immediately following my graduation from high school, I took a secretarial job at a large retail chain. Even though I was over 18-years-old and held down a full-time job, my aunt and uncle still only allowed me to go out one evening a week.

Of course, I complied. But I wanted to be with this incredible person every minute. Jonathan and I dated on the weekends throughout the summer. I was in love with a man who happened to look my way one day and gave me hope of having a life separate from my aunt and uncle.

About six months into our relationship, we made plans to go out to dinner with Jonathan's longtime friend Ted, who was in town on a visit. The two of them arrived to pick me up for dinner. I could see his friend behind the wheel as Jonathan and I approached the car.

Jonathan opened the back door of the car for me and I slid across the seat, thinking he would slide in beside me. I was taken aback when he closed the door and sat in the front seat with Ted. He'd gotten a date for his friend and we were on our way to pick her up.

I silently sat in the back, listening as they shared stories with each other. I wasn't part of the conversation and must admit I felt left out. Ted pulled up in front of her apartment. I was reaching for the car door to let myself out when Jonathan leaned across the front seat and said. "We'll be right back."

I watched them walk up the sidewalk to the girl's front door and disappear behind it, while I sat alone in the dark, overcome with feelings of foreboding and fear.

I remember thinking that this particular setting seemed faintly familiar to me. A long-forgotten memory of being a child alone, in a car in the dark tugged at my senses. After what felt like a very long time, the front door opened and all three emerged into the humid night air.

I was introduced to the girl, who sat in the front seat with Ted. Jonathan got in the backseat with me. When Ted started the car, I could see on the car's clock that they had left me outside alone for almost an hour.

I was angry at all three of them for leaving me in the car so long. Jonathan reached over, took my hand, and I gulped my anger down. He failed to show any remorse for leaving me alone. He gave no explanation and offered no apology, and I believed I didn't deserve either one. I turned my face toward the car window to hide the tears that filled in my eyes.

We married the following summer. I couldn't wait to leave my family's hypocrisy behind. They portrayed to the church and the world righteous perfection. But judgment, anger, and criticism governed their thoughts and actions. I was excited to be leaving them.

However, I took with me my own state of hypocrisy. I wouldn't be exposed to their judgment anymore; yet, I picked up right where they left off. I HAD to be perfect. If I wasn't perfect, I would not be "enough" in the eyes of the people around me. If I wasn't "enough", they would leave me.

My fiancé moved to another state a few months prior to the wedding to start a new job and find a place for us to live. Those months seemed like a lifetime, but he was coming home three days before our wedding. I couldn't wait to see him again.

After dropping off his luggage and visiting with his folks for a short time, he came to see me at my aunt and uncle's house. I wasn't allowed to go out with him that night. I was told that the temptation for us to have sex would be too great. Never once did I think to tell them I'd established my own values and convictions long ago.

Jonathan and I visited for a short while, in full view of my "guardians." I was devastated when he left to pick up his brother from the airport. I knew I wouldn't see him again until our rehearsal and dinner party the following evening.

The next day, I excitedly dressed in a beautiful rose-colored dress and matching shoes. I couldn't wait for Jonathan to pick me up. I was putting a final spritz of spray on my hair when my aunt joined me in the bathroom. She informed me that I would ride to the church and then on to the restaurant with her and my uncle rather than with my fiancé. Of course, I was disappointed, but as always, I said nothing. I'd be with Jonathan soon.

The dinner with our friends and family gathered around the table was nice. I felt like a princess seated next to her prince. I was so happy and thrilled to be marrying such an incredible man. In less than 24 hours, we would be husband and wife.

My excitement turned to disappointment when my aunt and uncle would not let Jonathan drive me home before his bachelor party. I slid into the backseat of my uncle's car, feeling like a child rather than a bride celebrating a joyous ritual with laughter and loved ones.

Looking back on that evening, I realized emotionally I actually was a child, an extremely naïve child, who had no will of her own and depended on others to steer the course of her life.

All I wanted in life was to be loved. My very humanity had been destroyed and I believed that this was my chance to finally have a home of my own and eventually a family of my own. My marriage wasn't to be a relationship of equality by any stretch, but I knew I'd never find anyone else who would want me.

Both of our families were members of the same church. Ours was a large wedding because both families had so many friends. I had no say in the wedding details or the reception, not even my gown. My aunt handled everything. While the wedding was lovely, it wasn't the wedding OR the gown that I would have chosen for myself.

Even though I didn't really know my brother and had only seen him once since our grandmother took him to live with her, I wanted him to walk me down the aisle. I believed having my arm in his might help me feel closer to my daddy whose presence, I desperately wanted to feel on that special day. However, I was told, in no uncertain terms, that my uncle would take that place of honor.

As I stood at the door to begin my walk down the aisle on my uncle's arm, I scanned the auditorium. My best friend, who was now dating my cousin, was my Maid of Honor. My cousin was a groomsman. Jonathan's side of the church was filled with friends and family. My side was filled with people who never took the time to know me.

I saw people who were kin to me, but strangers just the same. My brother was there seated a few rows in front of our drunk mother, who slumped against her sister. I suddenly felt very small and insignificant and for a moment, I wobbled.

But then, I set my eyes on Jonathan, my husband-to-be. He was waiting at the altar and the one person in the building who was truly there for me. My heart sank when I realized he wasn't even looking at me. I had hoped to take his breath away when he saw me, his bride, in all her glory for the first time, but he was looking elsewhere.

As we took our first step, my uncle looked at me and said, "This is the hardest thing I have ever had to do." I stoically stared ahead, but inside I crumbled. Needless to say, my fairytale walk down a fairytale aisle was dashed within seconds by the two most prominent men in my life. Yet, I lifted my chin and walked the aisle. I promised to love Jonathan forever while forsaking all others. Ultimately, "all others" would again include me.

The morning after our wedding, we loaded my meager possessions and our wedding gifts into a small U-Haul trailer hitched to the back of Jonathan's car. Waving a relieved goodbye to my past, I headed with the love of my life toward our new home far away. I was thrilled to be distancing myself from the misdeeds of my mother and from the judgment I bore because of them.

We hadn't planned a honeymoon, there was no money for one. I was so ecstatic to finally feel free to live my own life and be with Jonathan that my happiness overshadowed my disappointment.

Jonathan represented love and family to me. He was my hope for a new life, the foundation upon which I would build a home of my own. Marriage to him was a path that led me away from all the darkness and despair.

I was leaving my family's betrayals behind to live a new life with a man who loved me. I was ecstatic. No one had ever taught me how to be a young lady or a wife or a mother, but I was determined to teach myself as best I could. My future was filled with life, hope, and love.

As we drove north, I had a lot of time to think. I wanted my new husband to fill the emptiness inside me, an emptiness I didn't fully understand. By now, I had relatively little memory of my childhood, other than the loss of family and time spent in the orphanage.

I was so proud to be sitting in the car next to Jonathan, but I was nervous. I barely knew him, and we didn't communicate very well. I didn't know his likes, his dislikes, what made him happy, what made him sad. I didn't know who he was, and he knew very little about me.

The one aspect of our relationship I felt certain about was his dominance and power over me which felt familiar. Because I'd never seen how a healthy marriage functions, I perceived his dominance as love and willingly accepted his control.

The strong influences of the church certainly played a part in how Jonathan was raised. His mother was quiet and submissive. She believed that women should always hold a secondary position to a man. She raised both of her sons to believe they were superior to women and the church upheld that belief.

Three days after our wedding, we arrived at our new house, a small mobile home. But I didn't care; it was MY home. Jonathan had purchased the trailer fully furnished, so all I could contribute to making this house our home was to unpack the wedding gifts.

I immediately unboxed the kitchen items, filling the cupboards with our new dishes, flatware, pots and pans, toaster and mixer. I neatly folded our new bath and bed linens and slid them onto the linen closet shelves. Then I placed the beautiful Mikasa crystal candy dish on the little coffee table in front of the couch.

The sterling-silver picture frame went on the end table. When the pictures came from the wedding photographer, I'd slide one into the frame. As I topped our tiny kitchen table with a porcelain salt-and-pepper set, I made a mental note to find a tablecloth soon, maybe yellow to match the yellow, cream and orange curtains.

By early afternoon the next day, I'd unpacked everything and sat on the couch with a soda to admire my hard work. I was overjoyed to have a home of my own. Yet, a wave of pain washed over me as I thought back to the little girl who'd once been stripped of her family *and* her possessions.

The last time my life had been packed into boxes, I'd watched as their contents were spilled out all over the floor and divided among the other little girls in the orphanage. This time, I was determined to hang on to what I had and to put all that loss behind me.

We'd only been married two months when I was summoned back home to be the matron of honor in my best friend's wedding. She was marrying my cousin. My uncle and Jonathan got into an argument. My uncle insisted I fly back for the wedding, Jonathan insisted I not. The argument wasn't about the cost of the flight or the time I would be away. The argument was a battle of power, and which man had the most. They were battling over *me*. Two men used to getting their way. Two men who believed they owned me. Jonathan was livid and made his feelings known by not speaking to me, but he let me go.

I arrived at my aunt and uncle's house and put my luggage in my old bedroom. I stood in the middle of the room and felt a hot rush come over my body. Suddenly, I felt sick to my stomach. I brushed it off as stemming from the emotional goodbye to Jonathan and the emotional greeting to my "past". Perhaps, it was due to the litany of rules that were thrown at me by my aunt and uncle during the drive from the airport. Whatever was causing the physical reaction then, by the next day, I was also quite ill with a kidney infection. My aunt took me to her doctor who put me on a strong regimen of antibiotics. By the next day, the pain was not as severe, and I made it through the wedding okay.

On the plane back to Jonathan the following day, I desperately needed to use the ladies room. But the thought of leaving my seat mortified me. I didn't want anyone to look at me. I never wanted to be noticed. I felt safest when I believed I was invisible to others. So, I sat there for two hours, trying to take my mind off my growing need to use the restroom.

The first sight I saw when I de-boarded the plane was Jonathan's smile and waiting arms. I was so happy to be home, and he seemed thrilled to have me back. How could I tell him I needed to use the ladies room? Why was it so difficult for me to tell him I had a very human need?

As we stood at the luggage carousel, I tried to muster the courage. Jonathan was saying something, but I couldn't focus on his words. I had to find a way to tell him to please wait for me while I used the restroom. Our drive home would take over an hour. Before I could form the words, we were walking out the door to the parking lot and my bladder finally let go.

Jonathan never knew. He didn't notice when I placed the magazine I was carrying on the car seat before I sat down. He didn't ask why I hurried into the shower the moment we walked into our home, nor did he notice that I threw away the dress and shoes I was wearing. I still feel the enormity of my shame, and not feeling worthy to address my very human need.

~~*Shari*~~

I have a crooked "witch" finger. About three years ago, one of my fingers suddenly decided to veer off to the left just above my first joint. My once-straight finger now looks as if it's signaling to every person in the world that they need to take a sharp left.

Doctors confirmed my fear that I have the beginning of arthritis in my hands that will soon take over all my fingers and mangle them into a pile of twisted digits. At the age of 48, I have a healthy self-esteem and self-concept. I know who I am, and more importantly, I like who I am. I have come to accept my flaws and appreciate my deficits.

However, I was speaking to a group of therapists recently and noticed that a couple people in the front row were looking at my crooked finger. I could see their eyes follow my hand instead of looking me in the eyes. Even as I was speaking, I was acutely aware of the heat that began to rise in my cheeks and of how embarrassed I felt. I caught myself folding my finger inward and enclosing it in my balled fist. I felt ashamed.

I was transported back to a time when I was in kindergarten. I must have been five at the time, and I was swinging on the playground in my favorite green-checked dress. The girls I was playing with noticed I had on white underwear, what they called "baby underwear". My panties weren't colored or printed with flowers or princesses.

After school, I told my mom what they said. She cried and drove me to Walmart to buy a package of "grown-up underwear". However, my new undies didn't stop the taunting. For weeks, all the girls *and* boys made fun of me.

Their ridicule made me believe I was "less than." As a result, I acted "less than". I played by myself in the corner of the playground and didn't raise my hand when I knew the answer to the teacher's questions.

One day the teacher pulled me aside and said, "Get over it. This is not the last negative thing you'll hear in your life." I eventually did "get over it" but shame does not go away that easily. It haunts us until we banish it. Sometimes, we must banish it over and over again.

Shame--a simple word, yet it carries so much meaning. Dozens of books have been written on this topic. Shame is at the core of trauma work. I have found that people can heal rather quickly from the physical atrocities of their past but often have a hard time healing from the shame it evokes.

Brene Brown, researcher, and bestselling author describes shame in her book titled, *I Thought It Was Just Me (But It Isn't)*. Shame, she says, can be defined as "the intensely painful feeling or experience of believing we are flawed and therefore unworthy of acceptance and belonging." (Brown, 2007, pg. 5) I would add that shame is the cloud of invisible smoke we breathe in after we experience physical or sexual abuse, rejection or abandonment, disparaging remarks or even a demeaning look.

Shame is a feeling that takes residence in our spirits and clings on for dear life--after a beating, after being bullied, after receiving a diagnosis of depression, after standing in an elevator and watching a beautiful woman dripping in jewels walk in and eye our scuffed shoes.

Shame can take over and twist these events into a grotesque, foul liquid. It will soak into every fiber of our being and affect how we navigate our world. Shame interprets who we are at our core and spits out a verdict that usually sounds something like this: "You are ugly." "You have no value." "Hide this part of yourself because it is not acceptable." "You are too fat and unlovable to ever find someone who'll appreciate you for who you are." "You are not worth anyone's time."

The world doesn't understand shame very well and often confuses it with regret. Regret says something is wrong with my behavior or my decisions. Shame says something is wrong with *me*.

Healing from shame is hard because it requires us to look deep within ourselves and travel to our subconscious beliefs. Shame beliefs are hardwired into our brains. Our rational minds know they're incorrect, but the inner parts of our souls not only believe the shame but cling to it as rock solid, unshakable truth.

Shame is what makes us turn red with embarrassment when we're verbally attacked. It is what makes us throw away the colorful shirt we just bought after someone says, "That shirt reminds me of something my grandma would wear." Shame leads us to walk out of the gym in tears after someone tells us we've put on a few pounds. It causes us to walk through life thinking we don't deserve to be paid better, or to be given immeasurable love, or to experience happiness.

My mom couldn't use the airplane bathroom for fear of people looking at (and judging) her or tell her husband she needed to find a restroom because of shame. She'd been punished for so long for even her most basic and primal needs that a message about who she was, crept into her subconscious mind.

Expressing a bathroom need, when she was made to crouch down in the backseat of a car while her mother went on a six-hour drinking bender would have resulted in a beating. A persistent life-stealing message was coded into every cell in her body. "You do not deserve to have your basic needs met. You do not deserve to speak up and say that you need something. You do not deserve--to exist."

Dealing with our feelings of unworthiness is the most difficult but the most vital aspect of healing. My mom eventually tackled the demon of shame, but overcoming it required years of personal introspection and therapy. To confront our shame means we have to challenge, question and argue with the deep-seated messages and long-held beliefs that we're not worthy, and good enough, valuable, or lovely and perfect--just the way we are. We must rise against those beliefs, stare them down and stand tall as we tell them we are DONE! We must rip the leeches of shame from our souls and flush them down the toilet.

Purging ourselves of ingrained beliefs is painful because they've become so much a part of us. Our minds oftentimes don't know what to do when we get rid of what has become so solidified. People who do shame work often report feeling somewhat lost for a period of time. Some clients have stated that they lost their identity. Feeling shameful about themselves is easier than the emptiness of not knowing who they are. But when we start to replace shameful thoughts with the truth about who we are, we begin to blossom.

If you are someone who struggles with shame, the hard work will be to examine your deeply held beliefs about yourself. The exercise below will give you a guide for writing down the messages (both verbal and nonverbal) that you received in your life. At some point in your healing journey, you'll need to look at how YOU chose to interpret those messages. Then, the work of telling those beliefs to take a hike will begin. You can do this in your own unique way.

How we deal with relationships is largely influenced by the messages we received about ourselves (either spoken or unspoken) as we developed into adults. An understanding of the beliefs we hold about ourselves as a result of those messages is vital. If we don't heal from the damaging messages in our lives, they tend to creep into our relationships with our significant others, our children, our co-workers, our friends and ourselves. To be the healthiest version of ourselves, we must go back in time, discover the messages we were given about who we are, acknowledge the impact they had and replace those that no longer work for us.

Spoken or Unspoken message from my past	The Impact	Follow-Up message from myself
Example of a negative message: "You are not worth my time."	I continue to believe this and choose people to be in my life who validate this belief and can't "be there" for me when I need them.	"I am worth other people's time, attention and adoration. I will only allow people in my life who believe this to be true about me."

When I was first married, I went to lunch with my husband. I was so happy to be a new bride and to say I was "having lunch with my husband." I met him at work and we walked to a nearby restaurant. On the way back, I was giddy with excitement and reached over and grabbed his hand. He immediately and dramatically pushed my hand away, saying "Don't ever do that in public again."

That is when I heard her, that familiar voice I'd come to loathe. The one I heard way back in kindergarten. "Ha, you thought you were loveable. You thought you found someone who'd be proud to walk down the street with you. You foolish girl. You will NEVER be good enough for that. No one will ever love you like you want because you are simply not good enough."

Time and work were required to convince that voice to go away. But one day, it did. Several years after my divorce, I took a day off from work. I was a single mother, working a highly demanding job at a psych hospital, and I felt like I was losing my mind.

I'd been faced with some challenging decisions on the job and was visited daily by my old pal, Shame, who picked up every morning right where she left off each night. "You are so worthless. Why would you think you could run a program for teenagers, be a supervisor, and a good mother, all at the same time?"

I was sick of the sound of her voice. I was even sicker of my own willingness to hang onto her every word and incorporate it as truth. I sent my son off to school, told my staff I was taking the day off and drove up to the mountains, where I pulled over by the river and wrote a letter. It started like this:

"Dear Shame, I am done with you and your hopeless, destructive words for me. I see myself believing what you say and living my life according to your perceptions of me. You tell me I'm worthless, and I believe it. In fact, I AM an ineffective director and don't lead my employees well because I have taken in your lies as truth. I AM NOT the mother I know I can be because I have let you convince me that I'm not. I have no other choice. I have to murder you. Silence you. And forbid you to occupy space in my mind."

I sent this letter floating down the river in an old Bud Light bottle. There have been times when shame sneaks back. I can hear her start with her familiar barrage of insults. I can almost picture her standing outside my door, hunched over in the cold, pleading to come in.

Although I can still faintly hear her at times, I do not open the door. Instead, I turn the other direction and walk away. On days when I am feeling sassy, I point my crooked finger at her and tell her to get off my front porch!

~~*Jann*~~

As happy as I was to be back home after my cousin's wedding, I also dreaded the days of isolation. We had no phone. We had one car that only Jonathan could drive. He went to work every day and I stayed home, day after day.

I was unbearably lonely. I knew no one, I went nowhere. My life existed inside the four walls of our tiny mobile home. I had no money, and Jonathan did not allow me to work to earn an income. My existence depended solely upon him.

I sat inside the four walls of our home watching the clock tick and continuing my well-ingrained pattern of not asking for anything. I suppose I convinced myself that I didn't really need anything. I just wanted to feel safe.

But, I never felt safe. I just felt lonely and vulnerable and extremely dependent. I envied the life my husband had outside of me. He had friends, a car, a job, and independence. He had a sense of meaning and self-worth.

My days were long. I didn't read or journal. I didn't go to church or make friends. We didn't live near anyone, so I didn't even have neighbors I could visit with. My highlight was always the moment when I saw his car drive up the dirt path that led to our front door. Jonathan was my world, small as it was. I loved him more than anyone should love another person.

I was frozen in fear of disappointing him or making him angry, so I didn't voice my longing to have a job or to have money of my own. I wanted friends and a car to get around town in or at least a phone so I didn't feel so vulnerable.

I silently wished for something to fill my lonely days. I thought if I gave him what he needed, he'd give me what I needed. So, I patiently waited for my turn.

I kept from him my secret longing for independence and he kept secrets from me. Secrets that I fought desperately to ignore. Secrets that I continued to find out from friends many, many years later. I often wondered how a marriage could survive when it's built on a foundation of deceit, but I quickly erased the thought from my mind because I wanted my marriage to work.

I was learning how to cook for my husband. I was learning the foods he liked and didn't like, what seasonings he preferred. I kept our small mobile home clean and welcoming. When Jonathan came home from work, I was always standing in the doorway waiting for him.

Because we didn't have money to go out, we often had his friends over to play cards or games. I liked going to their houses because the outings gave me a different view than the inside walls of our home. I enjoyed the interaction with others and the reprieve from my empty days. Finding a church home, becoming involved, and making church friends was not an option at that time. Jonathan and I had both been disillusioned by the teachings of our former religion and taking a break from "the church" brought us both relief.

We were approaching our first-year anniversary and I was so excited to celebrate. Jonathan planned for us to go car shopping. I was elated. Apparently, we had money for a car and I could finally get out of the house. But that anticipation was crushed when he traded in his car for a brand-new sports car with a standard transmission I couldn't drive. Jonathan didn't discuss buying a new car with me. My feelings, wants or needs were never once considered. I was shattered by his total disregard for how I felt about such a large transaction, but I said nothing.

About 18 months into our marriage, Jonathan came home for lunch, which didn't happen often. He became upset with me about something and we didn't resolve it before he had to return to work. People being upset with me and walking out on me strikes a note of terror in my heart. I was convinced he'd decide I wasn't worth the trouble I was causing him and not return home after work.

I was driven by panic to go after him. I walked almost four miles in a snowstorm to get to his place of employment to make sure he wasn't going to leave me. My level of extreme anxiety overrode the bitter cold. I had never been to his place of employment and didn't know where his workstation was located. But when I approached the glass doors, I saw him walking down the hall with a lady he worked with. They were both laughing. For a moment, I envied her.

Jonathan felt badly about my anxiety, I think because he left work with me right then. On the way home, we stopped by the phone company and he ordered us a home phone. I had no one to call, but I had a phone. I was so relieved and happy to finally have a way to reach him if I needed to.

I saw an ad in the paper for a part-time position at a local car dealership. I was nervous to talk to him about it, but when I presented the idea to him, he agreed to let me interview the next day. I was hired on the spot to keep records in the parts department.

I loved having something to do to get me outside of the house. I had people to talk to, and I was a very good employee. I felt good about myself.

Jonathan drove me to my place of employment each morning and picked me up to take me home during his lunch hour. I'd been at the dealership for about six months when he arrived to pick me up and saw me talking with a male employee. Jonathan was furious and told me I could not return to work. That afternoon, I had to call my employer to tell him I'd just worked my last day.

I hated leaving my job without any notice, but I wasn't about to voice my regrets, my frustration or my anger. Once when Jonathan was angry at me, I tried to tell him how I felt. His reply, "If you don't like the way things are here, let me know. I'll pack your bags and put your ass on a plane!" A sentence that exited my husband's mouth and spewed my past all over me. The implied threat that reminded me of childhood threats prevented me from ever feeling completely safe for the duration of my marriage.

We never talked about having a family, and I didn't know if Jonathan wanted one, but I longed for a child. Beginning with our wedding night, I did nothing to prevent a pregnancy. I didn't know how to be a mother, but I prayed for the chance to be one.

We'd been married over a year when l went to a doctor who, after examining me, asked what had happened to me. I thought that was a strange question. He must have known by the confused look on my face that he should not pursue that line of questioning. I obviously didn't know what he was talking about.

He quickly moved on by saying I needed a procedure to remove internal scar tissue. I agreed to let him do whatever he needed to do so I could have a child. I didn't give further thought as to why I had scar tissue, and the doctor never again asked about the trauma that caused it. Sadly, Jonathan didn't either.

Jonathan took me to the procedure and knew the scar tissue was removed. He was also aware that my periods and sex were very painful for me, but we didn't discuss possible causes. I learned very young to keep my ailments to myself.

Shortly after that, we moved to another state to be closer to Jonathan's brother. We hadn't been there long when Jonathan decided to return to college, so I took a full-time job. Because we still only had the one car, he drove me to work and picked me up afterward. He attended classes during the morning and played golf often during the afternoon.

I loved working, but I had moments of resentment that it was permissible for me to work as long as it benefitted Jonathan. Me working had not been okay until he needed me to so that he could quit his job and go to school part-time.

Household chores weren't shared even though he was home more than I was. I cooked all our meals, I cleaned our apartment and I did our laundry. I was silent because I believed this was the way it was supposed to be.

After a year or so, I became pregnant. About six months into the pregnancy, I called for him to pick me up from work and take me to the doctor. I was having back pain and I was afraid I might be going into premature labor. After an examination and tests, the doctor determined I had yet another severe kidney infection.

I continued to work until the day our first daughter was born. I left work that Friday not feeling well. We had plans to go across the border to Mexico for the evening with Jonathan's brother and his girlfriend. But I just wasn't up for it, so the three of them went without me.

Not long after they left my contractions began and continued all night. By morning, they were quite strong. I wasn't due for two weeks, so I couldn't believe the pain was real. After lunch, Jonathan was taking a nap when I woke him to take me to the hospital. I was getting scared and needed to find out what was going on.

Jonathan was told to take a seat in the hospital waiting room and I was whisked off to the delivery room where our first daughter was delivered a short time later. I was over the moon delighted.

A nurse brought her to me swaddled tightly in a blanket. For a brief moment, I thought how strangely familiar the scene was. A nurse, a white blanket with pink and blue stripes wrapped around a tiny human being.

This was the first of many brief scenes I didn't quite understand that flashed before my eyes. I know now I was remembering the tiny babies I watched through the nursery window when I was hospitalized before going to the orphanage. On this special day, I quickly dismissed the mental picture as an annoying thought and reached for my baby.

She was a precious, innocent, angelic gift. I fell in love the moment our eyes met. She was perfect in every way. My heart overflowed with pure love, and I immediately knew the purpose of my life. I would protect this child with all that was in me.

Jonathan was proud of his daughter and he seemed content in his role as her father. He didn't participate in her immediate care, that was my role, but he enjoyed having her lie beside him as he watched television.

When our daughter was four-months-old, he quit school and we moved back to the same city we'd left a couple years prior. We rented an apartment and Jonathan found a job. I stayed home to care for our baby. The loneliness that had pervaded my life until our daughter's birth disappeared.

Sometimes during the night, I'd sit up in bed just to look at her sleeping warm and safe in the bassinet I kept within arm's reach. I was desperate to shield her from unknown forces. I didn't understand my intense desire to protect her, but I was certain something evil lurked in the darkness.

Now that I had this precious child, the days and nights seemed to fly by. I had a husband I loved and a daughter I adored. I had a family for the first time since my dad died. Life was perfect, except for the recurring kidney infections. After countless tests, the doctor told me one of my kidneys had atrophied and the pregnancy had taxed the fully functioning one that was left. He said I should not get pregnant again.

Despite the doctor's warning, I felt an urgency to have another child before it was too late. When I discovered almost three years later that I was expecting our second baby, I was ecstatic.

The pregnancy went well until the sixth month. I'd been running a high fever all day but couldn't put my finger on what was wrong until the back pain started. I went to the doctor, and sure enough, I had a kidney infection.

I was given an antibiotic and had started to feel better when about two weeks later, I began having contractions far too early. I was alarmed. The doctor told Jonathan and me that the pregnancy was in jeopardy due to the kidney infection. He gave me something to stop the contractions and sent me home. I rested in bed while Jonathan helped care for our toddler until he had to go back to work two days later.

The following three months were tenuous, to say the least. I desperately tried to hold on to the pregnancy by resting when I could and praying that God would allow me to deliver my precious baby. When I went into labor only two weeks before the due date, I was optimistic my baby would be safe to deliver.

I was in labor a long time, but when I heard the small, high-pitched wail erupt from the lungs of my second precious baby daughter, I wept with relief. I'd privately prayed for another little girl, and here she was, healthy and perfect. I wanted to hold her, but after delivery, my temperature took a sharp spike upward, and I wasn't allowed to see our new baby until doctors determined I had another kidney infection, not something contagious I could pass on to my newborn.

Several hours after delivery, a nurse brought our daughter to me. She was pink and beautiful with the biggest eyes I'd ever seen. I held her close, kissed her little turned-up nose and thanked God for her life. RaeLynn blinked her tiny eyelids as if she knew what I said.

Looking down at her looking back at me, I softly sang the old song, "You Are My Sunshine," because she WAS my sunshine. RaeLynn's grown now, and I still sing that song to her. She doesn't seem to mind, and a smile always crosses her face. Jesus fulfilled my prayer for one more child and I promised to shelter her with my very life.

Finally, the infection was under control. I was frantic to return home to our three-year-old daughter, whom I hadn't seen in a week. Jonathan's mother was caring for her during my hospital stay. I'd never before been away from her, not even for a short time with a babysitter. Our separation was difficult for us both.

I was thrilled when Shari ran to me, her eyes wide with excitement. But I wasn't prepared for the words that came out of her little mouth in a stutter. I remembered how I stuttered as a child and I was frenzied to help her. I grabbed her up, held her close and reassured her that I would not leave her again. Less than a week later, while I was tucking her into her bed for the night, she clearly uttered a full sentence and never stuttered again.

I was the happiest I'd ever been in my life. The scare of almost losing my second baby was replaced with gratitude that she was healthy and fast asleep in the next room. One short year after her birth, I had to have a hysterectomy due to the scarring that had built up from childhood abuses and caused me to hemorrhage. I was only 27-years old, and it was a sad day for me.

But I was grateful to have my two daughters. I held them both in my arms and whispered, "I don't ever want to let you down." They were my reasons for living and I devoted my days and nights to them and my husband. After so many years alone, I had a family of my own.

I finally had a purpose for my life. Two baby girls depended on me to lead them, teach them and protect them. But all I really knew how to do for sure was love them.

Leaving work to drive us to the grocery store and to doctor appointments became increasingly difficult for Jonathan. I obviously needed a car of my own, but I never brought up the subject.

Almost seven years after we wed, Jonathan surprised me with a car on my birthday. I felt liberated and immeasurably grateful to him. An immediate feeling of independence washed over me for the first time in my life.

The car was old and not very shiny anymore, but it was beautiful to me! At 27-years-old, I had my first car. I could now go to the grocery store and shop for my family. I could pile my girls into the car in the middle of the day and treat them to a picnic at the park. In the event of an emergency, I could drive them to a doctor. That realization brought with it a sense of comfort.

I cleaned the upholstery of that old car, vacuumed the carpets and oiled the dashboard. I needed to make it mine and cleaning it in my own way made it so for me. I didn't pick it out or even go through the steps of shopping for it, but I couldn't have been prouder of my very own car.

Jonathan was impressed that he was able to give it to me. I could see the joy on his face when he realized how happy I was. I could also see his fear. He kept me on a short leash, and now that I had a car, the tether was severed.

His insecurities created a tidal wave of mistrust. As a result, he established conditions that had to be met. I was to inform him of where I wanted to go and whom I wanted to visit. Then he would let me know if my proposal was acceptable to him.

A few months later, I started waking up in the middle of the night in a cold sweat. I'd go into the room our sleeping daughters shared and sit on the floor and watch and wait. I was convinced that if I didn't protect them, something awful would happen to them.

I imagined all sorts of horrible things and was sure if I drifted off to sleep, someone would harm them, so that was never an option. I became fearful and anxious and ultimately confused by this unwarranted behavior. I tried to stop my obsession, but the dread that engulfed me forced me out of my bed and into their bedroom every night.

I was overprotective of my daughters, sensing something bad at all times. I never let them out of my sight. If they went outside to play, I was right there with them. Living with such trepidation was agony, and I'm quite certain my constant worry wasn't healthy for the children.

I had no doubt they could feel my anxiety, but I couldn't seem to shake the apprehension that

was always present. At that time in my life, I had
no explanation for my intense fear. The abuses of
my childhood had been pushed to the inner recesses
of my mind.

I didn't share my feelings of doom about our
children's welfare with my husband. I knew he
wouldn't understand my apprehension, especially
since I couldn't rationalize it myself. I thought I
was crazy or at least GOING crazy. Because of my
grandmother, I knew what crazy looked like.
Thinking I might have inherited the odd workings
of her mind didn't require much of a stretch.

As our daughters grew older, my fears for
them dissipated more and more with each year. My
nerves finally calmed and I relaxed into the joys of
motherhood. I'd found my life's work, and I
reveled in it all. However, an unexplainable
sadness always hovered within easy reach.

~~Shari~~

Throughout my childhood, I loved hearing my mom in the kitchen. The sound of pans banging, the oven door opening and closing, and spoons clanging against bowls was my signal to sit on the counter and watch her create beautiful dinners. I spent hours in the kitchen with my mother.

We talked about life, and she let me lick bowls and beaters. In the kitchen, we shared a secret language no one else understood. We had our own inside jokes. For example, we often referred to ourselves as "Martha Stewart wannabes." We made up silly quotes and discussed what masterpieces we could make if we only had three ingredients in the refrigerator. I loved the way she would move from pot to pot, making sure everything was cooked to perfection at the exact same moment. As an adult, I have yet to master that skill.

When I was ten, I noticed my mother becoming increasingly sad. She was also gaining weight, and no one could understand why. I was baffled by this because I dutifully accompanied her to Weight Watchers meetings twice a week. And I watched her methodically measure out every portion of food.

She'd fix delicious meals for my sister, my father and me and then sit down to a salad without dressing. While we ate a bowl of ice cream each night before bed, she drank water with lemon. When the weight didn't come off, she became even more determined and started on an endless stream of cleanses and diets that included nothing but lemon juice. Yet, she continued to gain weight.

Desperate for answers, she began a year of appointments and testing with a panel of specialists at the medical university located in the next city. In her first meeting with the panel, she was asked if she'd suffered maltreatment as a child.

My mother had vague recollections of her time in the orphanage. She remembered that her father had died when she was young. But she'd stuffed most of her memories years ago in an attempt to forget the abuse and abandonment she had suffered at the hands of her mother and others.

Although snippets of violent scenes passed through her mind, she was so emotionally numb that at that time of the interview, she couldn't connect the dots. She wasn't yet ready to accept the fact that *she* was the main character in the horrific scenes that played out in her mind.

When the mind decides to forget negative memories and shove down painful emotions that creep up, the result can be that many years are lost and can't be easily retrieved. When asked what their childhood or adolescent years were like, so many of my clients over the years have responded, "I'm not really sure. I don't remember most of my childhood."

My mom was no different. She looked the doctors in the eyes and told them she hadn't suffered any maltreatment that she could remember. In her last meeting with the specialists, they suggested she find a therapist to talk with because her weight issues and depression were consistent with someone who'd suffered trauma.

Again, they asked if she'd experienced any abuse as a child. Again, my mother said she had not. And she believed she was telling the truth.

One night, my dad got fed up with her desperate attempts to lose the weight and her increasing level of depression. I was half listening to them talk about it in the kitchen and heard her begin to softly protest. When I walked in to see what was happening, they were both laughing as Dad shoved a cupcake in her mouth.

I laughed along too until I realized Mom felt ashamed and embarrassed but didn't know how to make my dad stop. Something down deep told me to help her. "Dad," I said, "stop it. She doesn't like what you're doing to her."

He replied through bouts of laughter, "She knows I'm just playing. I want her to eat." His behavior was so confusing to me. In my mind, my father was the almighty head of our household. He knew best. He was the epitome of what I wanted in my own husband one day.

That episode began an internal struggle in me that would last for years. I believed my dad's intentions came from a loving compassion for her plight. I also knew my mom needed to learn how to stick up for herself. There would be many instances where she would silently accept taunting and shaming from others without saying a word.

Shortly after the cupcake incident, I heard mom in the kitchen. As I rounded the corner in my pajamas to "help" her cook, I saw her at the sink holding a pan. When she turned, instead of her usual greeting, "Hello Pumpkin." she looked at me and froze.

She dropped the pan she was holding and continued to stare at me as if she'd suddenly become paralyzed. I was terrified by her actions and asked if she was okay. But she said nothing. She just stood there in the middle of spilled food that now covered the floor, tears in her eyes.

She was shaking, and I assumed I'd simply scared her. My mom had always been a jumpy sort of person. She was easily spooked and frightened by ordinary sounds like the doorbell, a car horn, or someone yelling. Only this time, she wasn't bouncing back quickly, like she normally did when frightened. She couldn't speak a word.

I called out to my dad and he immediately came into the kitchen. As if she'd traveled to a far-off land and was returning with gifts for all of us, Mom put a big smile on her face and cheerfully said, "I'm fine. I just got startled." And then she added, "I'll clean this mess and then get breakfast ready," as if nothing had happened.

Many years later, I learned what really happened that day. Mom had, in fact, been startled. When she turned around to look at me, she saw her mother. I apparently look like my grandmother.

She'd experienced flashbacks throughout her adulthood, where she caught images of scenes she didn't understand. But when she turned and saw "her mother," a tidal wave of memories from her horrific childhood came flooding back. At that moment, she remembered. She remembered the abuse, the neglect, the abandonment...the terror.

Soon after the frying pan episode, she started going to therapy to get what she thought would be a reprieve from the memories that were starting to surface. What none of us realized was that life, as we knew it, was about to drastically change. Darkness entered our home, perched on my mother's favorite chair in the living room, and decided to stay for a good long while.

~~Jann~~

To hold at bay the horrible thoughts I was regularly having, I stayed busy. Jonathan and I went back to church a few years after RaeLynn was born. I quickly began teaching Sunday school. I served as the PTA president at my daughters' school in charge of all related school activities and functions and volunteered in their classrooms. I kept an immaculate home and tended to the needs of my family which bordered on obsessive.

Even with all my activity, I had a yearning in my soul. I felt I was missing something in my life. My weight was a constant cloud over me and I struggled with inner demons I didn't understand. I longed for internal peace for my mind and heart.

I was anxious, I was empty, I was lonely, and I was in denial. My days were devoted entirely to my roles as wife and mother. I had no outside interests and no friends other than acquaintances at church. My involvement in PTA was merely a job I performed that kept me close to my daughters. My lack of self-confidence prevented me from viewing it as a social opportunity for me. I didn't form bonds with any of the mothers in the group.

Nothing I did was exclusively for me as an individual. I needed something that was mine, something independent from my roles as wife and mother, something that filled me up. But I had no idea how to have a life that was not centered around my husband and daughters.

MY life was THEIR lives. This emptiness and failure to validate myself as an individual with needs, wants, and goals of my own kept me from thriving. I was emotionally dying a little more each day. And I was haunted by constant flashbacks.

~~*Shari*~~

When my sister and I started to develop our own lives in school and my dad was busy in the restaurant, my mom stood by cheering us on. She celebrated our successes and took on our pain as if it was her own. When we were happy, so was she. When we were upset, so was she. Even as a pre-teen, I noticed that my mother's world rotated solely around our needs and desires and that she never expressed longings of her own.

A common occurrence for my sister and me was to walk into our bedrooms after school, only to be surprised with new outfits, shoes, book bags and purses spread out across our beds. When this occurs once in a while, it means a person is thought about and adored. When it occurs weekly, it starts to mean something else. People who build their self-worth solely around taking care of others, often end up losing themselves and don't have a barometer of their own yearnings, likes, dislikes, and passions.

My mother's reasons for creating bedrooms

that looked like the clothing department at Macy's was twofold. First, she was desperately trying to distract herself from the memories that were clawing their way to surface of her lonely life. Secondly, she had no clue who she was so she attempted to find her identity in us.

She was doing the things for us that she never experienced as a child. Because she'd been deprived of even the most basic needs, she was making sure ALL our needs were met and that we'd never want for anything. In her mind, if our needs were met, then the fact that hers were never met wouldn't hurt so much.

My mother still feels guilty buying something for herself and assuages that guilt by purchasing something for one of her daughters or grandchildren. As an adolescent, I began asking my mother, "How can you be kind to yourself, Mom?

My mother is a sought-after woman. Friends, colleagues, neighbors and family members call her when they've had a bad day, are experiencing discomfort in their lives, or they just need to talk. She spends hours listening to and comforting others. Many individuals take advantage of her sweet, attentive spirit.

For years, my mother worked late to finish job duties she couldn't get to during the day because everyone from the janitor to the CEO of the company dumped their trials and sorrows on her. They'd sit before her desk in tears over some calamity in their life, only to emerge from her office an hour later feeling like everything was right with their world again.

At the end of her day, her co-workers would tell her goodbye and leave work for the day and return to their families, feeling filled up. My mother would have to stay behind to finish her work, then return home late to care for her family, feeling completely empty.

Internationally known speaker and parenting coach, Aaron Huey challenges his audiences to ask themselves, "What does taking care of yourself look like?"

Today, when I hear about how mom has exhaustively poured into others all day, I ask her over the phone, "What does taking care of yourself look like right now?" She hems and haws for a bit and eventually says, "Well, it looks like having a glass of wine." I can almost see her smiling as she says it. She now has that question written on notecards in her car, in her kitchen, and on her bedroom nightstand.

Do not misunderstand. My mother was 50-years-old before she tasted any form of alcohol. She's never been drunk a day in her life. But she does enjoy a glass of wine from time to time.

Men and women, especially those who come from a life of not having their basic needs met, can spend so much of their energy pouring into other people that they aren't aware that their own cup is empty. When I talk to others about self-care and learning to embrace their identity, I am reminded of my favorite poem.

"When we become still as a lake,
we see where the ripples come from.
When we keep ourselves numbed out on chaos,
adrenaline and the needs of others,
we don't have a current gauge
of ourselves and our own needs."
~ Author Unknown

~~Jann~~

I loved that my husband and children could depend on me to be right there for them at all times and in every way. I basked in their love and dependence and the good times we had together, and I felt guilty for wanting more. By now, we'd moved into a small ranch house on a couple acres of land only minutes from the city. It had a country-living feel to it and we enjoyed the privacy.

We'd gone through some lean times when Jonathan lost his job. I drafted and sent out numerous resumes and request letters for months on end until he decided he would get into the restaurant business. It was slow in the beginning, so I continued helping him with clerical work. We made a good team, and before long his business was a success.

I admired his diligence and his work ethic. There was nothing he couldn't do if he set his mind to it. He was bright and very talented. I was in awe of him. I worshipped him in many ways.

He also frightened me. I feared his anger. I feared his silence. I feared his withdrawals that sometimes lasted for days. I feared his moments of callousness, like the morning we stood at the window watching as the girls climbed into the school bus idling in front of our house.

I was waving at them and they had such huge grins on their faces as they waved back. Suddenly, their dad did an atrocious thing that I knew would rock RaeLynn to her core. Rage smoldered in me because of the pain I knew she was feeling as she journeyed to school.

I normally stood at the garage door and watched as Jonathan left for work each day, but on that day I couldn't. None of us ever spoke of what happened that morning, but I am haunted by it to this day. One more thing to stuff down and one more thing to loathe.

~~*Shari*~~

My sister loved every living creature. She named all of our cows and considered them pets, despite knowing many of them would eventually become our dinner. She stopped eating beef (and hasn't touched it since) when my father announced we were eating Jake, her beloved steer. We both had cats, but my sister spent hours petting, cuddling and playing with hers. While I loved mine, I was easily bored by it and somewhat annoyed by its temperament.

One morning, when we hopped on the bus, my dad's goodbye wave took on a mean and sinister tone. He picked up my sister's cat by the tail and started to sling her back and forth. Even from a distance, we could tell the cat was in distress. As we sat in a seat together, we watched him through the window, horrified. He was not only torturing my sister's cat, we could tell he was laughing hysterically. Although I had witnessed him taunting my mother before, this was the first time I'd seen him do this with one of us.

My sister burst into tears and attempted to get off the bus to run inside the house to make him stop. But the driver said that once children were on the bus, they had to stay on the bus. As we drove away, I caught a glimpse of my mother standing beside my father, frozen in disbelief.

I spent the rest of the bus ride consoling my sister. I sat there with my arm around her, absolutely stunned at how my father, who knew my sister's love and tenderness toward animals, could be so careless with her emotions. I grew up that day and entered a harsh world, where the emotions of others could be stomped on and crushed in a matter of seconds. I didn't understand it at the time, but someone I looked up to was, in fact, very broken and allowed his own unresolved hurt to hurt someone innocent and pure. I only knew that the sister I adored was hurt beyond belief.

A pivotal moment occurs when a girl gets her first glimpse into what adulthood really looks like. For some girls, the start of their menstrual cycles is the moment they begin to see themselves as women. For others, the first time they have sex or the first time they defy their parents is the moment. My moment was the first time I realized that deep down, my father didn't like me.

My dad was a fierce protector. He made us laugh and was an excellent provider. He made sure my sister and I had everything we needed. He bought my first few vehicles and was patient and understanding when I proceeded to wreck every one of them. And, yes, those wrecks were usually my fault.

During my sophomore year in high school, I had a lead role in a play, taking on the character of a hardened and crass Russian matriarch. My mother was sick and couldn't attend the play, but I looked out in the audience and saw my dad sitting alone, intently watching my performance.

Afterward, he told me with tears in his eyes, that I really had talent and he was proud of me. I soared for months on that rare compliment from my father. When I had knee surgery in college and had trouble getting around my two-story condo, he stopped by with a bag of groceries. He'd always been a man I loved devotedly, but a man that, as much as I stretched my arms to him, was just out of my reach.

I think he loved me the best he knew how. However, he was very jealous of my relationship with my mother. I began to understand this when I started doing my own inner work and began to uncover the reasons for his distance. He grew up with a brother and a family that wasn't communicative, affectionate or attached in a healthy way. With two daughters, who both craved his attention, he was out of his element.

He and my sister shared several hobbies. She was the tomboy who'd play catch with him, run track, loved animals and spent hours with him working in our barn. The two could often be found in the pasture with the dogs and cows.

I had two things going against me. I was a girly girl. I loved wearing dresses, reading, and theatre, all things that didn't interest my father. Secondly, I was extremely close to my mother. We adored each other, and we still do.

We could talk for hours about anything and everything in life, go for long walks or shop together, and as mentioned, cook fantastic creations together. We often acted like two teenagers, giggling at our own inside jokes. In fact, I will never forget being called down to the office my junior year in high school and being told I'd been excused for the day and needed to drive home.

Mystified, I got my things from my locker and walked out to the parking lot, where my mother was standing by my car with a sly grin on her face. "I thought we should go get lunch." she said, "and spend the day shopping. School can wait."

I distinctly remember leaving my idyllic childhood behind, when I was 18-years-old. I lived at home during my first semester of college. I had a full load of classes, worked part-time and was involved in a church group. Because I wasn't the partying type, I was usually home on Friday and Saturday evenings.

One evening, my mom and dad were going out to our favorite Mexican restaurant. My sister was out with friends, so just the three of us were home that night. My mom asked if I wanted to come along and I jumped at the chance to do something other than study on a Friday night.

As we drove to the neighboring town, I could tell my dad was upset. He was quiet, but he had a seething way of broadcasting his anger. From the back seat, I could sense the tension building in the car.

Mom asked him what was wrong and he replied, "Why does SHE have to come?" This seemed odd to me for two reasons. First, he spoke as if I wasn't sitting a mere 12 inches from his seat. Secondly, although I had often felt as though my dad didn't want me around, he'd never stated it so plainly before.

My mother, who by this time was beginning to stand up to him and voice her needs, if ever so slightly said, "Because I want her here." Although soft, she spoke with a firmness that startled both myself and my dad.

I don't remember much more from that night, other than a sickening feeling in my stomach and a strong desire to melt into the restaurant's plaster walls. My father's rejection was life-changing for me. He planted a small seed of doubt that sprouted into an ugly weed that grew into mammoth proportions.

That weed clouded my self-concept and suggested no one would ever find me valuable enough to spend time with me. I felt what generations of women in my family had felt, and I allowed the self-doubt to consume my thoughts and decisions for years. Had I not made a conscious decision to change my mindset many years later, my poor self-concept would have continued to erode my being and extend the curse that had plagued my family for decades.

~~*Jann*~~

I was helpless to stop what was happening. My thoughts were haunting me and now my body was betraying me. For no obvious reason, I was gaining weight. At first, the extra weight didn't bother me. I thought it was water retention and would come off in a day or two. When it didn't come off, I reduced my calorie intake more, but my weight steadily climbed each week.

One morning after I'd finally found something loose enough to wear, I stood at the mirror looking at myself. Maybe if I lost the weight I'd gained, I wouldn't hate myself so much. Yet, my inner turmoil and self-loathing seemed to go beyond my weight gain.

Adding to my confused state were scenes running through my head as if from a play. I didn't know where the images came from, and I didn't understand them. Even more perplexing was the fact that sometimes my body reacted to those scenes with excruciating stabs of pain deep in my pelvic area.

After a battery of tests provided no definitive answers, the doctors strongly urged me to see a therapist. I initially rejected that idea but seeing another gain on the scales a week later, I felt I had no choice. What did I have to lose, except maybe a few pounds?

The dreams and flashbacks were unsettling, to say the least, and I wanted to find out how to make them stop. I remember awakening one night from horrible dreams that left me sweating and crying out loud in the darkness of our bedroom. My husband gently held me and told me everything was okay and that I was safe. But, why didn't I feel safe? Why didn't I feel like my children were safe? The torment HAD to stop!

Choosing the right therapist is similar to buying a pair of shoes. A shopper must try on a pair, put them back, and try on several more before they find the shoes that are the perfect fit and style. I tried several therapists, but I didn't feel safe enough with any of them to tell them about the frightening flashbacks that now haunted my days as well as my nights.

I could see familiar faces from my childhood. I could see the distorted features of my mother's face when she was angry. I was sure I was going crazy. None of this made sense to me. But I kept my fears and my very real pelvic pain hidden from my therapists and my husband.

Odd thing was, the little tidbits of information I managed to share with a therapist seemed to lighten the burden I'd been carrying all my life. In an effort to gain trust, I spoke to them about my low self-esteem, that I felt too worthless to ask that my needs be met. Saying those things out loud felt good, but I didn't know the source of those feelings. I was in utter turmoil and confusion.

One morning while dressing for an appointment, I dropped my pearl earring on the bathroom floor. When I bent down to retrieve it, I spotted the scale in the corner next to the cabinet. I pulled it out and with a deep sigh and heavy heart, stepped on it and was shocked to see an 11-pound loss.

WHAT was happening to my body? I hadn't been dieting. In fact, I'd stopped my futile dieting the same day I left the medical center. I'd gained weight for no reason, and now I was losing weight for no reason. Could those medical doctors be onto something with their therapist theory?

I lost weight as fast as I'd put it on and had the same amount of head-scratching confusion as when I was gaining. The more I talked to the therapist, the more weight I lost. I hadn't yet learned that the unrelenting stress I'd experienced my entire life had produced a chemical called cortisol, which can create weight gain when it's not released from the body. I also didn't know that releasing this chemical comes when one releases their emotions.

As mentioned earlier, Jonathan displayed his disapproval with my weight issues by shoving a cupcake down my throat. Joke or not, I felt degraded. And, once again, control over my own body was being taken away from me.

That incident wasn't the only time my daughters witnessed their dad's power over me. Another time, as we all settled in to watch a family program on TV, he wrestled me down onto the floor and started tickling me. I begged him to stop because I couldn't catch my breath.

I was on my back and he was straddled over

me. Suddenly, he reached down, grabbed my ankles and spread my legs wide apart. I pleaded for him to stop. I was only wearing a knee-length robe, fully exposed before my young daughters, and I was mortified.

The more I tried to wriggle out of his clutches the more he laughed. I didn't look at my girls nor did I ever speak of it with them. I was so ashamed. I can't imagine what they must have been feeling as they watched their mother being treated with such disrespect.

That was such an impressionable time for them. Privately, I told them to never, ever become doormats, to be strong and to always articulate their expectations and needs, to never submit to humiliation or abuse in any form. Despite my words, my actions taught them to do otherwise.

My example, no doubt, left a deep imprint on their minds and a scar on their spirits that they carry to this day. They looked to me to teach them what being treated with respect should look like. I failed them in this area. At that time, I didn't know how to forgive myself. Eventually, with my own healing came self-forgiveness.

The therapist I saw at the time used the get-in-your-face therapeutic approach that left me wishing I could sit in a corner and suck my thumb. His style of therapy only served to force me deeper within myself. An example of his aggressive style of therapy came when he pressured me to join a therapy group with other traumatized women.

He thought the group would push me to open up about my painful memories. I hadn't been able to access my trauma in a private session yet, so the thought of sharing with a room full of strangers seemed overwhelming to me. But I did as I was told, without stating my own fear of doing so.

After a few weeks, the ladies started criticizing me for not talking. They took turns expressing their anger toward me because I didn't participate the way they wanted me to. They accused me of thinking I was better than they were.

The therapist allowed the attacks to continue each week, apparently thinking I'd have a breakthrough and fight back. Well, I'd never fought for anything in my life. Their verbal assaults drove me deeper inside. I felt traumatized all over again and highly threatened. I regressed.

After one brutal session, I couldn't take it any longer. I picked up my handbag and ran out before my pent-up emotions came spilling down my face like a river. When I got to the hallway leading to the stairwell, my legs couldn't hold me any longer.

I slid down the wall to the floor and my sobs let loose. I wasn't there long when I heard the softest, kindest voice I'd ever heard. I looked up to see a beautiful lady kneeling by my side on the floor.

She asked if I'd like to come into her office for a minute before I got in my car to drive home. She told me her name was Neda, and she was a therapist. We ended up talking for a while, and I shared with her what had just happened. Talking with her seemed so natural.

Her kindness eased its way into my broken heart. What are the chances of such an encounter? Such timing? Such an opportune intervention could only have come from the hand of One greater than I.

~~*Shari*~~

When the brain is under stress, it regresses. When we STRESS, we REGRESS and go to our limbic brain. We don't have a lot of choice in the matter. We are wired that way.

As a society (and especially as therapists) we are conditioned to "help or fix" people with our words. When someone is stressed, we think we can help them by getting them to talk, to problem solve or to tell us how they're feeling. As a society, we're not properly trained regarding how to address someone who's stressed.

The key to helping individuals who are distressed is to not talk much at all. Think back to a time when you were under extreme, pull-your-hair-out, sucker-punch stress. Did you need for someone to ask you right then what your plan was to fix the situation? Would you have wanted to be pushed to share your thoughts at that moment?

Most of us can't problem solve or talk rationally about anything while we're feeling extreme stress. What we typically need is for others to just "be" with us, to offer us reassurance and safety.

When the initial threat or stress is gone, then we can think through our next move, verbalize our thoughts or come up with a detailed plan of how we're going to move forward.

Throughout my life, I've seen my mother anxious and terrified and operating from her limbic brain. I've also seen the same behaviors in my clients. But as much as I've witnessed their stress, my first tendency is to fix it. I want to get them to tell me what's wrong and how I can help. I move into action mode before they are ready.

I've had to train myself to recognize this and remember that when stressed, people cannot usually access appropriate words to describe what they're feeling. To remember this tendency, I think of babies.

Babies and toddlers do not have a developed language. When they indicate they're stressed or upset by crying or screaming, what do we do? We lower our tone and speak with a cadence. We soften our body posture and fold our arms around them. We say things like, "It's okay." "I'm here." "You're safe."

I've often wondered why therapists, counselors, psychologists, doctors, dentists, police officers, and EMTs are not better trained to offer safety and reassurance to people who are scared or stressed. When people know they're safe, THEN they can regulate their emotions, leave their limbic brain and tap into the "thinking" part of their brains. That's when they can talk, access their thoughts, come up with a plan or tell us how they feel.

The reason my mother connected so quickly with Neda, the therapist who met her in the hallway, was because she provided safety at a time Mom needed it most. Her former counselor's attempts to force her to talk before she was ready were inappropriate and unethical. Neda was able to see through my mother's fear and simply be with her, without judgment or expectations.

The work could come later and ultimately did. But until a safe relationship was established, Mom could not move out of her survival (limbic) brain because it was designed to keep her alive. Neda knew exactly what my mother needed. She softly approached her, knelt down beside her, lowered her voice and gently said, "It's okay. I'm here. You're safe."

~~*Jann*~~

Neda's patience and gentleness drew me in. The day we met marked the first of many years of therapy sessions. She allowed me the time I needed to feel safe in her office and with her. I didn't realize the magnitude of my need at the time, but safety was paramount for me.

I had a wounded child inside of me who was surrounded by layer upon layer of pain, pain that I'd spent many years denying and suppressing. I also denied that the small child in me even existed. I hated the child I once was. She was dead to me, and I was more than okay with keeping her that way.

I had so profoundly retreated into a life of secrecy, self-loathing, and denial of my own truth that a chasm was formed between my mind and spirit. Yet, I knew I had to cross that chasm in order to become whole. How was I going to manage that? I was too ashamed of my past to want to regurgitate it out for others to sift through and judge.

Jonathan allowed me to go to therapy, but it was out of his control, so it threatened him. He'd look for reasons for me to cancel my appointments, but I held fast to my need to go.

Neda allowed me to talk about what I felt comfortable sharing and didn't push me to reveal what I wasn't prepared to own. The flashbacks, which I was now experiencing more frequently, brought my memories to the surface so that I could access them. But the process of ownership of those memories was painstakingly slow.

I had tucked the memories away in a closed-off corner of my mind and hadn't thought about my childhood trauma in so many years. Those memories were not only the source of the terrifying flashbacks, they were also responsible for the pain my body experienced. To deal with the memories, I had to reveal the atrocities, but I had to be allowed to verbalize them in my own timing.

Neda's kindness and empathy were just what I needed to start the work of healing from such a violent past. The amount of patience my avoidance demanded of her, in the beginning is incalculable. I sat through entire therapy sessions talking about everything other than what I was there for, which was to access my past.

I talked about what my daughters were doing in school, I talked about the weather, I talked about my husband's work, I talked about the new recipe I was going to make for my family that night. One might think I was wasting our time, but trust was building and that was paramount for me.

She asked me to journal in between our sessions, to write down what I was feeling. For a person who had no idea how to feel, much less know what she felt, this was a monumental task. I wrote pages and pages with nothing but random words across them.

Just words, nothing more. I wasn't even able to string a sentence together to describe what I felt. When I look at those pages now, I'm astounded that today I am writing a book.

Asking me to step into my past again, even if it was only through my mind, was like rolling a boulder uphill. I didn't know how to begin. What was becoming evident to me was that when I closed away all memory of an event, I also closed away the feelings associated with that event.

Conversely, as I brought back the memory, I also brought back the pain inflicted on my soul and body. The physical pain in my body suddenly returned as I spoke of an ordeal, pain so real I felt like the brutality was happening all over again. Remembering was torture. I'm not sure which pain was worse, the emotional or physical.

Neda suggested that I look at a blank wall in her office and simply tell her what I saw as if I was relating the plot of a movie I'd seen the night before. That approach worked. I could give her some of my history without taking ownership of it, thereby keeping my feelings at bay.

I always spoke in the third person. I'd say, "She was held down by her mother as a man inflicted unbearable torture on her." In time, of course, I was able to tell the story in the first person. My own mother held me down and did nothing to protect me from what was happening, nor did she comfort me afterward.

~~*Shari*~~

What happened to my mother is common in all of us. Our bodies were designed to be in a balanced state of wholeness and healthiness. What we don't deal with emotionally tends to manifest physically when the negative memories, stored in our cells, muscles, and tissue begin to "act out." This is our body's way of saying, "I don't like this. The pain doesn't feel good. I want you to deal with it so it no longer lives in here and affects the way I function."

My mom's body was beginning to protest and alert her to the emotional healing work that needed to be done. While her mind struggled to make sense of the physical and sexual abuse she'd endured as a child, her body was yelling from a bullhorn, "I'm suffering painful memories here that you haven't dealt with. I want this gone, so I can get back to feeling normal and healthy again. I hurt because you haven't acknowledged the trauma, talked through it, cried over it and become angry about it."

When we face the source of our hurt, we begin to heal from it. Our bodies might whisper, but they will more likely yell, protest and plague us with pain until we pay attention to the prodding. They can be relentless until we answer one simple question: "What path am I going to take here? I could continue to deny what my body is signaling that I must deal with or I could choose the road that will challenge me to confront my hurt." They'll be even more insistent until we offer one simple answer: "I choose healing."

I had always been a dramatic, charismatic and inquisitive child. I loved to question things and debate topics. I knew I wanted to get an education and deepen my understanding of people.

My dad, on the other hand, did not have the affinity for education that I did. He often made fun of people who wanted to gain a college education that fell outside of learning a trade. Although he went to college for a brief amount of time, he dropped out and called those who finished, arrogant and self-absorbed. My mom encouraged me privately, but she never contradicted my father. The message my parents passed on to me was that women were not supposed to be strong or have their beliefs and ideas heard.

I did go to college, but the week I signed the enrollment papers, I got a massive sore throat. In fact, I was plagued with one sore throat after another for the first two years of college. After I graduated, I married a man who had no interest in hearing what I had to say, and I again had trouble with my throat.

This time, I could not get food down my throat, as hard as I tried. Doctor after doctor shoved cameras through my esophagus to find out what was wrong, to no avail.

Finally, when I started my own healing work and began to challenge my negative beliefs about being a strong woman with a voice, my throat problems stopped. The irony of turning my destructive beliefs into a career where I speak for a living does not escape me.

Our emotional issues and woundedness will manifest physically and alert us to the work that needs to be done. Our job is to pay attention. If we don't, our bodies will betray us by turning our physical pain and discomfort into disease and illness. We owe ourselves the opportunity to heal our hearts so that our bodies can be free to do what they were designed to do. If we don't, our bodies will act like temperamental toddlers to get our attention.

~~Jann~~

I tried to act as normal as possible when I returned home from a therapy session. But many times, the effort to smile and pretend my internal world was not threatening to implode and swallow me up was difficult. My husband rarely discussed my therapy sessions with me. He never asked me questions, so I assumed he wasn't really interested.

That perceived lack of concern was disconcerting. People in my past had only had time for me within the context of what I could do for them, and I was beginning to see this same pattern in my current relationships. I gravitated toward people who were needy. I gave my attention and energy to fulfill their need, and I walked away empty.

I'm sure my husband was waiting on me to start the conversation, but due to my conditioning, I was unable to presume he wanted to know anything about what I was feeling after a therapy session.

I worried that my two precious daughters

might notice the sadness in my eyes and this was of deep concern to me. What they might be thinking in their innocent young minds caused me pain. I didn't want them to know anything about my childhood or that the world could be an unsafe place. But Shari was 15-years-old and due to her precocious nature was already beginning to see through my pretense.

~~*Shari*~~

In a rare moment of confidence, I stood tall, regal even, completely embodying my Russian-speaking character, (the one I performed when my dad stated he was proud of me.) She was caustic and hardened, and I loved her. Theater had been a part of my life since I wrote and directed my first play in the third grade. Acting allowed me to enter a different world and step out of the shy, insecure little girl who couldn't stop worrying about her mother.

Even though we were rehearsing the school play, and I was in sweats and leg warmers, I felt the long flowing robes my 60-year-old character would have worn. As I plodded back and forth across the stage, feeling the swish of those robes and reciting my perfectly executed monologue, I saw him.

He was seated in the middle of the theatre, a menacing grin on his face. I was only slightly annoyed that his stare seemed to bore its way into my soul. Being a budding, professional actress, (at least I thought of myself that way), I was accustomed to distractions.

When I came to the most dramatic part of my monologue, I looked right at him. That was a move I most likely would not have executed, had I been Shari, the insecure, shy 15-year old and not Esmerelda, the 60-year-old Russian matriarch.

He stuck out his tongue and started moving it up and down in a sick, sexual motion. His accompanying gestures revealed his immature adolescence as well as his intention. However, his behaviors weren't what got me; rather, his evil grin was what turned my stomach. I haven't seen such a menacing smile since, other than in movies where the killer is about to murder his prey and is relishing his impending conquest.

I had seen the boy at school before but never talked with him. He was the new kid and didn't fit in with any of the established cliques within the school. I had thought something about him was odd but nothing more than that.

Now, watching him smile at my discomfort, I imagined he embodied Satan. Everything about him was dark and menacing. I somehow fumbled through the rest of my monologue, but I was never the same. This one small, inconsequential incident would change the next two years of my life and send me tumbling down a confusing, fearful, and isolating path.

From that moment on, the world became dirty, literally crawling with germs and infested with bacteria waiting to attack and bring me to my demise. Almost overnight, I went from a carefree girl who rarely thought about germs to a prisoner trapped inside a world where everything was suddenly filthy. I couldn't bring myself to touch many of the objects in my world.

My mind made up stories about this boy, places he might have gone and things he might have touched. I told myself that if he'd ever been anywhere near the school cafeteria, I couldn't enter it because his germs would get on me. I believed that any pencil, desk, book or doorknob he touched would not just contaminate me but eat away at my skin like a slow-devouring disease.

I could no longer enter certain places in the school. The library was off limits because I'd seen him studying in there. Certain desks and chairs in classrooms were forbidden because he had sat in them or next to them. Even the school bus was not safe because his bus was parked right in front of mine in the lineup at school. Surely, his germs would flow out of his bus windows and find their way to me. I dealt with this reality by turning away from the bus window and sucking in my breath until I couldn't hold it any longer. I repeated this pattern until the bus carried me away from the hazardous air.

I became a master of lies, telling my teachers I'd injured my back and needed to stand at the rear of the classroom during lectures. I told my best friend I had to study during lunch and couldn't eat in the cafeteria. I often made up excuses to leave class, so I could hide out and watch the boy's comings and goings.

I needed to know which classrooms he entered, what he touched and what objects he passed, so I could avoid them. I became quite skilled at sleuthing and no one at school seemed to notice. Even if they did think I was acting weird, my peers were too involved in their own teen angst to worry about my idiosyncrasies.

What became increasingly difficult to navigate were the phobic patterns unraveling in my house. Initially, when I returned home from the mounting "contamination" at school, I entered a safe haven. However, in my mind, my sanctuary slowly became just as germ-infested as the school. The clothes I'd worn that day had surely been infected, so I removed them the moment I got home.

But then, the floor where I'd dropped my clothing also became infected. If I picked them up to wash them, my hands became contaminated. So, I'd wash them two or three times. My twelve-year-old sister, who was three years my junior, thought this was odd behavior and often confirmed what I already believed, "You're such a weirdo!", she'd say in her most annoyed tone.

As I stood there scrubbing my hands until they were red, my demented mind told me I missed a spot, so I needed to wash them again. I washed my hands incessantly. On a good day, I was able to leave the bathroom after washing eight or nine times.

When I finally felt as though they were clean enough, I dried them with a tissue, for the hand towel must have contained millions of germs, just waiting to attack me. After drying my swollen and chapped hands, I usually had a short-lived moment of bliss that I was finally clean. Until that is, I had to turn off the light switch, which of course, was now polluted due to flipping it on when my hands were dirty. As a result, I'd start the process all over again.

I got to where I couldn't sleep at night. Convinced only certain spots on my bed were clean, I'd contort my body to avoid hazardous regions.

But then, the realization I might roll over in my sleep and touch a contaminated part haunted me. Eventually, I found the easiest way to deal with the problem was to lie awake all night without moving.

The germs, of course, weren't just confined to my bedroom and the bathroom. I had certain paths in the house that I couldn't walk or places on the couch I couldn't sit because my sister had sat there. She went to the same school I did and, therefore, had also been exposed to the germs. The kitchen table was a safe spot to sit because we all had our own chairs. I could sit in mine only if I had taken a shower before sitting there, assuring myself it was clean if I was clean.

Within the year, my parents started to worry that what seemed like an odd adolescent phase was turning into something serious. In the early 80's, much had yet to be learned about Obsessive Compulsive Disorder. My behaviors scared my parents, and I'm sure they wondered if I was descending into full-blown craziness.

After a day of running errands with me in the backseat, my parents sat me down for a talk. Not only did I require a tissue to touch the car-door handle, I held my breath when we drove past places in town I was sure were poisoned. My mom and dad said they were afraid I was slipping into mental illness and asked me to go to therapy to get help.

The thought of therapy both scared and mortified me. "I'm not crazy!" I insisted. "I don't need a shrink!" I thought my mom going to therapy was a good thing. However, I knew beyond a shadow of a doubt I was NOT going.

I was learning in my school psychology class, how people that society deemed mentally ill were often sent to hospitals for intense treatment for five to seven days. In my mind, therapy meant I'd be ripped away from my family and sent away. I was terrified. My answer, at the age of 15, was to become my own therapist. My parents reluctantly agreed to give me a month to fix my behaviors.

I read what few books existed at the time regarding excessive handwashing and germs phobias and learned about Obsessive Compulsive Disorder. My mom printed every article she could find on the topic, read and highlighted them, and placed them on my bed. With a new-found understanding, I wrote out the first of a thousand or more treatment plans, I'd write in my lifetime-only this one was for myself. I plastered the plan on notebooks, so I could see it throughout the day. It included small, attainable goals that looked a lot like this:

Goal #1: Only wash hands two times in between classes.

Goal #2: Pick one "forbidden" place at school or in the house to walk, even if it makes you sick. Do it, anyway!

My treatment plan was impressive if I do say so myself. Slowly, I was able to overcome my fears and reenter the world of the living. I transitioned from soap to hand sanitizer to nothing at all.

Years later, in college psychology classes, I began to understand what prompted such extreme behavior. To my astonishment, my OCD had nothing to do with the strange boy in the theater, who triggered my fear and mental anguish. He was simply in the wrong place, at the wrong time with his offensive sexual gestures. I didn't recognize until later that those gestures sucked me into my mom's world of pain and abuse.

As Mom faced her sexual abuse in therapy, I became more and more curious about what she was experiencing. Even though she didn't supply details, she began to disclose some of her abuse to me.

The decision to share her past did not come easy for her, but I was curious and relentless with my questions. After agonizing over how to answer those questions, Mom asked her therapist what to do. Neda told her that "not knowing what happened" would allow my naïve and fragile mind to make up all kinds of horrendous stories. So, Mom began to tell me very limited details of her abuse.

I was a sheltered, over-protected child and very close to my mother. When she shared even very benign pieces of her story with me, I filled in the holes with imagined atrocities. Later in life, I'd learn that what I envisioned my mother enduring was very close to what *actually* occurred. But at 15, my clean, wholesome, pure world came crumbling down. In its wake was a world filled with germs, shame, and disgust. I had to wash the filth off and make the world a pure place for me and for my mom. If I could make everything clean enough, Mom wouldn't have to wade through any more muck.

The griminess of our lives can go away, but not by washing it down the drain. Dreadful memories and beliefs are neutralized when we make a conscious choice to alter the way we view the traumatic or dirty aspects of our lives. We become clean and whole again when we make a choice to see ourselves as clean and whole.

I've often been asked if my mom telling me about her abuse was a bad idea. As a therapist, I only recommend doing so with certain children at certain ages. I was so concerned about what was happening with my mother that I needed to know some of what she was going through. Each child is unique and how they process information is just as varied.

I wish I'd gone to therapy back then, which would have helped me process my mother's pain and provided an outlet for expressing my fears verbally. I still have times when I reach to shake someone's hand and I hesitate, wondering what germs I'm about to encounter. I still cringe when I touch a wet doorknob. I still run for the hand sanitizer in my car after I leave the doctor's office. But I have overcome the thoughts of contamination and fear that used to consume every part of my being. I have power over my thoughts, and I can change them before they change me.

Suggestions for therapists, counselors, life coaches, teachers and anyone who wants to understand the dynamics of seeking therapy:

In this society, clinicians are quick to give a diagnosis or a label. We want to understand what is going on with a person, so we can categorize their behavior and develop a treatment plan based on the number of criteria a person meets.

"The Diagnostic and Statistical Manual" (DSM) is used by clinicians to diagnose and treat mental health disorders. Within the pages of the DSM are diagnostic codes used for billing purposes and data collection. Each disorder listed in the manual features a specific set of diagnostic criteria that must be met to qualify it.

Ask your clients to fully explain who they

are emotionally, physically, spiritually, mentally and socially to get a clear picture of what is going on in their lives. Had I gone to a therapist who simply looked at my symptoms, I might have been given a diagnosis and put on medications. I would have dutifully followed any intervention the therapist suggested. What I needed, though, was someone to question me about all facets of my life and uncover the fact that my actions were a result of my contextual environment. I needed a therapist who would partner with me to build creative and self-driven interventions that worked for me.

If you are a non-clinical person reading this book and think you may have a behavior that is getting in the way of living a full and meaningful life, or if you care about someone who's struggling in life with a certain behavior, I would encourage you to find a therapist who will do the following:

1. Prior to meeting with you, take time to answer your questions about how they do their clinical work.

2. Conduct a thorough intake that includes discovering who you are emotionally, physically, mentally, socially and spiritually.

3. Obtain a timeline of your life and a thorough family history.

4. Talk less than you do.

5. Partner with you to come up with interventions and strategies that will fit YOUR lifestyle, beliefs, culture, and personality.

6. Check in with you throughout therapy to ensure your needs arc being met.

7. Refer you to someone else if they feel they are unable to help you.

~~*Jann*~~

I am a very disciplined person, so I took my therapy and the homework I was given very seriously. However, as I mentioned earlier, I usually spoke of my childhood in the third person. I suppose it was my way of keeping the horror at a safe distance. Once I was able to say, "This happened to me," my healing journey truly began.

Neda talked to me often about my need to integrate my "inner child" with my adult self. She felt I needed to claim the wounded child inside me in order to become whole. Weekly, she had me close my eyes and envision myself as a small child, and picture how I looked back then. She encouraged me to visualize my little self at the door and to invite her into the room, into our sessions.

I didn't want to resist her words, but I just couldn't embrace the child I saw in my mind's eye. I hated her. She was the reason I was abused. She was the reason I was unloved and forgotten. I wanted no part of her. I'd made a new life and she held all the pain, suffering and ugliness of my old life that I'd spent years denying.

Neda didn't let my resistance amend her belief that this symbolic scenario was crucial to my healing. For several years, we ended each session with her gently coaxing me to accept Little Jann, as we now called her, into the room. But for years, I symbolically closed the door on Little Jann barring her from the entrance.

One day, in an emotional breakthrough, I invited that broken little girl in. I allowed her, in my mind's eye, to come over close to where I was sitting. For a long while, I sat in silence, tears streaming down my face. I saw a precious and innocent child, who'd been born into a life of rejection. Little Jann looked at me with such empty, longing eyes. I was lost in the scene I'd created in my mind.

Neda sat in silence as she watched the scene unfold. I'm sure she wondered what was going on inside my mind and heart, but she let the connection unfold without interrupting it. As I looked at that little girl with the mesmerizing brown eyes, suddenly I could see her bruises, her burns, her emaciated body. I could see her shattered heart, and I felt her terror and loneliness. I silently communicated with her as if she were standing right there in the room with Neda and me.

I finally understood the power in Neda's unwavering insistence that I experience this symbolism. I reached down and picked up that innocent child and put her on my lap. I held her, promising I would not abandon her again. When I opened my eyes, I saw that my arms were folded across my chest, tightly embracing my adult self. Little Jann was wrapped inside my arms, inside my heart, filling up my very being. She would forever be a part of me. At that moment, I became whole again.

We can learn from the past, we can claim the past, and we can become far greater than our past. But we cannot deny it existed without denying who we are.

Shortly after reclaiming the little child in me, I was lying in bed one night about to drift off to sleep. Suddenly, I was startled by the feeling of a presence in the room. I opened my eyes to see three demonic visions, close enough for me to touch if I had mustered the courage to reach for them. Jonathan was watching television in the den. I was alone with the visions, and I was afraid. My eyes were locked on them. I didn't move.

One was much larger than the other two. He was fierce and had red eyes surrounded by yellow edges. His back was hunched, and his shoulders were broad. He had fangs of extraordinary length, and he growled ominously.

On the opposite side of him stood two relatively smaller forms. They, too, had red eyes, hunched backs, and fangs. Cowering between the three of them was the silhouette of a small child, a little girl with haunted eyes.

I watched in wide-eyed terror as the beasts grabbed her arms and pulled her this way and that. They battled over her with such fury I was certain they'd tear her body apart. She tried to get away, but they were too strong for her. I didn't want to look, yet I was helpless to close my eyes to the scene that unfolded before me.

My heart pounded in my ears. I silently prayed for the girl, who was fighting for her life against the frightening beasts. I prayed with such urgency that one would have thought I was pleading for my own life. I prayed, I cried, I began to perspire, I couldn't catch my breath. Instinctively, I reached for the child, pleading with God to free her from the beasts' talons.

As I did, the demonic creatures vanished, trailing a faint stream of putrid smoke behind them. Minutes passed before my breathing and heart rate normalized. The terror didn't subside for what felt like hours. But when it did, a beautiful sense of peace filled the room. I could clearly see the face of the precious little girl. The hollow eyes she had minutes ago were now shiny and bright. She was me. Neda was the only person I ever shared the vision with, until now.

Integrating my child self with my adult self was not the only hurdle in my recovery process. The next hill Neda had to drag me up involved facing the debilitating messages I had received in my past life, along with the ones I was receiving in my present life. She wanted me to see the similarities between the then-and-now messages. I needed to unravel all the negative beliefs instilled in me and replace them with positive ones to become the person God meant me to be.

~~*Shari*~~

The reason why many people avoid therapy is because they know it will be difficult and could disrupt their lives. Reliving the pieces of our pasts that we've worked hard to forget, can be painful.

We've all heard, "The past is in the past." Yet, the past can't settle into the past until we reconcile it. We MUST walk through the painful moments of our lives again in order to get to the other side of them. The other side offers healing and a healthier way to live our lives.

Painful memories stay stuck in our bodies until we unearth them, feel the hurt, and make a conscious decision as to whether or not we will allow them to rule our lives. Will we let them keep us scared, guarded, self-doubting, critical, anxious and angry? Or will we demand they set us free?

People often believe they're unaffected by their pasts, but they're wrong. We were wired to live as whole, healed, peaceful beings. Buried painful parts of our lives eventually present themselves mentally or physically. They creep up and affect our relationships and our ability to live the way we were designed to live.

The therapeutic work my mom did was hard. Feeling the emotions of the abuse she experienced as a child was agonizing. She'd worked so hard to forget those memories, and now she had to not only talk about them but acknowledge the feelings she had about each incident. This is the point where many people leave therapy. They don't want to feel sad, rageful, lonely or lost again.

Courage is required to power through the pain, but the result is truly worth the anguish. When we accept our WHOLE story, own it, reconcile it, feel the emotions of it, and make a decision regarding how to live as a result, we experience healing. And when people are healed, they become the best version of themselves.

As a professor, I'm committed to teaching the theoretical frameworks, evidence-based interventions and the philosophical arguments that have driven my profession for years. I enjoy imparting the basics of Cognitive Behavioral Therapy, Dialectical Behavioral Therapy, Psychodynamic theory, and Gestalt. I lecture my students on the importance of having a solid understanding of these theories, their origin and when it's best to use them.

I tell my students to learn all of it and to learn it well. And then I dramatically slam my teacher's edition textbook shut and I tell them to unlearn what I just taught them. Of course, I want them to keep those academic gems in the back of their minds. But I also want them to realize that sometimes what people need isn't found in a textbook.

I credit Neda for much of my mother's

healing. My sister and I sometimes accompanied Mom to her sessions. We were made comfortable in the waiting room with books and games, while she disappeared into an office with her therapist.

What happened behind that door was a mystery to me, but Neda's soft voice and kind eyes reassured us Mom would be safe, even though her eyes often showed fear. As my sister read books, I would scamper over to the door, press my ear to it and try hard to hear what words of wisdom my mother's therapist imparted to her.

I so desperately wanted to understand what happened in their meetings. I HAD to know what made my mom cry for hours after some sessions. I also wondered what caused her to eventually carry herself with new strength and confidence. Not until I started my own undergraduate and graduate programs, did I understand that much of what Neda challenged Mom to do couldn't be found in any textbook. Believe me, I looked.

One day following a therapy session, my mother walked in the front door with a bright yellow bat in her hand and a determined look on her face. She kissed my sister and me on our foreheads and told us she had some homework to do for therapy. She'd be outside for a little while.

Curious, I peered out our back window to see what she was going to do with the bat. At first, she strolled around our beautiful backyard, slowly swinging the bat from side to side. She'd stop now and then, stoop down, and pull a weed. When she'd accumulated a huge pile of weeds, she laid the bat next to it and came inside.

I watched this unusual ritual for several weeks. After therapy, she'd head to the backyard with that resolute look on her face. I was sure something dramatic was about to unfold, only it never did. She'd simply set the bat down and commence pulling weeds.

I'd almost abandoned my perch at the window, when one day Mom walked out to the backyard, bat in hand, right past a new crop of dandelions. She stopped in front of our biggest elm tree. Her first whack at the tree was a half-hearted attempt. I could tell she barely tapped the trunk.

But then something happened. She hit the tree harder the next time and even harder the next. With each wallop, she yelled, the first scream a soft squeak that grew into a wail.

As the expression goes, she beat the living tar out of that tree. My sister heard the commotion and came running to the window. "We need to go see if she's okay!" she cried. After further discussion, we agreed that although what Mom was doing was weird, she was okay.

We understood enough at that point to know our mom had tapped into something raw, emotional and scary--and healing. The tree seemed to understand because it took the blows, absorbing the impact and her soul-crushing screams without so much as a dent.

To watch someone timid, scared and silent unleash such wrath is bewildering. I couldn't help but feel a little nervous about my mom's actions. But I was also relieved by her display of aggression, for I knew what it meant. Mom was beginning to get in touch with her anger. She was beginning to heal.

Now, one could argue that this technique is something taken from several therapy approaches. But my hunch is that Neda knew intuitively that my mother needed a tangible, physical, experiential way to "feel" the anger she'd stuffed for so many years.

For many years, there were three amazing male therapists who worked in the facility I directed. I was awed by their clinical skill. They'd been trained in all the psychotherapy modalities and techniques, but it was when they tailored their interventions to their specific clients that I saw true progress in the kids.

One of the men, Chad, was a large, stoic-looking man, whom I begged to come to my facility to work with some of the most traumatized youth in the state. He said he'd come over and give it a try and stayed for 10 years.

One afternoon, I walked by his office and I saw this large man sitting cross-legged on the floor, facing the wall. His large frame was folded inward, his shoulders drooped, and his head was down. His client, a tiny little blonde girl, sat in a chair by the door.

She was wearing his badge on her blouse and talking. Chad nodded ever so slightly now and then in solidarity. This pattern continued every time they met.

I made every excuse to leave my office during their sessions to catch a glimpse of their interaction. After six weeks, Chad was finally "allowed" to sit in a chair on the other side of the room, facing his client. After three months, she gave him permission to wear his badge again.

Through sobs, that little girl looked him straight in the eye and told him of her physical, sexual and emotional abuse. When she was finally ready to be discharged from treatment, the gentle giant and the little girl who'd been in treatment for a year, stood outside in a long "goodbye" embrace.

They both wiped tears from their eyes as she thanked him for being the only male in her life to give her safety and hope again.

Daniel was another excellent therapist. One day when I walked by his office, I saw a young boy curled up in one of his desk drawers. The drawer was large, but I was still amazed that any human could fit inside of it. At the youth's insistence, every week for six months, their sessions were conducted with the boy curled in the sheltering confines of the drawer.

Finally, I asked Daniel how I was going to explain to the state's monitoring team why one of our clients was stuffed in a drawer for therapy. Daniel's answer was very simple. "Tell them that's exactly what the boy needs to feel safe."

The child had been abused and abandoned repeatedly for most of his young life. He had trouble attaching to anyone, a self-protective measure to keep his fragile heart from being shattered again.

Youth with a diagnosis of Reactive Attachment Disorder find it hard to connect with others or feel safe in their environment. However, this little guy felt safe talking about the horrors of his life when he was securely tucked away in his drawer, protected from the outside world.

One day as I drove into the parking lot, I saw one of the kids with her therapist, Ned, standing on top of a dirt mound. He'd had her walk around for two days with a pile of rocks in a backpack she strapped on every morning when she woke up. They'd been talking about the emotional "baggage" she'd been carrying.

That baggage had been deposited into her psyche by her parents, siblings and other family members who constantly told her she was ugly, damaged and disgusting. Although this 16-year-old was one of prettiest teenagers I'd ever seen, she wholeheartedly believed her family members' messages. As a result, she carried their condemnation with her everywhere she went.

Those negative tapes played constantly in her head and kept her from loving herself or anyone else. A hardened gang member who wreaked havoc on her community, she was an angry, tough kid who retaliated against the world.

However, she adored her therapist, another big, burly guy with a long mountain-man beard. Ned looked more like someone from "Duck Dynasty" than the tenderhearted therapist that he was with a life goal to patiently and compassionately help children heal.

As I watched from the parking lot, this beautiful girl took the rocks from her pack one by one and hurled them into the nearby field. With each hurl, she screamed at the top of her lungs. "Take back your lies, Mom!" "You're the one who is pathetic, Dad!" She "gave back" the negative messages she'd received and believed all her life. When she walked back into the facility, her head was high and she was lighter, both literally and figuratively.

I'm not saying any one exercise mentioned above completely healed these children of their painful pasts or that my mom beating the sap out of a tree healed her deep wounds. But I am suggesting that each of these interventions helped an individual glue another piece of himself or herself into place. We are all on a journey to heal our broken and cracked souls.

Sometimes, we end up with a splintered

work of art that's been glued back together again to create a whole and complete masterpiece. Other times, we are so shattered that we construct a new design altogether. We discover the parts of ourselves we want to keep and discard the parts we no longer want or need in our lives.

Each intervention was based upon the needs of a client in an attempt to create a sense of safety, validation, and empowerment. While some of these interventions fall under certain therapeutic theories, they were inspired by empathetic, compassionate therapists who truly understood their clients' needs.

~~*Jann*~~

I felt guilty for the money we spent on my costly therapy. When Jonathan said he might have to sell his pickup to pay for my sessions, I cut back. I didn't want my husband to lose his pickup. He needed it for his work.

I didn't understand why our bank account was running low. As far as I knew, we had the same amount of income and outgo as always. Jonathan kept track of our finances, so I didn't question where the money was going. However, I assumed the shortfall was my fault.

About that time, we started getting strange calls on our home phone. When I answered, an evasive male voice would ask to speak to Jonathan. If he was not available, the man would hang up without leaving his name or number. I was curious about the calls, but Jonathan always blew them off as work-related.

As time went on, I discontinued therapy altogether. It was not worth the drain on our bank account, and I could tell the expense troubled Jonathan. He was relieved when I told him I quit therapy and said he'd been considering what he could sell to keep us afloat. I sank to the sofa in tears, feeling terrible for the anguish I'd caused him.

We were in the kitchen one morning when the phone rang and Jonathan quickly answered it. His side of the conversation sounded very odd. I wondered if it was the stranger who never left his contact information. When the call ended, I confronted Jonathan about the strange calls.

After much questioning, I learned the truth about our financial predicament. The mysterious phone calls were from his bookie. Jonathan had a gambling problem and had gotten in over his head.

I wanted to be angry at my husband for what his addiction had done to us financially, but it was obvious he already felt deep remorse. My anger would just heap guilt upon guilt. Even though I held my tongue, the secrets and lies made it hard for me to trust him.

I had placed Jonathan so high on a pedestal of perfection that his fall into a vice was a serious blow to my reverence of him. I never mentioned his gambling after that day, and as far as I know, he never gambled again. But his deceit left a hole in my heart. The only way I knew to get past the pain was to pretend it didn't happen. I wasn't sure what he would do if I told him how much his dishonesty hurt me or that it initiated a crack in the foundation of our marriage.

I felt my anger was justified, but I feared his anger more. Jonathan's control diminished me every day, but his anger froze me in my steps. I knew all too well how vindictive he could be toward those who crossed him. I was afraid to be on the receiving end of his vindictiveness, and that fear kept me in submission to him. It also kept me silent.

~~*Shari*~~

While the foundation of my parent's marriage was beginning to crack and my mom was questioning what unconditional love for a spouse meant, I was starting to date. Now, I can clearly see the dysfunction in my parent's union, but when I was a naive young adult, I set out to create a similar relationship. We humans tend to recreate what we're used to.

I didn't date much in college, but the boys I chose were possessive or simply couldn't "be there" for me. I rarely spoke about my one-sided relationships. If asked, I defended my boyfriends and justified their mean, insensitive behavior. "He's so angry because he's passionate. Passion is a good thing!" "He'll learn how to communicate over time." "It's okay that he doesn't know anything about me. He's so busy with work."

At the time, I couldn't see that I was doing what I'd been taught. I grew up watching a possessive, insensitive father, one who kept secrets and mistreated others and a mother who never objected to his callous conduct. To me, their relationship seemed perfectly normal.

I've heard clients say, "My father has never been in my life. He wasn't around much to influence me in any way. So, why do I keep attracting partners who are just like him?" Our caregivers, whether they're physically in our lives or not, leave us with messages about our worth and value.

My mother's mom abused and neglected her, which told her she was unwanted and unloved. Her dad died when she was three, which left her with a message that love and safety can disappear instantly. Without understanding death, she assumed his absence was her fault and tried to be perfect so that no one would ever leave again.

We gravitate toward the familiar. On a subconscious level, we seek what we experienced at a younger age. The key is to examine past events and consider how we might be recreating them in our lives. Then we can decide to discard whatever is not good for us or those around us.

Parents have said to me, "I will never treat my children the way I was treated by my parents." And yet, they end up telling me through tears, "I've become the very thing I hate." Deep down, we might tell ourselves things will be different with us, but then we find ourselves being or doing what we swore we'd never do.

Why? Because our brains like patterns. Patterns enable young children to learn how to do things. When food slides off a child's fork, someone shows the child how to hold it and makes him or her try again. We watch how our parents hold their forks and we copy them. And that pattern becomes ingrained.

We also watch the way people relate to each other. How our mothers and fathers or caregivers treated each other and how we were treated as young children become an ingrained pattern in the fabric of our souls. Tearing that fabric apart to form something different takes a deliberate and conscious effort, every moment of every day.

Intentionality is the ONLY way patterns change. We must choose consistently, to do something that, at first, feels awkward and strange. But, we do it anyway, over and over--until one day, we have established a new pattern.

Our conscious minds have a filtering system. We take in data, mull it over and decide what works for us and what doesn't. Our subconscious minds, on the other hand, do not have filters. Everything that enters our subconscious minds is, to us, the truth.

My mother learned from her caregivers that she was worthless and didn't matter. She believed them and incorporated that lie into her subconscious as truth. Subconscious beliefs become self-fulfilling prophecies, of sorts.

I've met people who proudly proclaim to everyone who'll listen that they love who they are. They often follow up with, "If others can't accept me as I am, well, they can take a hike." or another version of this with expletives attached. If those statements are true, wonderful for them!

But if such an assertion is a facade to cover up something inside that hasn't fully been dealt with, such as a core belief that they're ugly, dumb, inadequate, boring, or bossy, what they shout from the rooftops doesn't matter. They'll invariably end up attracting people who'll treat them the same way they feel deep down.

Because mom believed she was unlovable, she married someone who couldn't truly love her, which validated her belief. Because I believed I wasn't worth a man's time, on a very subconscious level, I sought out men who didn't have time for me. We believe what we've been taught. We create what we believe.

The work many of us must do in order to heal from our pasts has two parts. First, we must tackle our beliefs. Secondly, we must go back in time and give ourselves the beliefs we should have had in the first place about who we are.

We have to re-parent ourselves, become friends with ourselves and whisper new beliefs into our psyches over and over again. Those words sound something like this: "Every day, in every way, I am lovable, valuable, adorable, worthy of time, love, patience and grace. I am a warrior, and I have incredible strength. I was uniquely designed to be a gift to the world."

Those who desire to replace old, negative beliefs about themselves must spend time every day creating new beliefs. Let's say, I asked you to close your eyes and envision what your childhood bathroom looked like, you'd likely remember where the sink was in relation to the toilet and the bathtub. Was it because you took a conscious inventory of where everything was positioned every time you walked in?

No, you remember where everything was located because your subconscious mind "saw" the arrangement and memorized it. Your conscious mind was busy looking in the mirror for new zits, while your subconscious mind scanned the room to make sure everything was the way it should be.

Our subconscious minds seek out the patterns in our lives and constantly check to make ensure everything is in its proper place.

Beliefs about ourselves are monitored in the same manner. Our subconscious minds constantly assess our beliefs. Do we still believe the way we're "supposed" to believe? Do our actions reinforce those beliefs? After all, our subconscious is used to certain patterns. When we start to challenge those beliefs, we upset the applecart, so to speak.

When a person tells themselves every morning, "I am a gorgeous work of art, with a powerful voice and a sweet spirit," their subconscious mind panics. "Alert, Alert!" it shouts. "This is new! I'm not used to this, and I don't know what to do here."

However, as with all patterns, the more we incorporate a new truth, the more it becomes ingrained. When we begin to believe we are gorgeous works of art, we start to act that way and ultimately seek out people who also believe that about us. Our brains become used to this new way of thinking and behaving and push aside the old patterns to make room for the new ones.

I suggest to all my clients that they put sticky notes on their car dashboards, refrigerators, closet doors and bathroom mirrors with the beliefs they want to cultivate. For the first week or so, they notice the lists and repeat the mantras aloud five times each time they see them. But after a while, they stop reading them.

Yet, the subconscious brain continues to receive those messages. It "sees" them just like you "saw" where everything was in your childhood bathroom. The brain receives these messages and records them as data. This data spits out a new truth, one that informs us of who we really are. And a new pattern is born.

~~*Jann*~~

Not long after the gambling incident, I fell into a deep depression. I managed to get up each day and go about my responsibilities, but inside, I felt dead. I called Neda. She was concerned for my safety, so I returned to therapy. I desperately needed the outlet to my pain that therapy provided. My sessions with her were the only time I spoke of the turmoil that haunted my every waking minute.

Shari and I were the early risers in our family. Each morning, we'd quietly meet in the dimly lit living room, so as not to awaken Jonathan and RaeLynn. I'd have my coffee black with a packet of sweetener. Shari, not yet a teen, had a small amount of coffee with a large amount of milk and sugar.

This was how we started each day. Our morning talks became a special time we both looked forward to. Shari was worried about the emptiness in my eyes, and the sadness my smile couldn't hide. When I shared brief snippets from my past with her, she hammered me with questions.

I told Neda about my daughter's concern for me, and she suggested both of my daughters go in to see her. After that visit, Neda said I should explain some of my childhood to my oldest child because what she was imagining was probably worse than what I would tell her. I found out later that Shari thought I was dying.

Neither of us could have known that the talks we had would culminate in her future career. However, sharing pieces of my past and telling her I was dying on the inside, not the outside, was not without a heavy price. My story robbed her of her innocence.

The world was no longer sunbeams and rainbows. It contained dark corners where scary people lurked. This new information resulted in behaviors that are with her to this day.

I made a promise I would shelter them from everything ugly in this world. I told them portions of my childhood, and I was grieved when I saw the shock and pain on their faces. I wanted to take my words back, but they were embedded in their souls.

With time and perseverance, I made healthy strides in therapy. As I became stronger, Neda incorporated some tools to enable me to access the anger I could not express on a consistent basis. She suggested I buy a plastic bat, find a quiet, private place, and beat the bark off a tree!

When I finally convinced myself to attack a tree, I screamed, I cried, I raged as one face after another appeared on the trunk. Facing my abusers proved to be a difficult but cathartic experience. Until that day, I had not been able to feel anger or a sense of injustice about the way I'd been treated.

Neda also encouraged me to indulge the part

of me who never had a chance to be a child. I took Little Jann to the park to swing. I took her to a Disney movie, and bought her ice cream, even when I knew it would ruin her dinner.

These actions might seem mundane or irrelevant to someone who didn't have their childhoods stolen from them. They gave me permission to feel and to have fun and to recognize I was deserving of both. To this day, I sometimes go out and buy something I absolutely do not need, but only WANT, and then I tell my daughters that Little Jann asked for it and we smile.

Eventually, I told Jonathan parts of my history. But I couldn't read the expression on his face to tell how he was receiving the information, so I was selective with the degree of detail I shared. Neda felt that Jonathan's participation in my healing process was crucial and invited him into a therapy session or two with me. Throughout the sessions, she voiced her concern for his lack of family interaction, his dominating personality and his need for control. But when she realized that he was unwilling to make changes, she focused her sole attention on nurturing a more assertive side of me. All the while, she warned me that as I became stronger, the dynamics of our household would shift and possibly create chaos. Well, that was an understatement.

Sitting on the backyard porch with Jonathan one evening, I mentioned that I wanted to get a job. His business was thriving and he required my help less often. The timing for me to broaden my identity outside the home seemed perfect. He adamantly opposed the idea. I continued to express my desire. When he finally relented, he closed the discussion by stating that I should not expect him to share the household chores just because I was working. I assured him that I understood.

I quickly found a job and loved how working outside our home made me feel about myself. I opened my own bank account, as Neda had suggested, and began to feel some long-overdue independence, which had been her goal from the start. I was promoted from receptionist to a manager's assistant in less than a year and the responsibilities gave me confidence in my abilities.

But, having a job I loved didn't fulfill my desperate need for someone I could talk to on a deep, personal level. I wanted a close friend and realized my husband couldn't or wouldn't fill that need for me. His dominance was so large that I felt very small by comparison.

Jonathan was outgoing in public and told others about how much he loved and adored me. He said I was the greatest thing in his life, but inside the walls of our home, he was different. Sometimes he shut down and didn't talk to me for days. Other times he seemed bored with me. His words to friends never matched how I felt inside our home.

His image to the outside world appeared to be more important than the well-being of his family. In time, I came to the painful awareness that a healthy relationship must have trust, honesty, and equality. A couple cannot walk side-by-side when one person is elevated so far above the other.

Our marriage had no romance, no emotional intimacy. We never had enough money to travel, so we rarely got away from our daily routines. We didn't talk to each other about anything other than the children and money.

Even special holidays were uneventful. Every year, he sat in his recliner, watching TV while the girls and I decorated our Christmas tree. He would hurry through Christmas dinner to get back to the football game on TV. I grew more and more resentful, more and more angry, and more and more lonely.

I developed a friendship with a lady at work. We connected the moment we met as if we'd known each other all our lives. I'd finally found a friend, and her name was Maria. Now, I had someone to do things with. We shopped, had lunch, and went to outdoor music concerts together. I felt like I was fulfilling a missed childhood experience that I never got to have growing up.

Maria was just what I needed, a girlfriend I could relate to, someone who understood me, someone I could confide in woman to woman. She was outside the family unit, and she was *my* friend. Jonathan had friends to go to coffee with and play golf with, but that kind of socialization had been missing from my life.

Unfortunately, Jonathan detested Maria because she was gay. And he detested the time I spent with her. Her alternative lifestyle was not a problem for me and my being straight was not a problem for her. We shared a friendship, a sisterhood, and a commonality that was pure.

However, Jonathan felt threatened by her, and his insecurities blinded him to everything else, like the fact that I was deeply in love with him. His jealousy and mistrust of me were so great that he couldn't allow me to open my heart to friendship with anyone else.

I had finally become emotionally strong enough that most all my memories had surfaced. Therapy was arduous and grueling work that tore at every part of me. The layers of my soul had to be peeled back in order to rebuild myself from the inside out.

The process was almost more than I could bear at times. I was angry with God. I felt He had left me. To endure the abuse once was bad enough, but to have to go through it again was too much to ask of me. I raged at Him one minute and prayed to Him the next. Some pain is so great that a person cannot endure it without someone to hold them up.

Because my husband had pulled even farther away and I did not have his support for my friendship with Maria, my therapy or my work, I reached for God's hand. Jonathan did not know how to be present for me during my times of despair, pain, and brokenness. He hadn't learned that from his parents, who had a cold, distant relationship. I adored his parents, but their marriage was not cemented in emotional intimacy or closeness. Jonathan's apathy was killing me.

The physical pain I felt was matched only by the emotional pain I suffered. I did not yet have the tools to cope with the magnitude of my internal and external pain. My precious daughters were my life, but my "demons" convinced me I was going to ruin their lives if I remained with them.

While I knew they loved me, I doubted my husband's love. I wanted to die, and those dreadful thoughts erased any reason or logic I had. I decided to remove myself from my family before I destroyed their lives.

The day was Shari's 16th birthday. Naturally, I was overjoyed she'd reached that milestone in her life, but a treacherous darkness was bubbling to the surface of my mind. I sent my girls off to school with the same phrase I'd recited every school day since they started elementary school. "I love you, be safe, and walk with Jesus!"

The moment the school bus drove away, rather than get ready for work, I baked a birthday cake for Shari, prepared dinner for my family, decorated the house, set the table and arranged the gifts by the sofa in the living room. Then I climbed into my shower and sobbed as the warm water spilled over me. I had landed in the bottom of darkness, alone. I didn't want to die, but I desperately needed out of the pain.

~~*Shari*~~

A girl's 16th birthday is a big deal, possibly because it marks the end of student-driving and the beginning of independence. She can begin to explore who she is as she leaves childhood behind and steps into adulthood.

I remember riding home on the bus on my birthday, excited to take my driver's test the next day and have a sleepover at my friend's house. All my friends would anxiously be waiting to know whether I passed the test and if I'd be the first one to drive us around town. We couldn't wait to jam to music and not be bothered with the constraints that come with having an adult in the car with us.

This milestone represented a day I will never forget, not because I failed my driver's test, but because of what I saw when I returned from school. With my sister staying behind for band practice, I bounded off the school bus and ran into the house, eager to see what Mom had prepared for our family celebration. She always baked our favorite cakes, set the table for our favorite dinners and piled our presents in the center of the room for a night of family festivities.

When I walked in, I saw all of that waiting for me. I even noticed the pink-and-red paper plates and balloons lined up on the counter with a precision that only my perfectionistic mother could achieve. I called, "Mom. I'm home." expecting her usual, "Happy Birthday, my sweet little 16-year-old angel."

And, that is exactly what I got, but something was off in her voice. When she met me in the living room, I detected a change in her eyes. She wrapped me in her arms but not before I noticed a white piece of tape sticking out from the cuff of her shirt.

When I asked about the bandage, she said she'd had a little accident, but she was fine now. We played the usual cat-and-mouse game we'd played many times before. I asked, she gave a vague answer. I kept prodding, she attempted to distract me with another topic. I got frustrated, and she eventually relented and told me what she'd done that morning.

I didn't understand the distorted thinking and warped emotional rollercoaster she was on when she climbed into the shower that morning and cut her wrists. I couldn't fathom such a thing until I began working with suicidal clients and delved into the psyches of people who thought ending their lives would have no emotional impact on others. Such individuals don't comprehend that those they love, the ones they leave behind, will have to try to make sense of the tornado of loss and grief that rips through their lives.

I somehow walked through that night. We

did what my family did best--we ignored the reality of our lives and pretended everything was just fine. We had dinner, opened presents, and ate cake, I blushed in embarrassment as my family told me how much I meant to them. Then we watched a movie and went to bed without so much as a word about how Mom tried to take her life that morning.

I was in a fog all the next day. When I had to tell my friends, I wouldn't be the one to drive them around town, they didn't know how to comfort me. But that didn't stop us from eating the cake they'd baked with "Congratulations" written in icing on top.

We raised our glasses of lemonade, I told them I'd pass the test next time, and we went on with our slumber party. However, as everyone stretched out in their bags on the floor, I was haunted by my mother's fake smile that seemed to be "enough" for the rest of my family. Although I knew the truth, I was almost fooled into believing her ridiculous story about a "little accident."

The truth was, she'd prepared dinner, baked my cake, wrapped my presents and carefully placed the decorations in a manner that would rival anything Martha Stewart could put together. She did all of this so that after we found her dead body in the shower, we could have her hauled away and continue with the evening's celebration.

This rationale was steeped in a false perception that none of us would miss her, grieve her, or even notice she was gone. Her sick reasoning couldn't have been further from the truth. My mom didn't think she was worthy of love, so she had no understanding that her family would be devastated by her decision.

Over the years, I've worked with many a

client who, like my mom, formulated detailed suicide plans. Wounded, desperate individuals don't consider the ripple effects of their deaths or the gaping holes they'll leave in their loved ones' hearts. Their logic is overshadowed by a powerful desire to make the pain stop.

From my birthday party experience, I learned that "faking it" was not only a way to deny my own truth, but a way to keep people at a distance. I didn't have to be vulnerable. I didn't have to share the deepest, darkest corners of my heart.

What happens in one generation tends to get passed onto the next. I learned from my parents that communicating on a surface level and never addressing real issues is the way people relate to one another. As a result, I struggled for years not knowing how to be real and authentic with others.

In fact, I spent most of my young adulthood telling my friends that life was great when it wasn't. My denial allowed me to work with dangerous and mentally unstable clients during the day but lie to my young son at night. Over dinner, I'd ask him how his day was and then say, "Mommy's day was great." when in actuality, it wasn't.

Thinking back on that awful day my mother tried to kill herself, the unspoken words are what I remember. And the sideways glances my sister, father and I shared with one another. And the worried looks we tried to mask so we could play along with mom's charade.

I remember the tension that hung in the air as we pretended to celebrate my coming of age. Eventually, I concluded that *faking it* is destructive and minimizes who we are at our core. Pretending denies our reality and teaches our children that truth is so insignificant that it should be whipped into silence.

When I came to this realization, I changed the way I lived my life. I made a decision that I would always discuss the elephant in the room. In doing so, I would teach myself, my son and maybe even my mother to be authentic and connected to who we really are.

I instituted feeling words in my home. My son learned that being vague would not be allowed in our conversations. For example, if I asked him how his day was and he said, "Okay," I would keep digging. Our discussions often sounded something like this:

Me: How was your day, son?

Son: Fine.

Me: What does "fine" mean?

Son: That it was okay.

Me: Well, having an okay day can be a good thing or a bad thing. What made it okay?

Son: (with a sigh of frustration) I passed my test.

Me: Awesome! You worked hard studying for that test. What made the day okay instead of great?

Son: My teacher is a jerk.

Me: What did she do that was jerk-ish?

Son: She made fun of me in front of everyone.

Me: She made fun of you? Wow, I imagine that made you feel humiliated. Tell me what she said.

You get the drift. Is this redundant? YES. The point is that we owe the people in our lives an opportunity to drill down until we get to the real emotions. I've found in my work that we often miss the opportunity to dig deeper because people give us clear signals that they don't want to talk.

We want to honor and respect their privacy. However, we humans are wired to share the things in our hearts that cause us pain, whether they overwhelm us, humiliate us, confuse us, make us sad, or bring us joy. If we don't dig deeper with our children, our spouses and our friends to peel away the layers of the onion, we don't learn who the people in our lives really are.

This creates a world where children are raised to be adults who fake their emotions and hide behind the trivial "I'm fine" answer. We teach people that being real, transparent and authentic is something to avoid rather than a sacred thing. My mom's suicide attempt taught me to go deeper in all my relationships.

Faking it was a coping mechanism that worked for my mom for years. In many ways, it allowed her to survive. As a child, if she'd told an adult she was not fine, she would have been beaten. From watching my mom's struggle to be authentic, I've learned to take time every day to connect with myself and pay attention to what I feel. I owe myself honesty and transparency. To be the truest, most honest version of myself and to acknowledge who I am and what I feel is to acknowledge my human experience on this earth.

If you'd like to connect on a deeper level with the people in your life, be intentional about "checking in" with them. Ask yourself, your family and your friends questions. Here are some suggestions:

What was your high/low of the day?

Tell me about your happiest/crappiest part of the day?

How did I/you feel when this happened?
What will I/you do about how I/you felt?

The key is to be consistent and predictable and to dig deeper into the answers you receive. In asking the question, you've sent a strong message that tells the people in your life their feelings matter to you. If you live alone, you're connecting your experiences to emotions and validating who you are.

Let these question/answer sessions become something you practice every day. Do it night after night, even when your children become teens, roll their eyes and tell you "this is stupid." Do it anyway.

When your loved ones respond with, "I didn't have a high or a low today," that's okay. Sometimes, they may not have anything huge to report. Tell them that if they don't have any highs or lows, then you'd like to share what the high and low points of your day were.

Be consistent with your questions and attentive to the answers. Don't allow anyone in your life to always just be "fine". Ask them to tell you more. Show them you're interested in hearing WHY they're "just fine".

We live in a society of individuals who cannot connect to their emotions. We don't know how to be real. As a result, we're robbing ourselves of the unique opportunity to experience our humanness, our authenticity and our magnificence.

~~*Jann*~~

After the suicide attempt, I was more determined than ever to heal my emotional pain. I was also determined to push through the physical pain that came hand-in-hand with the memories, pain that became more pronounced during sexual intimacy with my husband. Pain that almost took my breath away at times, pain I held inside during each encounter. I had to get to the other side of that pain, so it couldn't hurt me anymore, because my body remembered the abuse as clearly as my mind now did.

My therapy had advanced to the point that facing my mother was an obvious next step. I had not seen her for many, many years. Jonathan and I planned a trip to our hometown. Our daughters could spend some time with their paternal grandparents whom we hadn't seen for a while, and I would visit my mother in the nursing home, where she now resided. Alcohol had taken its toll and she could no longer care for herself.

The day I was slated to see her, I was filled with fear and dread. I couldn't eat, my hands shook as I tried to dress. When we pulled into the parking lot, I was a nervous wreck, I wasn't sure my legs would hold me up.

I spoke to my uncle that morning about my upcoming reunion with my mother and he quickly reminded me of the commandment to "Honor thy father and mother." He didn't hang up until he had made sure I was chastised for wanting to confront her in the first place, stating that my desire to do so was a sin I would ultimately be punished for. I didn't hang up until I reminded him that I had already brought her honor by the way I had lived my entire life.

Jonathan stayed in the car with our daughters, who insisted they tag along. The three of them knew I was dreading the visit with my mother. They wanted me to feel their support but understood I needed to do this alone. I walked into the foyer and approached the front desk, where two staff members manned the station. One lady turned and asked who I was there to see, and I told them.

When I announced who I was there to see, the woman furrowed her brows, glanced at the other lady, and they both looked back at me. I was puzzled by their demeanor.

One lady pulled my mother's file from the gray steel cabinets that lined the back wall. After thumbing through the contents inside she said, "Martha doesn't have a daughter. She only has a son."

With sadness, I simply said, "Well, she has a daughter too."

As we stood there staring at each other, I heard a shuffling sound and turned to see a hunched little lady, with long white hair, dressed in a gown and robe, slowly walking toward the desk. She was a pathetic individual, and it was plain to see that life had not been kind to her. Her face was marked by deep wrinkles and scars. Her eyes were a dull brown and looked so sad.

I could not have asked for more precise timing, for the bent little old lady was my mother. I watched in disbelief as she approached. She no longer looked menacing. She no longer had the larger-than-life presence I remembered from my childhood. She was frail and pitiable.

The nurses at the front desk were silent as they watched the scene unfold. I walked a few steps toward my mother, met her where she now stood and asked, "Do you know who I am?"

Without hesitation, she replied, "Yes, you're Jann."

We went to her room, unhindered by the astonished nurses. I sat down beside her. Before I lost my courage, I told her I'd come that day to give back to her everything she'd given to me to carry all my life. My monologue went something like this:

"I thought because you didn't want me, no one else would. I believed because you didn't love me, no one else could. I suffered greatly at your hands and at the hands of others as you watched without doing anything to help me. I thought the things that happened to me were because I was a bad person. But what happened to me was about YOU, not me. Today, I give the abuses and the messages they sent back to you. They do not define me, and I will not carry them any longer." I paused. "However," I added, "I want you to know that I forgive you."

She never uttered a word, and her eyes never left my face, but she stared without emotion. I wasn't sure she'd heard me until tears formed in her eyes and one solitary tear spilled over the rim and rolled down her wrinkled cheek, it stopped when it pooled in a scar by her lip. A bell rang, which I assumed summoned the residents to the cafeteria. As she got up from her chair, clearly implying the visit was over, she asked, "Will you be coming back?"

I replied with only one word: "No."

I'd gone to see her without expecting to hear her tell me she was sorry or that she loved me. But as I walked away, tears filling my eyes, I knew how very much I wished she'd said those words. On the way out, I overheard one of the nurses say to my mother, "Your daughter is beautiful!"

And then I heard my mother's reply. "You think so?"

That day was one I'd dreaded; however, it was a step in my healing, the first tangible step off the path someone else had chosen for me. The first step onto one that offered a completely different journey. I had to unburden myself from the messages my childhood had carved into my heart. I had to destroy the beliefs I carried about myself to make room for new ones, healthy ones.

Before opening the doors that would lead me outside and away from my mother, I turned one last time to watch her walk out of my life, AGAIN. That moment was the last time I saw her.

I walked toward the car. I could see the concern on the faces of my husband and daughters. I tried to assure them I was okay, but they could see the hurt in my eyes. I told them what happened, and then we rode to my in-law's house in silence.

The road trip back home was a good one

overall, but such long hours in the car were very uncomfortable for me. For some time, I'd been dealing with a piercing pain in my buttocks and spine. When I could no longer sit, I knew I had to do something about it.

X-rays revealed I had a badly broken coccyx (tailbone). The orthopedist asked me when the break occurred. I replied. "When I was a small child." I'd felt the odd bone protrusions at the base of my spine since I was a little girl but couldn't remember what caused such a severe injury. He said my tailbone had to be removed, or the pain would worsen, and scheduled surgery for two weeks later.

He felt the procedure would be simple, but when he got inside and could see the bones clearly, repairing the damage proved to be more complicated than he'd anticipated. Over the years, my body had attempted to heal itself by creating layer after layer of calcium that had now grown into the muscle and had to be cut out. The tailbone itself had been deformed by the buildup.

As I awakened from the anesthesia, the pain felt familiar to me. Through a drugged fog, I saw clearly what had caused my injuries. My mother had invited a man over, and they were drinking. I'd been in my room most of the day when I decided to venture out to the living room, where they were. I was only in there for a few minutes, when I was told to go outside and play.

My mother left the room and went into the kitchen. And in a rare moment of defiance, I planted my body at the threshold of the front door, but I didn't go outside. With my mom in another room, I felt braver than usual.

Without warning, I was hoisted into the air by a man I'd only seen once before, perhaps a week prior when we'd driven to his house and stayed the night. He flung the screen door open, whispered in my ear that I should have obeyed my mother, and threw me outside. I landed on the concrete porch just before he stepped back inside and closed the door.

As soon as I could catch my breath, I crawled off the porch and around the corner of the house, so no one could hear me cry. I covered my mouth to try and silence the pain. I never told anyone about what happened because I didn't want to get in trouble.

I hadn't remembered that event with such clarity until that drug-induced moment. I saw myself landing squarely on my bottom on that unforgiving surface with my legs straight out in front of me as my tailbone shattered.

As I lay on the gurney in the recovery room, I felt the shock of pain as it had coursed through my small body back then. I remembered it all. Closing my eyes, I drifted off, praying I'd forget again.

Several hours after I was moved to my room, my husband and daughters arrived for a visit. A nurse came in and instructed them to leave and not return, but that was all she'd say. In the elevator, a policeman stepped aside to make room for them. Jonathan demanded to know what was going on.

The officer told him the hospital had received a bomb threat. My husband got our children home safely and promptly returned to the hospital. I'm not sure how he got through security, but I'd long ago learned that no one told Jonathan "no".

He marched into my room and said, "I'm taking you out of here!" He was packing my things when a nurse entered the room and told him he could not take me from the hospital. I was barely out of recovery and I had not been up to walk yet.

Despite her warning, within minutes Jonathan had loaded me into the front seat of our car. A nurse chased him down the sidewalk to sign release papers, absolving the hospital in the event I suffered complications because I'd not been officially discharged.

I was settling into our bed at home when the doctor called. Jonathan let him know I would not be returning to the hospital. The doctor gave Jonathan some instructions and said he'd ordered medication at a local pharmacy. I was nervous about being moved so abruptly from the nurses' care, but I knew better than to argue with my husband.

Jonathan had removed me from perceived danger at the hospital, while simultaneously risking my recovery. He'd been genuinely frightened for my safety, although we later learned the bomb threat was not legitimate.

Jonathan expressed most of his feelings through sexual intimacy. Whether he was angry, happy, worried or frightened, he released his feelings the same way. The hospital scare was no different. Even though I wasn't healed, telling him "no" was not an option then…or ever.

This was not my first surgery and would not be my last. I went on to have seventeen major surgeries besides the tailbone removal and the earlier hysterectomy. I hated being in the hospital because I was alone most of the time. Jonathan's visits were sporadic and brief, and he only allowed our daughters to visit for a short period of time. My time with them would have alleviated much of the loneliness.

As much as I needed to see our girls and they needed to see me, I didn't feel I had a right to ask him to take the time to bring them to visit me.

My hospitalizations took a toll on both girls. RaeLynn was younger and didn't show her emotion as easily as her sister, but I could always see Shari's anguish on surgery day as I readied for the hospital.

Visiting with my daughters would have been a welcomed distraction. The medications lowered my defenses and my typically stoic demeanor crumbled. I cried a lot.

During another hospital stay, a nurse heard me sobbing and came in to check on me. She called Jonathan and told him he needed to be with me. However, he was busy purchasing a new pickup right then.

My pain, my losses, my loneliness, and my emptiness always threatened to engulf me after the surgeries. The medications prevented me from keeping my heartache at bay. When I felt overwhelming emotions at home, I could tear apart a closet and re-organize it. By the time I put it all back together, I no longer felt anything.

If I couldn't organize the chaos of my internal emotions, I could feel a sense of calm by organizing the kitchen cabinets or my dresser, anything to not feel. I cleaned our house every other day. I ironed my husband's jeans, his t-shirts, all of my daughter's clothes and mine. I did whatever I could do to keep my demons away. The more memories I faced in therapy, the more agony I had to face at home.

~~Shari~~

I grew up not knowing from day to day if I'd ever see my mother again. As a young child, I watched her undergo several surgeries to mend the toll the years of abuse had taken on her body. After my mom's suicide attempt, I wasn't sure if in her devastating depression, she'd make another effort to end her life. I began to worry about her incessantly when I wasn't with her.

Due to the broken bones, sexual abuse and malnourishment she suffered during her sad childhood, I watched nurses wheel away my mother in her hospital-issued cap and gown over and over again. I never handled those separations well. In fact, I was an emotional wreck until I was able to see her again.

I've got a vein on my face that travels from my forehead down my right temple, past my eye. The vein swells when I'm stressed and pulsates when I'm under extreme stress.

When I was in my teens, I'd break out with

acne along that vein each time my mom went in for another surgery. My friends knew when they saw the line of red bumps down the side of my face that my mother was back in the hospital.

The older I got, the more I insisted I stay in the waiting room until I heard mom was safely in recovery, rather than see her off and return to school to wait for word from my dad that all had gone well. When I was finally allowed to stay, dad and I would sit in silence with him reading a golf magazine and me praying.

Each time, I feared Mom would not survive the surgery. As a result, I became somewhat compulsive in my prayers. I'd pray for her to be okay and then think I hadn't prayed hard enough, so I'd pray again. Then I'd wonder if I should pray differently, in case God didn't think I was serious.

This ritual would usually deteriorate into a chant I repeated silently to myself over and over to make sure God received my message. "Please make her better. Please make her better. Please make her better."

The doctors and nurses would do everything they could to ensure Mom's physical pain was under control. They'd have her scale her pain from 1-10 and provide extra pillows, warm blankets, and more medications, based upon her number. While I was grateful for this level of concern, I was always struck by the fact that while her physical pain warranted and received so much attention, her mental anguish went unacknowledged.

She'd lie in the hospital bed, the purr of monitors in the background, watching the IV bag. Its methodical drip-drip-drip seemed to flow in unison with the tears that fell from the corners of her eyes. I knew the physical pain wasn't what caused her tears.

The emotional pain that had long ago burned its way into her soul was still smoldering. Memories of being alone in a strange bed, in a strange building, with strange sounds caused her tears, as did the emotional pain tied to the abuse her doctors desperately tried to repair. To compound her misery, not having her family with her brought back all the abandonment she'd ever felt.

Why as a society, are we so compassionate and caring about the physical pain others suffer but at a loss for words regarding emotional pain? Or when we do have words for them, why are they disparaging? Why don't we try to understand their pain?

We wouldn't tell a person who has to take an insulin shot before going out for an evening of fun, "Come on, you're not just doing this for attention, are you? You just need to try harder." We wouldn't say to someone with a broken leg, "You're being a Debbie-downer. If you can't learn to deal with this better and get rid of those crutches, people aren't going to want to hang out with you." We wouldn't suggest to a hearing-impaired person who uses sign language, "You're acting a little dramatic, aren't you? Can't you just try harder to hear? Find a group that helps with that kind of thing and join it."

The above are messages that people who struggle with emotional issues hear again and again from misinformed and maybe even well-meaning people. Why can't we as a society, notice when someone is emotionally hurting and take the time to listen, really listen, to their struggles? So much shame is tied to emotional pain. In fact, we often label such suffering as "emotional baggage," which gives it a negative connotation. I wish I had a dime for the times I've heard my clients say, "He/she broke up with me because I had too much emotional baggage."

I "scale" with my clients (and friends), just like doctors and nurses do. When I know the people in my life are struggling with emotional pain, depression, anxiety, etc., I tell them I WANT to hear how they're doing, what they're feeling, what obstacles they face. I ask what their challenges are, and I ask them to tell me on a scale of 1-10, how bad the pain is.

As a clinician, the scale gives me something to gauge what level of intervention my clients might need. As a friend, it signals the amount of distress or hopelessness my loved ones are experiencing and helps me identify ways I can be there for them.

I beg anyone who'll listen to not shy away from emotional pain. My hunch is if someone mentioned at a party that they couldn't eat the pineapple because they'd been struggling with abdominal pain, others would jump right on it. They'd ask questions and offer opinions and names of doctors. But if a person said they'd been struggling with depression lately, the room would go silent.

We are not trained well as a society to know how to talk about emotional pain. We tell ourselves, "That is personal and I don't want to make them feel uncomfortable." My guess is that they already feel uncomfortable and risked their pride to reveal their pain in public.

We all want to be comforted, understood and accepted. My mother's family, neighbors, teachers and others who saw her, surely noticed the emotional pain she lived with every day. They may have even seen the bruises. But no one investigated the source. If anyone had, her life might have taken a completely different trajectory.

Dig, ask questions, drill down, inquire, show empathy, exude compassion and let those brought into your path know that A) you notice their emotional pain, B) you do not judge them for it, C) you want to hear about it, and D) you'd like to be a support person, if they're open to your encouragement. In doing so, you might just save a life.

~~*Jann*~~

Our daughters were active and popular in high school. They were both involved in cheerleading, drama, art club and the track team. I loved seeing the beautiful young ladies they were turning into. They'd been such easy children to raise and never caused me concern. I had no doubt that, left to their own devices, they would always choose wisely.

Jonathan and I and the girls were all very involved in a church that adhered to an oppressive hellfire-and-brimstone religious persuasion. It was the same type of church and had the same rigid rules as those my grandmother forced upon her offspring and me. It was the same denomination as my in-law's.

Because our church believed dancing was a sin, we were faced with a dilemma when our daughters wanted to go to prom. Jonathan and I saw nothing wrong with them going to prom, but their participation would have been met with condemnation from our church elders and church family. Neither my husband nor I truly embraced the church's doctrines, but we were so brainwashed we couldn't escape it either. We believed we'd go to hell if we didn't attend church three times a week. Jonathan and I reached the conclusion that forbidding dance was a church rule and not God's so our girls attended prom.

Shari was graduating from high school, and my husband's parents came for the occasion. I was so moved and proud of our daughter. This was the first of many accomplishments that she would attain.

But, it was also a very, very difficult day for me. I was trying to hide something horrible from everyone, including myself. I smiled and laughed for the sake of everyone. This had to be a day of joy! I was accustomed to holding my pain inside, I knew I could do this.

~~*Shari*~~

Once a week, I drove out to Missy's home. She was a 15-year-old handful of a girl I'd removed from an abusive household and placed with a foster mother. My purpose was to do individual therapy sessions with Missy and to provide support and guidance for her foster mother, a tired woman who had little experience dealing with the issues Missy had brought with her.

As I pulled into the driveway, the foster mom was standing there, waiting for me. I knew something had happened. I braced myself for what I thought I might hear and got out of the car.

All too often, I'd witnessed well-meaning foster parents who were ill-equipped to understand the immense pain that surrounded the children they'd welcomed into their home. I expected the foster mom to say, "I can't handle this child" or "She can't live here anymore. She's tearing my life apart."

The woman hurried toward me with a

worried look on her face. "She doesn't feel pain," she said. I replied, with my usual therapeutic, intellectual rhetoric. "She's learned to hide her emotional pain as a way to protect herself."

The foster mother shook her head. "No, she literally doesn't feel pain. Last night, we had a lasagna dish in the oven at 400 degrees for an hour. She pulled it out without using pot holders. Her hands are scalded but she doesn't feel the burn. She did the same thing a few days ago with a cookie pan. What does that mean?"

Unfortunately, I knew exactly what that meant. My whole life, I'd seen my mother's lack of sensitivity to pain. She felt physical pain, but it had to be extremely intense or it didn't register with her brain. I remember doctors' being in awe of how she didn't require the same levels of pain medication that other patients required after surgery. They'd say, "Jann, you are so lucky to have such a high pain tolerance." Even as a young child, I knew luck had nothing to do with it.

Mom tolerated high levels of pain because acknowledging her pain, whether physical or emotional, would have provoked others to ridicule, shun or beat her. As a result, her body learned how to absorb the pain and, to some degree, "numb out" from it. Again, the brain has a fascinating way of adapting in order to survive.

Missy and so many other children I worked with learned to do the same. The problem with "numbing out", as I call it, is that the brain can't always tell the difference between physical and emotional pain and will numb both out. The result is an individual who doesn't have a trustworthy gauge to tell them when they're tired or hungry, have a toothache, feel sad or need to care for themselves.

Thousands of people walk this earth who've ignored their needs for so long that they simply don't know what those needs are anymore. These people can care for others very well. They can show concern, encourage their friends to get some rest, instruct loved ones to be sure to take their medication, but they cannot do the same for themselves. They have become numb to their own needs and put pets, coworkers, neighbors, friends, and family above themselves.

Sadly, I have often felt exasperated with my mother. When I see her in pain and completely ignoring her own needs, I want to cry out, "MOM, please take care of yourself!" I've watched her take care of other people's pets, host a party, suffer through a long conversation or spend an entire weekend doing household chores without stopping for a moment to do something as simple as taking an aspirin for a pounding migraine.

I've had temper tantrums when Mom visited the doctor in need of an antibiotic and returned empty-handed because she hadn't provided an accurate picture of her illness. Now, in all fairness, she's improved greatly in this respect over the years. My sister and I now roleplay with her prior to a doctor's appointment, so she knows what to say.

I have become a broken record, often asking, "Mom, what are you going to do for yourself this weekend?" My hope is to alert her to her own needs. Caring for herself has been a struggle for her, one that was first highlighted when my grandparents came for my high school graduation.

I loved my father's mother dearly and

cherished every moment with her. We were emotionally tethered to one another and had a relationship that completely blinded me to her flaws. All I saw was a dainty, soft-spoken, older angel who adored me.

Most high school seniors ended the last day of classes by hopping into their cars and driving to the first party of a long string of celebrations that would last well into the night. I hopped in my car and raced home to see my grandma. I knew she'd be waiting in the driveway for me.

That night, we barbecued and had a picnic in the backyard. We had a wonderful time. Then, my grandma suggested I put on my cap and gown for some pictures. Everyone took turns posing with me as I hammed it up for the camera.

My grandma wanted a picture of herself and my parents, so I told her I'd take the picture. But as I steadied the camera, I saw the hollow look on my mother's face. She was blinking back tears and swallowing hard as if to push down emotion welling up inside her.

By this time, I'd become used to my mother's expressions of sadness and I knew this was something more than simply a mother mourning the loss of a daughter who'd be starting college in the fall. Later in the night, I asked her what was wrong. She gulped hard, blinked away tears and said she was just emotional about her baby growing up.

I knew she was lying, but I'd grown weary of trying to discover what was going on emotionally with my mother and trying to help her sort through her true emotions. That night, I didn't want to expend the energy to uncover what lay beneath the surface. My self-absorbed teenage self just wanted to relish the fact that I was center stage and finally graduating. I wanted my family's attention and accolades to be on me.

I still feel guilty about not nudging my mother to tell me more. I knew something was terribly wrong. I also knew she wasn't going to tell me the truth. And she didn't, for many years.

I was in my mid-twenties before I learned that before my mom arrived home that day, she'd been raped by someone she knew and trusted. She didn't want to spoil my graduation and, therefore, hid what happened. Even though she was in great emotional and physical pain due to that attack, she never acknowledged her needs.

Additionally, she didn't report the crime to the police or any other authority. Such behavior made me sad and angry. Even as a naive teenager, I knew something was wrong with hiding emotions.

That event motivates me to teach others to acknowledge their pain. Identifying our needs and attending to our bodies and minds is vitally important because such actions declare to us and to everyone around us that WE MATTER! Paying attention to our "human-ness" says we have value and worth.

Our self-respect teaches our children how to care for themselves. It also establishes boundaries and guidelines for others to treat us with the same respect we have for ourselves.

Suggestions for therapist, counselors, life coaches, teachers or anyone who works with clients who struggle to identify emotional and physical pain.

Ask your clients how they experience physical pain. Ask how they attend to their needs.

These questions are often not included in a typical intake questionnaire. Yet you'll discover valuable clues in the answers to the questions that will help you formulate strategies to implement with your client.

For clients who don't have an accurate gauge of their physical/emotional pain and/or their needs, you may want to begin with exercises that encourage body awareness. I often have clients chart in their phones what they notice about their physical sensations throughout the day and give each sensation a rating of intensity from 1-5.

When they become more aware of physical sensations, we move into tracking emotional states. I ask them to text themselves an emoji they can relate to during certain moments throughout the day. And then we later review their emoji texts together.

As clients become more in touch with who they are as physical and emotional beings, we begin working to establish a "container of safety" to help them handle the emotions that surface. We develop coping skills correlated to each sensation.

For example, when clients begin to actually "feel sadness," the intervention might be to call a friend or write a letter about the sadness. Each sensation has its own coping strategy, which we write down. And then I ask my clients to take a picture of the plan, so they have it on their phones. This "working document" becomes part of every session. We review it and role play how to implement these new strategies repeatedly so that a new context is built and can be remembered.

~~*Jann*~~

Due to Jonathan's disdain for Maria, I tried
to forge a friendship with a lady I knew from our
former church. Developing a friendship with her
took a while, but over time, we became close. Our
families got together for dinners. Shari baby-sat
their children.

Soon, we were inseparable. She was a
lovely lady. I envied her confidence and beauty.
One day, I went over to her house for a morning
coffee and girl chat. Seated in her sunlit kitchen,
enjoying coffee and muffins, we talked about
anything and everything.

As we talked, my trust in her grew. I told
her more and more about myself until her
expression changed. I'd taken the risk to share a
portion of my childhood with her. Apparently, she
had not been exposed to such degradation in her
life. I knew immediately that exposing my past to
her was a mistake.

But once the words left my mouth, I

252

couldn't reel them back inside. I knew she came from a very pristine family, but we were "sisters in Christ." I didn't expect judgment from her. However, to say she was shocked is an understatement.

I panicked and couldn't grab my purse and keys fast enough. I wanted out of there and away from her condemning eyes. The next evening, our family attended the midweek service at our church. I saw my friend in the foyer and approached her, but she turned as if she hadn't seen me. I brushed off her behavior, but when it happened again the following Sunday, I asked her what was wrong. Without hesitation, she told me she'd spoken to her father, an elder in the church, he'd said she needed to stay away from me.

In his opinion, my coming from such a dismal childhood could only end badly, and he did not want her to be exposed to me. I was stunned and humiliated. Following the judgment issued by my friend's dad, we severed ties.

Shortly thereafter, we left the church. Not solely because of this incident, but Jonathan and I were both beginning to question the church's teachings. Breaking away from that religion would prove to be as critical to my spiritual healing as facing my trauma would prove to be for my emotional and physical healing.

In time, I re-read the Bible cover to cover because I wanted to hear how the pages spoke to me. I soaked in the history written in each chapter, but my focus was Jesus' mission while He was on earth. He didn't preach hellfire-and-brimstone as the church so often did. He preached love. I realized this was the Jesus I knew and loved as a child. I also realized I'd stepped away from Him,

but He'd never stepped away from me. These
realizations firmly set my feet on a new spiritual
path that I continue to travel today.

I wish I could have considered my husband
my best friend, but without emotional intimacy,
such a foundation cannot be built. He was far too
inattentive for us to be "besties". I was on a quest
for a friend in whom I could confide. I needed
someone in my life with whom I could be real,
someone I could share all the things I held so tightly
in my soul.

Now that my daughters no longer needed me
as much and my husband had a life outside the
home, I threw myself into my job. It gave me a
small sense of worth. My low self-esteem
continued to plague me, and I was doing whatever I
could to overcome it. Therapy was progressing, but
clearly, until I found independence and
assertiveness, my healing was impeded.

Neda was right about the dynamics changing
in my home life as I became healthier. I was
beginning to feel that my interpersonal growth
would come at a hefty price. The taller I stood, the
more threatened Jonathan felt.

I now had independent thoughts and
feelings, and I slowly began to speak them for the
first time, I voiced my likes and dislikes. This
newfound behavior unsettled Jonathan. Just as I
earlier equated his dominance and control as love,
he equated my late-blooming as the lack thereof.
When I displayed any form of individuality, he
perceived it as rejection, and it created contention.
He withdrew and wouldn't speak to me or he'd cut
me down in some way. Sometimes, I'd stand up to
him and defend my emotional growth. Other times,
I remained quiet.

What is profoundly sad to me is that I wasn't falling out of love with Jonathan, I was simply falling IN LOVE with myself. I still needed and wanted him in my life, but I wanted him to be beside me rather than over me.

This shifting of the imbalance in our relationship must have been very difficult for him. Reworking our union was certainly a confusing time for me. I'm still saddened that Jonathan failed to understand he was going to have a better, healthier version of me in the end. All those years of marriage, and I still had not revealed my authentic self to him, partly because I had no idea who my authentic self was, and partly because I was afraid to do so.

Jonathan had fallen in love with someone who was compliant in all areas. When I became less compliant, he was shaken. He didn't know the woman who was developing her own identity. I was no longer the submissive young girl he'd married.

I had accomplished so much in therapy and a new strength grew from my changing internal beliefs and messages. However, I had one last big hurdle to overcome in therapy, the trunk I had in the orphanage. That trunk was so very important to me. Neda and I had discussed it often, but I was about to find out what her obsession with my trunk was all about.

One morning, she leaned forward in her chair across from me, and with tenderness in her voice, she asked, "With all that was stripped from you in the orphanage, how did you come into possession of a trunk full of jewelry?"

I replied, "Oh, I, I, I..." Stunned and frantically trying to remember, I just fell silent. I'm sure she could tell by the shocked look on my face that I'd never questioned the reality of that trunk or how I acquired it.

As I internalized the fact that my trunk and all its contents were not real, I broke into a deep guttural sob. My admission to myself that my trunk was an impossibility sent a shockwave of panic through the heart of the child crouched inside my soul. Neda felt I was strong enough to handle the truth, and she was right. Yet, I experienced all the panic of that forgotten child who'd been abandoned in an orphanage. Without that trunk, she had no hope of defining her value or seeing her family again.

Even though I was facing difficult realities in therapy, it centered me. I was growing emotionally and learning who I was. My home life had the opposite effect.

The college Shari attended was only 20 minutes away. She lived in an apartment, but she still came home on weekends to catch up with RaeLynn, who still lived at home, and with her dad and me. I really missed our morning chats and loved having her with us again.

But Jonathan didn't seem to want her there and she knew it. He was critical of her and everything she did. His fault-finding broke my heart because I knew it was breaking hers.

This was still Shari's home, and I wanted her to feel welcome. Naturally, I wanted peace with my husband as well, so I was constantly torn by the tension her arrival created. I could see the pain in Shari's eyes as she endured her dad's rejection. Jonathan had felt rejected by his dad, and he'd told me how it hurt him. I wonder why he couldn't see he was doing the exact same thing to his daughter?

Jonathan never took the time to know or understand her. He didn't support her desire to further her education. He didn't support her goals or dreams. In short, he didn't accept her, and she knew it.

He was closer to RaeLynn when she was a child. She adored him and spent time with him outside. But, she was growing up as well, and he had a difficult time relating to his grown daughters, who had minds of their own. RaeLynn was a senior in high school and I could see him starting to pull away from her as well.

RaeLynn and I were selecting graduation cards when she received a phone call. I watched as her face turned ashen and then she dropped the phone and began sobbing. I picked up the phone. Her boyfriend's mother was on the line. She'd just found her son in the basement of their home, an obvious suicide.

I offered my condolences and got off the phone to attend to my wounded daughter, who was reeling from the news. The death of her first love spiraled her into depression, confusion, and unjustified guilt. Shari and I worried about how his suicide was going to impact the rest of her life. As it turned out, it impacted her in a significant way for many years.

We all seemed to be struggling to find our own way amidst the changes in our lives. Shari was studying and planning her future, RaeLynn was trying to make sense out of a senseless death, my husband wondered how to get back the unassertive wife he'd married, and I was desperately trying to stay on my path to greater healing without losing my husband and daughters in the journey.

After distancing myself from Maria, and

being shunned by my friend from our church, I wasn't sure I wanted to be close to anyone again. But Maria and I found our way back to each other and drew closer as the time passed. Unfortunately, our friendship caused a wider gap to grow between Jonathan and me.

I had missed so many steps growing up. Taking them now felt strange. I had no clue what I liked, what I wanted, what I needed, nor did I have any idea what it felt like to hear my own voice. But as I took baby steps in my self-discovery, I began to hold my head higher. I was in my 40's, and finally growing up...about time.

Sometimes, I feared I'd lapse into who I'd been for so many years. One such evening drove that fear home when Jonathan wrapped his arms tightly around me and said, "I wish I could take you to a place where no one knows you, so I could have you all to myself!"

Apparently, as I became healthier, strings that tied me to my husband snapped, the kind of invisible strings that bind a child to a parent rather than an equal partner. I could see the fear growing in him. How was I going to find myself without losing my husband?

Maria, who was moving needed a temporary place to live, so I told her she could stay in Shari's room until her apartment was ready. Of course, I told her I'd check with Jonathan. But I didn't see how he'd mind because he'd let some of his friends stay with us over the years.

When I mentioned that I wanted to help Maria by giving her a place to stay for a couple weeks, he clearly was not pleased with the idea. But he conceded to my wish to help her out. However, his silent treatment told both Maria and me that she was not welcomed.

Again, I found myself trying to make my husband happy while trying to be kind and welcoming a guest into our home. Maria's time at our house was constantly overshadowed by Jonathan's lack of acceptance. I didn't understand why everything I wanted or needed in my marriage meant I had to choose between it or my husband. I became so stressed over the situation that by the end of the two weeks, I was relieved when she moved out. I couldn't take the tension any longer.

Now, it was RaeLynn's turn to graduate. Her graduation was also a celebration, but it was clouded by the still-raw grief of her boyfriend's suicide. He should have graduated with her. She was a talented artist and could have received an art scholarship, but she wasn't sure how she could apply that to a career, so she declined it.

She chose to attend cosmetology school, putting her artistic talent into a skill that would open career opportunities for her. Within a year, she became a highly successful stylist in a nearby salon with more work than she could handle. New clients clamored for an appointment with her because of her exceptional skill.

She was slowly finding her way out of her depression and even dating again. I was so proud of the young women our daughters had become. Things looked hopeful for them, their futures looked bright.

Maria and I continued with our friendship. Having a confidant during the daytime was rewarding because my evenings with Jonathan were mostly spent in silence. Eventually, he seemed to accept when I went to lunch or a concert with her, but I was oblivious to the fact that he was stalking my every move. During an argument over Maria, he confessed he had been shadowing me.

He'd sit outside her house, repeatedly calling her home phone while I was there. She didn't answer because she'd been in a dispute with a relative just before I arrived, and thought it was her calling over and over. There was no caller ID then. I knew Jonathan struggled with our friendship, but the thoughts he had surrounding my relationship with Maria were way off base. He thought we were having an affair.

While spreading my novice wings, I tried to stop bending to my husband's every feeling, mood, and attitude. But when he suggested Maria and I were having an affair, the accusation threw dirt on our friendship and covered us in blackness. She moved to another city, and I never saw her again.

I was heartbroken. That relationship was very symbiotic for me. I needed someone to love me without wanting anything in return, and Maria filled that need with her supportive, unconditional love.

I grieved the loss of my friend. But in time, I discovered who I was as a person and established my own journey. I felt like I was 16, learning about life and what I wanted to get out of it for the first time. I laugh now as I remember how I tried to find my identity at the age of 40+ rather than my late teens.

In hindsight, I'm glad I didn't pierce something I would have later regretted or dyed my hair purple or embarked on a vision-quest to the top of a mountain. I tried to remain conventional in my pursuit of wholeness. My worth was still strongly linked to other people's likes and dislikes because I wasn't convinced I would be accepted if I differed from them. And, my own likes and dislikes were not yet grounded. I was so fickle. One day I liked brown, the next day I liked purple. But I was determined to find my way.

I hadn't been to therapy for about two years. I had wanted to try life on my own. Neda and I kept in touch, but it was important for me to use the tools she'd given me and to rely on my newly embraced inner compass to guide the rest of my journey.

I was gaining emotional strength, but at the same time, my marriage was weakening. For me to find my own courage, my own sense of self and my own value while losing the man I loved was a daily battle that shook me to my core. I was losing respect for Jonathan and he was losing his footing.

Rather than walking hand in hand to a higher ground, he pulled away and flailed. As I found my voice, he silenced his. Clearly, we were traveling different paths.

Our daughters married within six months of each other. I longed for them both to have mutually respectful, loving partnerships like I had long hoped for myself. But, who was I kidding? I'd modeled an unhealthy marriage to them. My failure to show our daughters the importance of finding someone who valued them played out in the partners they chose.

Shari chose an emotionally unavailable man. RaeLynn chose a kind man, but he didn't display strength. Because her father was such a dominating force in her life, her husband's perceived weakness felt unsafe for her. To cope with an insecure situation, she developed a serious health issue.

I discovered this condition when I went to her house one day to hem some slacks for her. She'd always worn large shirts, which was the style at the time, so I hadn't really seen her body until that day but seeing how emaciated she had become propelled me to take the first huge step in standing my ground with my husband.

I decided to take RaeLynn home to help her regain her strength. She'd developed an eating disorder. Jonathan adamantly disagreed and announced, "I cannot believe I have a daughter so screwed up." I knew I had a battle on my hands, but I dug my heels in because I was fighting for the well-being of our precious daughter.

I devoted months to taking care of RaeLynn. She was my priority. When she started to improve, I was elated. But the enormity of what my determination to help her did to our marriage was evident. While I desperately worked to save our daughter, Jonathan withdrew. When she was well enough to return home, his rejection and the pain I felt from his lack of support burned within me.

One night while sitting with him on the sofa, I noticed he'd taken off his wedding ring. I asked him about it and he said it bothered him at work. I wondered why, after 25 years, the ring suddenly bothered him at work, but I let it go. I mean, why would he lie?

He also began going away on weekends. This had never happened in 25 years, either. I didn't question his absences, because why would he lie? The phone would ring at night and he'd be secretive about who he was talking with. I briefly considered he might be gambling again, but he'd promised that was over.

One call came while we were in bed. He claimed that there was a problem at the restaurant and he needed to check it out. He left and didn't return until morning. That had never happened before and it seemed strange. But I shrugged it off, because why would he lie?

A friend of his came over one afternoon and I was introduced to him for the first time. My hair was and always had been black, but he asked me, "When did you dye your hair? The last time I saw you in Jonathan's car, you were a blonde."

I laughed, wondering how he could have made such an odd mistake. When I asked Jonathan about it later, he said he had no idea what the guy was talking about, and I believed him. After all, why would he lie?

Jonathan planned a golfing trip with some of his buddies. He didn't tell me where he would be staying and said that his cell phone would not have reception. I thought the golf club surely must have a landline, but I didn't question him, because why would he lie?

In hindsight, I should have questioned everything! But he'd always been aloof, and I'd never questioned him or what he did. I never once thought to question him now, which would prove to be my downfall.

~~*Shari*~~

My parents' marriage started to crumble the same way many relationships do. Their beliefs and values collided. You often hear people say, "We just drifted apart." or "We outgrew each other." Most likely, one partner's deeply held beliefs changed and living with the constant collision of beliefs became too difficult to continue.

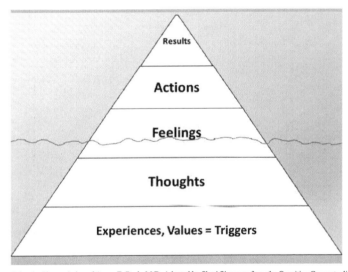

Printed with permission of Aaron T. Beck, M.D. Adapted by Shari Simmons from the Cognitive Conceptualization Diagram Worksheet.

If we think of ourselves in terms of an iceberg, we can see the stages we go through that eventually lead us to the results we get in our lives. Cognitive Behavioral Theorists (CBT) often refer to a diagram that illustrates this pattern. What we believe (usually born out of our life experiences, both good and bad) produces our thoughts. Our thoughts then lead to our feelings. Our feelings create our actions. Ultimately, our actions, behaviors, and decisions produce results. These results carry positive and negative consequences.

In therapy sessions, I often draw this on a board with a waterline. When discussion hovers at the surface level, I ask clients to try to go beneath the waterline where the deeper issues lie. The waterline is drawn through the middle of the feelings section to show what happens with us as humans.

The world gets to see *some* of our feelings. Our friends and loved ones see when we are frustrated, angry or elated. But only a select few in our lives get to see or hear about the feelings that occur beneath the surface. We only share our deep-seated fears, self-doubts, insecurities, etc. with people with whom we feel safe. Those feelings usually stay beneath the waterline, where they lurk unseen in the dark. Relationships are like two icebergs floating along together.

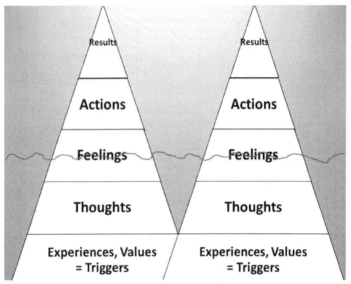

Printed with permission of Aaron T. Beck, M.D. Adapted by Shari Simmons from the Cognitive Conceptualization Diagram Worksheet.

I saw the cracks in my parents' marriage before they ever realized they had a problem, although, at the time, I didn't understand what was happening. My dad loved to make my mom laugh. The problem was, he often did this at her expense and in a way that showed his dominance over her.

He'd come into the living room when she was watching TV or reading, grab her by the ankles and spread her legs wide open. He'd tower over her, laughing at her discomfort in being exposed in front of her girls. He'd laugh hysterically, and because my sister and I were young and still revered him, so did we. My mom would laugh too, as someone does when they are being tickled, but obviously, don't like it.

This humiliating maneuver happened frequently. When we saw the panicked look on our mother's face as she struggled to break free, my sister and I would beg our father to stop. One such time, we both ran to unlock his fingers from her ankles. He walked away laughing, but I saw the tears in my mom's eyes.

She was trying to swallow the lump in her throat and to steady her breathing. And she said something we'd never heard her say before, "I don't like that." Her therapy work was still in its infancy stage, but she had been introduced to the idea of her own self-worth.

She hadn't learned how to engage her voice and establish her boundaries yet, but she was beginning to identify small pieces of what she did and didn't like, after a lifetime of others dictating her likes and dislikes to her. I ran to find my dad to tell him Mom didn't like that.

He retorted with, "Of course she does. She knows I'm playing. You saw her laughing."

More time and therapy passed before she could make her boundaries and feelings known to my dad. Her beliefs about how she should be treated were changing and, as a result, beginning to clash with his. Our struggles with others are usually because our beliefs collide with theirs.

However, we tend to focus on what we can "see" rather what's going on beneath the surface, at the bottom of the ocean floor. My dad could see my mother was showing signs of unhappiness. He also saw that her actions were changing and she was responding negatively to things she accepted before.

As time went on, she became unwilling to embrace the relationship as they'd once known it and established a life where she had some control. She started working and going out with friends. He isolated himself from her and his family and developed his own secret, private life, one that ultimately destroyed their marriage.

As seen in the illustration above, their Actions and Results were miles apart from each other. They did not address their true Feelings and Thoughts, all because their Beliefs were clashing in the cold, dark, murky waters in the depths of their ocean.

~~*Jann*~~

My little grandson was born amid bright lights and warm hugs. I noticed my husband's distance in the hospital but brushed it off thinking he was overwhelmed by the birth. I certainly was.

During the car ride home, I tried to engage him in a discussion about the day's beautiful events. But he said nothing. I had no idea how to reach this man I'd lived with for so long.

And I was furious at him for making my healing process such a dismissal of himself. I still have trouble thinking about the times I just wanted to fall back into my old self-deprecating ways, just to make peace in my marriage. I wanted my husband to accept me, but to do so meant I'd have to become invisible again, and I was not going to do that.

I delighted in seeing our grandson every chance I had. My heart was so full of love for him. I was confused at Jonathan's mounting detachment to anything that had to do with our marriage or our family. I grew angrier and angrier because I felt I had to defend the love and devotion I felt for our daughters and grandson. It was as if my love for them invalidated my love for him.

One morning as I was leaving for work, I asked him if he loved me anymore. He replied, "I could never love anyone as I love you." I assured him I loved him, too. I kissed him and left for work with hope filling some of the cracks of my heart.

Over the next few weeks, I asked him that question often because I sensed something was dreadfully wrong. One afternoon, as he worked on his car in the garage, I walked out and stood beside him as he worked. Afraid of the answer, I mustered the courage to ask the question differently. "Are you still IN love with me?"

Without stopping what he was doing and without looking up at me he simply replied that he didn't know. At that moment, every rejection, abandonment, and loss I'd ever experienced came flooding down on me in a torrential downpour of excruciating pain.

My very soul exploded. I walked inside to our bedroom and sat down on the bench at the foot of our bed. I opened my mouth and doubled over. Grabbing my stomach as if doing so would somehow ease the agony I felt. Suddenly, I heard a blood-curdling scream that didn't even sound human. It was me.

He'd followed me into the house, but I wasn't aware of his presence until he said, "I love you. I will always love you." I'm sure he must have been hurting as well, but this time I couldn't take care of his feelings. I was now grappling with the uncertainties of my life with him and my growing awareness that what a person says must match how they treat the other person. Love is not just a word, it's an action!

I finally went to bed in utter exhaustion. I cried all night and tried to figure out what my next move should be. I knew myself well enough to know I could not stay where I was not wanted, but I had no idea how I would make it on my own. By the time light began to fill the room, I was already up and dressed.

Jonathan, who looked as damaged as I felt from the reality of the night before, got up, pulled me into his arms and said, "I love you."

I didn't want to hear him say that to me after he'd told me last night he didn't know. I couldn't even be sure what those words meant from him. Now, I needed to know if he had someone else in his life. He assured me he did not.

I believed him because…why would he lie?

Nothing was clear to me. I couldn't feel my legs. My heart was pounding, but it didn't feel like it was in my body. This could not be real.

The words of my therapist burned in my ears. "As you get stronger, the dynamics in your marriage will change and cause chaos." That was an understatement. I was going to have to revert to who I'd been, or I was going to have to leave my marriage. I had no idea how I was going to find the courage to just walk away, but I learned how. I would do it one step at a time.

Because of my childhood rejection, I knew I couldn't remain with someone who questioned their love for me. I felt like a caged animal, desperate to get out and, as far away from the rejections as possible.

I called Shari and we went in search of a place for me to live that very morning. When I returned home from house hunting, Jonathan and I talked for a few moments. He said he didn't want me to move out. He wasn't sure what was going on with him, only that he didn't want to be a husband or a father or a grandfather.

I asked him again to go to therapy with me to work on our relationship. He said he didn't need therapy, I was the one who was damaged. He was right. And, at 49 years of age, it was time I started to glue myself back together again. The "gluing" would begin with me leaving a toxic marriage.

Jonathan packed a small bag and left for the night. I didn't know when or if I'd see him again, but he returned the following day. Within two weeks, I was packed and moved out of our house. My haste shocked Jonathan. I don't know if his reaction was because I took the choice from him or because he wasn't ready for the marriage to end. But he'd forced my hand, and I was in control at that moment in our life together, for the first time.

As I stood in the doorway of our garage after putting the last of what would fit into my car, I faced Jonathan and asked, "Why did you treat me like you did for thirty years?" Without hesitation, he answered, "Because you let me."

~~*Shari*~~

Throughout my childhood, I watched my mom literally swallow her feelings. She'd actually *gulp down* the emotions rising in her chest and blink away tears she hoped my sister and I couldn't see. My dad would say something hurtful that wounded her spirit. Rather than risk saying what was really on her heart, she'd draw her lips into a firm line, swallow her emotions and will herself not to cry.

This reaction was not exclusive to my father. She did the same thing with friends, family members and coworkers who sometimes said cold, callous things to her. I even saw her swallow her emotions with my sister and me when we spoke out of line. Rather than chastise us and stand up for herself, she gulped down the pain.

This pattern unfolded so many times in my life that I saw it as part of who my mom was and how she responded to her world. When I later viewed her behavior from a therapist perspective, how she handled emotional pain spoke volumes and told a story I believed for many years.

The story went like this, "Even though I tell you to be strong and to share your real feelings, I am not strong, and I will shove my feelings down at all costs." This mixed message was difficult to grasp. I heard my mom telling me the kind of woman I should be, but I saw something very different, until the day she left my dad.

I married at twenty-three. Still naive, I hadn't quite emerged from my very sheltered upbringing. I was still in college when I met my future husband in the restaurant where I worked. I wasn't particularly attracted to him. He wasn't charming, nor was he charismatic. In fact, he was socially quite awkward.

He did, however, walk into the restaurant one day and tell me he'd packed a lunch for the two of us. If I was interested, he'd like for me to join him during my break. This gesture seemed so kind and romantic to me. That a man would take the time to think about me, pack a lunch for me and want to spend time with me was something my soul longed for.

We dated for a year. Throughout that time, I ignored how he wouldn't respond to me when I tried to talk with him about my feelings. I ignored how he made fun of me when I tripped or fell or hurt myself. I ignored his rude behavior because I'd been taught to ignore it. I swallowed my feelings and accepted that my role as a girlfriend, fiancée and eventually, wife, was to be silent. I learned my feelings were not valuable and, therefore, should never be expressed.

When we choose to ignore the red flags in our relationships, our decisions about what paths we'll follow can have grave consequences. My mother and father are not to blame for what they taught me regarding relationships. They did the best they could with the tools they were given. They taught me what they knew.

However, our time on earth is short, and in that time, we have decisions to make about what we want to pass down to future generations, whether we have children or not. Nieces, nephews, cousins, and children who don't even belong to us, soak in information from ALL the adults they watch. Believe me, they watch. Watch them watching you the next time you're sitting at a restaurant or are in line at Starbucks.

Six months after that lunch, we were engaged. Six months after that, we were married. But our marriage was void of love or adoration. It's difficult to feel adored when your husband sleeps in the living room most nights. It's hard to feel loved when he throws all the gifts you made for Christmas into the street in a fit of rage or taunts you with mice when he knows you're terrified of them.

Like myself, my husband's behavior was learned. He carried around a large load of justified resentment and anger he frequently dumped into my lap so he could be free of it for a while. I didn't take the load willingly. I argued with him and tried to reason with him regarding his irrational behavior. He wanted to love me, but he'd had no loving role models, and therefore, resorted to what he knew, ambivalence.

Prior to our wedding, I recorded a song to surprise him with during our ceremony. As we stood in front of a crowded church, lighting candles, my song played. I smiled at him and asked, "Do you know who's singing this?"

He responded with "Yeah."

Knowing all eyes were on us, I whispered,

"Do you like it?"

He looked at me and paused for what felt like an hour and then whispered back, "It's okay, I guess."

Blinking back tears, I swallowed the hurt, just as I'd been taught to do.

Life as newlyweds set in, and I noticed something that felt familiar. My husband became increasingly jealous when I was around my family, especially my mother. While he seemed to be in awe of my bond with her, he was also resentful.

His behavior took on a bizarre twist before family gatherings. He'd provoke an argument and yell for hours about how I needed to grow up and leave my family behind. When his yelling didn't stop me from seeing them, he resorted to making his point when I was asleep. I woke up one night to him pushing me with his feet to the edge of the bed and then laughing when I fell off.

Another night before my parent's relationship crumbled, my husband was angry with me when we went to bed. I was awakened by him pouring a pitcher of cold water on my head. Flabbergasted and hurt by his behavior, I threw on my clothes and drove to my parents' house. My wet hair and tears froze in the cold night air and my mind reeled from the shock. I couldn't believe my husband would resort to such tactics just to make a point.

My parents kindly climbed out of bed, gave me towels to dry my face and hair and sat with me in the living room. That's when I noticed myself doing what Mom always did. I swallowed hard, blinked away tears and gulped down my sadness for fear that if I let it come to the surface, it would surely wash me away.

I hated watching my mom walk through her life without the esteem to demand respect from others; yet, here I was, caught in the exact same dynamic. I'd learned that women didn't have the value to be treated with fairness and although I'd swore I would not marry someone like my father, I'd chosen a man who validated my inner belief that I wasn't worth a loving, respectful relationship.

Children will usually pick the path their parents and grandparents and even great-grandparents walked because that road is all we know. It's familiar and we know how to navigate it. Not until something negative happens in our lives, like getting drenched in water, do we begin to question which way our life is going. In these most powerful of moments, we are forced to decide how we will live and what we will model for others.

With my mother making changes in her life, I slowly but surely followed. As she began to capture control of her life, I took mental notes and forged a new way for myself. Although, it took a few years to implement, when I was ready, I pulled those mental notes out and started to take action.

Two years later, I gave birth to our son, Dakota, in what would prove to be a harrowing adventure. My 5'2" frame was not prepared for the eight-pound, three-ounce baby I carried two weeks past his due date. When there was no sign of my little boy wanting to make his way into the world, my doctor decided to induce labor.

After 15 hours of labor, she decided to break my water. Three hours after that, she looked at my baby's heart rate, saw it had taken a significant dive and calmly, but somewhat eerily, said, "Okay Shari, let's get that baby out now." By that, I learned she meant yanking him out forcibly.

I gave birth to a dark-blue baby, who was still not breathing several minutes later. While nurses were trying to get air in his lungs, my mother, who was in the room with me and my husband looked at me in horror. Dakota was a color he shouldn't have been and I was bleeding profusely.

In the hour that followed, the nurses whisked away my baby boy and put him on a ventilator. They also whisked away my mom, who'd almost fainted, to an adjoining room to lie down. In the hallway outside the birthing room, I could hear my doctor and the surgeon who'd been called in to review my case, arguing about the absurdity of allowing me to give birth to such a large baby rather than have a C-section.

After that heated debate, the surgeon, whom I'd never met walked in, obviously upset, and proceeded to give me the 350 stitches required.

Due to my stitches and my son's rough start in the world, we both stayed in the hospital for four days.

On the second night of my hospital ordeal, I was holding my sweet little boy in my arms when my husband looked at me with a familiar angry expression on his face. He was enraged because he wasn't "getting enough attention" and because our son didn't look like him. He was sure I must have cheated on him. The fact that squishy, red newborn babies barely resemble anything human at all, much less their parents, must have escaped him.

Accusations, belittling, and anger spewed from his mouth. The nurse assigned to my room came bursting in and told my husband to stop yelling. She already had an idea of what he was like after I pushed the "help" button the night I gave birth and asked her to help me walk to the bathroom.

My husband had sat on the bed they'd rolled out for him and laughed as I struggled to get my still-numb legs to hold me upright. When she came in the room, she'd looked at him in disgust and said, "Are you going to just sit there and watch her struggle?"

After she sent him out of the room due to his yelling, she sighed, obviously frustrated. I said, "I'm sorry," completely mortified that she was witness to the inner sanctum of a relationship in shambles.

She said, "No honey, I'm the one who's sorry."

I was touched by her tenderness and protection of me. At that moment, I felt validated. That was the first time in my life someone implied the way my father treated my mother and the way my husband treated me was NOT how a man should treat a woman.

A flame ignited in me that would grow stronger over the coming year. As I looked down at the little boy I was holding, I saw he was watching me with huge, brown eyes that bore into my very soul.

His little brow scrunched as if he was concerned. I will never forget that look because it seemed so mature, so knowing. To this day, I don't know if it was an actual look of concern or just a typical newborn reflex.

I cried. I cried for him and I cried for me. I cried because, at just three-days-old, he'd already been exposed to a dark, ugly side of a relationship that had not been grounded in love but instead was shrouded in fear. I cried because I was repeating the same pattern my mother followed in her marriage. I cried because as I looked down at this perfect little child, I knew what I had to do, and it terrified me.

Three months after bringing our son home from the hospital, my mother came over to watch him so I could go to a therapy session with my husband. We'd seen this therapist throughout our marriage, but things had escalated since our little family became three. My husband seemed entertained by our baby but also grew bored with him rather easily. His disdain for me continued to grow. He had become so angry with me that he'd stopped speaking to me for an entire month.

That's right--30 days without him saying hello, replying to my questions, answering my pleas to talk things out. I told him I was going to therapy and he could come if he wanted. He showed up, but when confronted by the therapist about his anger, he left.

She leaned forward in her chair and looked me straight in the eye. Her words seemed so chilling at the time. "Get out." She repeated the words over and over. "Get out. G...E...T O...U...T!"

A few months later, I got a call from my sobbing mother. She'd decided to leave my dad and asked if I could accompany her to look for a place to live. I was stunned. Never before had I seen my mother take a stand against my dad. She sounded devastated and yet, for the first time, she had a strength, an unwavering resolve in her voice. She would not change her mind. Her decision was final.

I hung up absolutely wrecked that my mother's 30-year marriage to my dad had dissolved. I hurt for her pain. I hurt that my dad had been so reckless with her emotions and the life they'd built together. I was relieved and livid at the same time. I had long hated the way my father dismissed my mother and took for granted the love she constantly poured on him.

Mom's strength empowered me. I'd grown up watching her allow everyone in her life to take advantage of her, belittle her, use her and sabotage her. This time, I heard an unstoppable force well up in her voice that has grown stronger every day since. Her "take the bull by the horns" attitude opened my eyes and gave me strength that I too would need in my own life.

That first Thanksgiving after my mom moved to a condo and began establishing a life on her own, she came to our house for Thanksgiving dinner. After eating Mom's mouth-watering holiday feasts since I was a child, having her come to my house felt odd. And it must have felt odd to her, too. When she walked in that day with her famous banana pudding, her eyes were puffy and red.

Despite her heartache, she smiled and talked sweetly to Dakota, who reached for her the second he saw her. He was only nine months old, but he gave her the same worried look he'd given me right after he was born.

His forehead furrowed in concern, he sucked his binky and stared into his grandmother's eyes. I heard my mother whisper in his ear, "I'm okay, baby son. You make everything okay again."

None of us ate much that Thanksgiving. Mom, my husband and I, and my sister and her husband were quiet and awkward, unsure how to proceed with this change of tradition. But the baby in the room was the one who knew exactly what to do.

He looked up from playing with his mashed potatoes, peered at my mother and made the most hilarious face I've ever seen on a child. He held his breath until his little face turned red, balled up his chubby little fists and made what we now call, "the monkey face". His combination smile and grimace provoked a roar of laughter from everyone at the table.

My son was aware of the laughter, but his eyes were locked on his grandmother's face. When she laughed at him, he too started to laugh, only to make the face again. He'd hold his breath so long I thought his little head would explode. This scene went on for 45 minutes until we all hurt from laughing so hard. My little boy saved Thanksgiving and brought happiness into an uncomfortable holiday that went down in our history books as the "Monkey Face Thanksgiving".

That's when I realized my mother and my son were kindred spirits. They understood each other. The Monkey Face Thanksgiving was the beginning of an incredibly close bond that has continued even as my little boy has grown into an adult man.

Four months later, I filed for divorce and moved myself and our one-year-old into a small condo. Before I left, my husband and I divided the items accumulated in our short six-year relationship. He wanted the dining room table and living room furniture. I wanted my son and his crib. We both got what we wanted.

I credit three women for giving me the strength to leave an emotionally and physically abusive marriage--the nurse who stomped into my hospital room, the therapist who told me to get out, and my mother. I watched her blossom in the months following her divorce. She smiled, she danced, she attended concerts, traveled, tried funky restaurants and funky foods. She played and laughed and even walked differently.

Her shoulders straightened, and she was able to look people directly in the eye. She grew into a brilliant, articulate, brave, strong woman, and I admired her immensely. I began to see that what my parents taught me about relationships was wrong. My mother was replacing those lessons with new ones about charting one's path, not tolerating abuse and not only finding one's voice but using it.

Finding one's voice can be a hard concept to grasp if a person isn't used to hearing themselves speak with confidence. In my clinical work, I've found that establishing a sense of strength comes with replacing the thoughts and tapes we play in our heads. My mom and I both had to alter our thoughts about ourselves, and when we did, a new voice emerged. A tool from the Cognitive Behavioral Theory called the Trigger Cycle challenges thought patterns. It's a simplified method to help us understand how our thoughts play a significant role in determining what feelings, actions, and results follow.

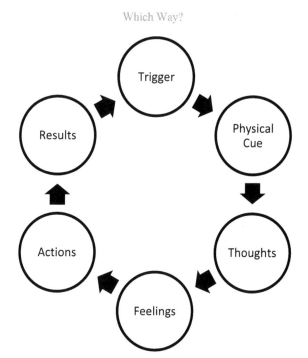

Printed with permission of Aaron T. Beck, M.D. Adapted by Shari Simmons from the Cognitive Conceptualization Diagram Worksheet.

Cognitive Behavioral theorists believe if we change our thoughts, our feelings and actions will also change. Therapists use the circles shown below to challenge their clients' thinking. When my ex-husband stopped talking to me for a month, I was "triggered" because my father often withheld affection from my mom by shutting down and refusing to speak.

Even as a therapist and professor who teaches this concept to students, I still get triggered when someone in my life refuses to speak to me.

My tendency when this happens is to shut down myself. Or, I can go to the other extreme and get intense, demanding that the other person engages with me.

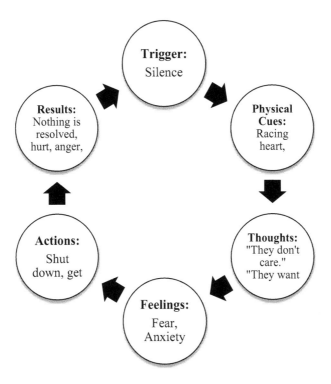

Printed with permission of Aaron T. Beck, M.D. Adapted by Shari Simmons from the Cognitive Conceptualization Diagram Worksheet.

This not-so-mature behavior from someone who should know better initiated my search for a healthier way of dealing with triggers. Knowing silence is something that will likely always be a trigger for me, I must control my thoughts if I want my feelings and, ultimately, my behavior to change.

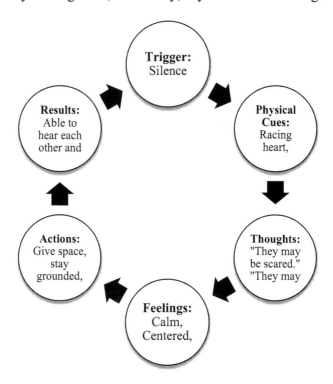

Printed with permission of Aaron T. Beck, M.D. Adapted by Shari Simmons from the Cognitive Conceptualization Diagram Worksheet.

One can see the sequence of events that potentially occurs when triggered. This picture illustrates what typically happens in the brain. When we change our thoughts, the entire cycle changes and we become far more in control of how we respond to our world. In the blank circle below, fill in the triggers in your life, your resulting "negative" thoughts, feelings actions and results. Then, write down what might happen if you replaced your negative thoughts with "positive" ones.

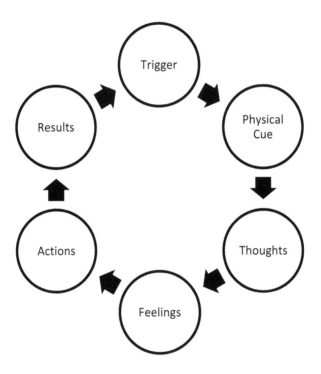

~~*Jann*~~

The day I moved into my new condo was a sad day. My two daughters and their husbands came to help me. I was very grateful for their support and for my six-month-old grandson, who offered us his constant grin. He was the only bright spot in the day.

When I felt as if I'd come completely undone, I'd look at his precious face. He'd see me looking at him and his little legs would start kicking, and he'd break into a huge chipmunk-cheeked smile.

I sat next to Dakota while we ate our fast-food lunch of burgers and fries. Without thinking to ask his mother's permission, I placed a fry into his chubby fist. He raised it to his mouth, and a love affair was born.

I don't believe Shari was ready to introduce salty fried foods to her baby's diet, but seeing his excitement gave us all a moment of joy we desperately needed right then. She kindly forgave my lapse in judgment.

Way too soon, everything was unloaded, my family left, and I was alone. I stood in the tiny kitchen and looked out the patio door, feeling like I was the only person left on the planet. I sobbed...for days.

Shortly after the move, Jonathan's mother, who'd been ill for some time, took a turn for the worse and her family was told she didn't have long to live. I was very close to his parents, so her illness was difficult for me, especially now. I'd lost her son, and now I was losing her. Almost from the moment of my engagement to Jonathan, we had a family joke that if her son and I had a conflict, she would take my side, not his. I was the daughter she never had.

Mother, as I called her from the beginning, asked to see us, so Jonathan requested I fly home with him to visit her one last time. I agreed to go, not for him, but for her. We drove from the airport straight to her nursing home.

As we walked the hall toward her room, my heart ached. How was I going to pretend I was still living with her beloved son? Jonathan hadn't told his parents about our separation.

I stood on one side of her bed, holding her hand, and Jonathan stood at the foot of her bed. She looked at us and weakly said, "You two make such a beautiful couple." I smiled and gently squeezed her hand and did not reveal our sad secret.

She died not long after our visit, and never knew the truth about us. I was not invited to attend her funeral and my name was not listed as one of her survivors. I was devastated. After all she'd meant to me and I to her for 33 years, after giving her two grandchildren, my existence was not even mentioned at her funeral.

That first year of my separation from Jonathan was dedicated to finding a reason and a will to live. My daughters, both divorced during this period of time, so dealing with my own emotions gave way to being present for them as they went through their own hell.

Shari conducted therapy sessions with clients one evening a week. When I got off work, I'd drive to her condo to spend time with my precious grandson. His smile was what kept me going. As I parked in the driveway, I could see him standing at the screen door, waiting for my arrival. He'd jump up and down as I approached the door. Inside the house, he'd take my hand and joyfully say, "Come Nana!" and lead me to a toy.

His pure, unfiltered jubilation at my presence was fresh and new in my life. Like an invisible salve on my open wounds, his love assured me that I was important to him. He didn't want anything from me other than my time.

As mentioned, both of my daughters' marriages ended during my year of separation from their dad. One evening, RaeLynn called to say she thought her husband might be involved with someone. I couldn't get off the phone fast enough.

I, along with Shari and Jonathan landed on her doorstep within an hour to present a united defense. Jonathan and our son-in-law walked into another room to talk as the three of us women talked in the living room.

RaeLynn was beside herself with suspicion and grief. My heart broke for her. My own wounds were still raw and bleeding, as were Shari's. RaeLynn had a beautiful home, but like her sister and I experienced in our marriages, something was missing for her.

Later, when I approached the room the guys were in, I overheard my son-in-law say he was not having an affair, they were only friends. Jonathan replied, "I would completely understand if you turned to someone else." I was stunned by his words and confused as to why he'd say such a thing. I quietly walked away without being noticed. I re-joined my daughters down the hall but didn't tell them what I'd heard.

After Raelynn's divorce, we helped her settle into a condo. When I was sure she was going to be okay, I picked up my own baggage again to deal with it. Jonathan and I had been separated for a year, yet we were no closer to resolving our situation than when I first moved out. We regularly spoke to each other, but not about the marriage.

Sitting alone in my living room one day, my mind went back to Jonathan's comment to our daughter's husband. I called him over to my place to ask him if he had "turned to someone else". Before he could answer I asked, "Are you having an affair?" He assured me he was not. I believed him, because why would he lie?

A week later, I received a call from a man whom we'd met at a Christmas party several years ago. He blurted out that my husband was having an affair with his wife and that it had been going on for a long while.

Suddenly, I couldn't breathe. My whole body violently shook. He was wrong, he had to be wrong. Not Jonathan. He'd never do such a thing. He had too much integrity. Besides, I'd asked him if he had someone else and, he'd said no other woman was in his life. I never doubted that he was being anything other than honest with me. He respected me too much to lie to my face!

I immediately confronted Jonathan with the proof I had, and this time he admitted the truth. I looked at him in disbelief. I didn't even recognize the man who sat before me, admitting to what was culminating in the demise of two marriages, the shattering of two hearts who never saw it coming. I was left to make sense of the infidelity somehow.

Jonathan and I had both made mistakes, but I couldn't believe he did this to me and to our marriage. Not an ounce of me ever expected him to betray me. To stop loving someone is a matter of the heart, but betrayal is a matter of the spirit that leaves scars so deep a person carries them forever.

Jonathan was my husband who'd vowed to honor me and forsake all others. Even in the wake of his terrible confession, I didn't want to believe it was true. In the end, however, I had to acknowledge reality. He lied to me!

In fact, as I sat there staring at him. I wondered if he'd ever respected the sanctity of our marriage. Did he ever love me at all? Had over thirty years of marriage been reduced to one lie after another. I questioned everything about our life together. Most of all, I questioned myself.

I wasn't sure how to come to grips with this soul-shattering development. Jonathan didn't know what to say nor did I, so I asked him to leave my house so I could find my bearings. When the door closed behind me, pain ripped through my body like a knife. I literally felt a stab in my heart.

I thought about his admission for one brief day, and before going to bed that night, I picked up the phone to call Jonathan. It was the most difficult thing I'd ever had to do, but I knew the time had come to end the long trail of abuses that had defined

my life.

Jonathan answered on the second ring, told him I wanted a divorce. He said he wasn't if he was ready to make that decision. In a surg courage, I told him this decision was being made him.

During the legal mediation, I told our attorney I did not want half of Jonathan's successf business, nor would I accept maintenance. The attorney advised me that I was making an emotiona decision. While that may have been true, I felt like I could not take my husband's money, not understanding at the time that it was *our* money. I had contributed to the success of his business, and even though the law required him to give me half, I refused it. I didn't want to be tethered to anyone, who in any way used lies, deception, and control to manipulate.

Finally, the divorce was official. What had begun as my idealization of love, family, devotion and leaving behind a childhood of pain and loneliness, ended in the greatest pain of all. When we divorced, I lost the "perceived" safety of a loving, devoted husband.

His dominance in our marriage kept me child-like. Though I'd grown a lot over the past few years of therapy and striving for independence, the divorce knocked the breath out of me and left me stunned. Jonathan's choice to have an affair felt like I was being thrown away in favor of someone who was more worthy than I was. Suddenly, I was an unloved orphan again whose little-girl heart was shattered...one more time.

For the next three years, I did little more than go to work and spend time with my children and grandson. But, I knew I needed to get back into

therapy to unravel the web of lies that permeated my 31-year marriage.

I went to a male therapist this time. On my first visit, he asked me what I enjoyed doing. I looked at him with a blank stare and scrambled to come up with an answer so I didn't come across as a complete idiot. But I couldn't think of one thing.

He said with such kindness in his voice, "No one has ever asked you what your wants are, have they?" My affirming nod resulted in him assigning me the task of going through magazines, cutting out any words or pictures that piqued my interest and pasting them to poster boards. He instructed me to not analyze the things I chose. "If they catch your eye, just cut and paste."

This began my quest to learn what was important to me (like the precious face of a child), what I enjoyed (like travel or breakfast with someone I cared about), what interested me (like learning to paint, reading and studying history), what I didn't like (like war, human suffering, injustice).

Other than trying to find my way out of the darkness, my children and my adorable little Dakota became the center of my universe. In our grief, we spent a lot of time supporting each other and doing things together. The three of us locked arms and forged a united front. We held tightly to each other until we could be sure the others could stand on their own.

With the guidance of my new therapist, I diligently processed my marriage, and my divorce and all the emotions the traumas of my past created for me. I had a lot of emotional processing to do around Jonathan's affair. Friends told me many heartbreaking stories about his infidelity, which I

should have noticed, and which made me feel like a fool because I didn't.

I trusted my husband and closed my eyes to his behavior, even when I suspected something was amiss. Twenty plus years since the divorce, I continue to hear stories of his flirtations with other women throughout our marriage. Each time I hear a new one it reopens my wounds, and I feel the humiliation and disrespect all over again. Everyone in town knew how Jonathan conducted his life--everyone but me?

My therapist was succinct but gentle in his guidance, although he pushed me at times. I was so much stronger now than when I was with Neda, and I could take a more robust approach. When I got stuck, he'd remind me that I needed to use different words.

He'd have me repeat after him, "I understand the act of betrayal: what I don't understand is how a person can turn their back on their own integrity in order to commit it." He reminded me that my confusion and pain was because my own character would never have allowed me to hurt someone I claimed to love in this manner.

The fact that I was betrayed by my husband was reminiscent of my past and the betrayals I'd endured by the people who were supposed to love me. My struggle with Jonathan's betrayal rested smack in the center of the complete and utter disregard he had for me as a human being who deserved more.

I will always care about my ex-husband and desire the best for him. I don't blame him for the divorce. I blame him for the deceit, which left a mark on my soul as deep as the ones left by my abusers. Like them, he had no regard for me or for what he inflicted upon me. When we occasionally see each other today I'm kind to him. He's the father of my children. We shared a life together that spanned 33 years.

During those years, we laughed and cried together. We had children together. We worked and played and loved. I think the greatest hurt came when he acted as if none of it mattered.

Yes, I have been scarred by my past. My scars tell me where I've been. But, I have decided, they will no longer define who I am.

~~*Shari*~~

After my parents' divorce, my sister and I decided to meet our father. By now, he was happily living his new life with a new wife. Occasionally, he'd reach out to us to ask why we never called him. He was always cheery over the phone and even suggested we get together for lunch as if what had occurred in our family was insignificant.

My sister was seeing a therapist at the time who suggested the three of us have a family therapy session to talk about our feelings regarding the divorce. RaeLynn desperately wanted her relationship back with our dad. I desperately wanted to confront him about the lies and deceit. He had not acknowledged the part he played in the demise of a 30-year marriage, and sadly, he still hasn't.

To be a therapist and go to another therapist for help feels odd. Yet, I think everyone in the helping profession should do just that. I recommend to every student in every class I teach that they avail themselves of therapy so they can in turn, become healthier for the clients they serve.

At that time in my life, I didn't quite understand or value the cathartic release that can come from talking to an objective person. Someone who is trained to both listen and ask the right questions can bring a person to the answers they had inside themselves all along. I knew all that, but the session was awkward, and I wasn't sure how to act.

As my sister and I sidestepped what we really wanted to know, the therapist finally asked my father to talk about his relationship with each of us. He looked at my sister and said, "I have always felt close to you. We've been buddies from the start, and I have great memories of us hanging out at the barn and playing catch. We are a lot alike, you and I."

When it was my turn, my dad shifted uncomfortably in his seat. With a smirk I don't think I will ever forget, he said: "Gal, I have just never really liked you."

Although his words hurt, and I felt something akin to shell shock, I was also relieved. Experiencing both emotions at the same time was like my inner child declaring, "I told you so!" and lying on a battlefield trying to stop my own hemorrhaging.

I now understood what I'd always felt. With time, I came to realize that on some level he did love me, but he was jealous of my relationship with Mom. Sometimes, jealousy can be the stronger emotion.

All the times I was confused by my father's distance and bewildered by his angry silence toward me began to weave together a blanket of understanding. His statement allowed me to snap the misunderstood pieces of my life with him into a puzzle that began to finally make sense. My father loved me AND he disliked me.

His internal struggle with these two emotions must have been difficult. I was his daughter, his firstborn. I was loyal, a hard worker and a compliant, respectful child. He loved me for that. But I challenged his thinking and decided to go to college, even though he thought that anyone who obtained a degree was pompous and arrogant. The most significant aspect of his feelings toward me was my close relationship with my mom. He hated me for that.

His resentment centered around the fact that I had a bond with my mother that was sacred and special. Only when I wasn't around, could he have her completely to himself. She adored me, and in my father's eyes, that meant she didn't adore him.

To someone with a fragile ego, everyone is a threat. I threatened my father's ability to be "okay" with himself. My mother made him feel validated, strong and secure. If he could control my mother and have all of her attention, he knew his place in the world.

The dissolution of my parents' marriage was also marked by the painful realization that one of my parents didn't adore me the way every little girl wants. I had to accept my father's flaws and his mixed feelings for me. I had to accept his betrayal of the family unit he'd told others he cherished. I had to accept his lack of truly understanding the unique personalities of his two daughters. Once I accepted all that, I could own my own life story.

However, my story is not unique. Millions of people carry the unfortunate baggage that comes with having a less-than-ideal relationship with one or both parents. This emptiness in one's soul can take on the form of distance and guardedness in relationships with significant others, friends, and children. The pain of having a parent who doesn't shower us with the love we're born to crave can create a protective shell around our hearts that keeps us from showing others what we truly feel and who we truly are.

So many clients have sat with tear-filled eyes in my office and said something like the following: "I'm not sure why I can't have a deep, connected relationship with my spouse, my child, and my parents. I have trouble opening up and being vulnerable."

We're wired to protect our hearts but shielding them can be a double-edged sword. As children, protecting our heart can keep us from feeling the penetrating pain and confusion that comes from a parent whose love is always out of our grasp. By erecting a wall of bricks around who we really are and what our hearts really desire, we can merrily zip through our childhoods relatively unscathed.

When we become adults, this wall can create problems. The protectiveness can become a roadblock in relationships and cause us to struggle to be our true, authentic, vulnerable selves. Our partners, our friends, and our children always want more of us. They wonder why we keep ourselves closed off emotionally from moments that could be tender and beautiful.

We act this way, oftentimes unknowingly, because on some level we're trying to keep ourselves from being hurt again. We tell ourselves the false message that, "If I don't give all of myself, then I won't lose all of myself when this relationship ultimately ends."

Unless we have truly examined our childhood relationships and acknowledged our unmet needs, we grow up to be adults who innocently try to recreate our painful childhood relationships. Though we are wired to have healthy, happy relationships, all we know is what we experienced as children.

If our needs were not met then, we grow up to be adults who gravitate toward individuals who are just like the people in our childhoods who didn't meet our needs. We subconsciously do this in an attempt to "re-do" our early relationships. In my case, not feeling wanted by my dad propelled me to choose a husband who didn't really want me.

We do this because we think, "If this person (who is like my parent), loves and cherishes me, I can finally believe that I matter." And my childhood pain will be resolved. We do this dance with ourselves because we're trying to mend old wounds. The problem is that when we select people like those who hurt us, we typically get the same response we got when we were young. We hope we will get a different reaction, but typically, we do not.

As humans, we have several basic emotional needs. Different experts and theorists identify different words to describe these needs, but they are usually some version of the following: Safety, Self-Worth, Freedom, Control, Consistency, and Connection. If any of those were missing as we grew up, we search for people we think can meet those needs for us. These basic needs are so important that most of our adult arguments and behaviors center around getting those needs met. In fact, I'd like to suggest that EVERY human behavior is based upon one of the six needs above.

A couple who came to me for therapy loved each other, but their fights usually deteriorated into some version of two needs. She wanted to feel safe because she hadn't felt safe as a child. He wanted to have some control in his life because he had an overbearing, possessive mother. Everything they disagreed about led down a winding path to these basic needs that they desperately wanted the other spouse to meet.

If we find someone whom we think can meet our needs, we assume their presence in our lives will negate the pain we carry deep within. This "thinking" is usually done at a very subconscious level, where we say things like, "I usually attract men who just can't commit." Or, "Why do I always meet women who are selfish and only care about themselves?" The energy we put into the world attracts those people because we have unmet needs we're desperately trying to fill.

Because my dad didn't acknowledge my self-worth, which as a child, I really needed from him, I grew up seeking out men who also did not validate my sense of worth. I attracted men who were workaholics or gym-aholics, men who couldn't connect to their emotions or who had fragile egos and therefore, couldn't fill my need for connection and validation. I was trying to recreate what I didn't have with my father.

"You have to learn how to love yourself" was a clichéd line I read in self-help books and heard from my own well-meaning friends over the years. In the facilities where I worked, I heard these words from other clinicians as they sat next to young women who couldn't leave their abusive boyfriends or adolescent boys who raged about how the world was "out to get" them. I always thought the platitude was wimpy and an empty directive from someone who had no idea HOW to guide someone to actually "love themselves."

The sad truth is that for many of us, we have to go back in time and re-parent ourselves. This takes some work and is something that needs repetition, but if done with consistency, we will wake up one day to find that a small seed of self-love has sprouted. If we continue to water and nurture that seed, it will grow into something that resembles acceptance and compassion.

I never thought my mother would get to a point where she loved herself. She had so much self-loathing that, as I grew into an adult, I worried about her incessantly. But I watched her break free from her past, and I saw the positive messages she journaled to herself.

She began to say things like, "I'm going to go to Italy by myself because I deserve to see it." "I'm taking myself to dinner and a movie tonight." "I've decided I'm redecorating my entire house in colors and a style that makes me happy." I witnessed her put my father in his place when he ridiculed her for buying a new car. "I bought a new car," she said, "because I've never had anything new, and I'm worth it."

Learning "how" to love yourself and meet your own needs for Self-Worth, Safety, Control, Freedom, Consistency or Connection can take on many different forms. If you grew up needing Connection but didn't have it, surround yourself with people who are like-minded and love doing the things you do. If you grew up needing Control but didn't have it, plan a trip, create artwork, plant a garden that you oversee. If you grew up needing Consistency but your life was unpredictable, develop routines that bring you peace. If you grew up needing Safety but didn't have it, make your home a peaceful sanctuary.

Creating these behaviors will teach us that we can fill the parts of our lives that were empty. When we meet the needs we have in healthy ways, we send messages to ourselves about who we are. Do these things repeatedly until your soul begins to incorporate them as a truth. Only when we cherish who we are and replenish the needs others could not or would not, do we live the life we were created to live.

Another way to love yourself is to write love letters to ourselves, reciting all the strong and beautiful things about who we've become. I often give my students an assignment in which they are to write letters to their "little selves." I suggest they apologize for any negative things they have done to themselves over the years. I also encourage them to write down their vows to honor who they are and only bring people into their lives who treat them with the respect they deserve.

Some clients have recorded themselves saying positive things about themselves. Some even include music. I recently started writing in my daily planner the following statement: "Shari, do only what makes your heart soar today!" I'm amazed by how setting that intention each day can alter the decisions and choices I make. It's my way of honoring my needs and telling myself that I am worthy of having a splendid day.

Below, you will find a letter-writing exercise. Just telling yourself that you love who you are is not enough. Our hearts need to hear "why" we are loveable. If you haven't heard this from a parent or a loved one, you owe it to yourself to give yourself the messages you longed to hear.

Picture yourself at a young age. If you have a physical picture on hand, great. If not, remember what you looked like as a child. What are you wearing? Do you have peanut butter on your face? Is your hair in a ponytail? Are you wearing your favorite Nikes?

In your letter, allow your adult self to tell your younger self the things you wish you'd heard growing up. Your letter might read something like the below example.

Dear little self,
I want you to know how valuable you are. You are kind, smart, funny and simply adorable. I'm sorry you were not told that more often when you were little. I am making you a commitment that I will no longer bring people into your life who perpetuate a negative and false belief about you. When you were small, you couldn't escape negative, false and sometimes mean words, but that is not the case now. I'm here to tell you I will do my best to only let people and circumstances into your life that honor "us" and recognize "our" true beauty.

~Love, adult self

Dear_____,

_____
_____
_____
_____
_____
_____
_____
_____
_____
_____
_____
_____
_____
_____
_____
_____
_____
_____
_____
_____
_____
_____
_____
_____
_____
_____

With Love, _____

~~*Jann*~~

Regardless of what I wished our marriage could have been, it was over and I needed to move on. I remained in therapy for about a year and worked through the next phase of becoming my own person. I was learning to embody my beliefs, once I discovered what those beliefs were. I was formulating my goals and dreams and desires.

For me, healing from my divorce was a time of self-discovery. However, growing up at 51 years of age was not without its challenges. Though I stumbled like a toddler taking her first steps, I was determined to never stop growing, learning and evolving into all my Creator had in store for me. Rather than looking backward and holding on to a past I couldn't change, I reached forward to my future. I was on my way, and my first stop would be…ROME.

At that point in my life, I had not driven outside my small city limits alone. When a person's boundaries are confined, some trepidation is associated with venturing out. But, here I was, facing one of my fears while sitting on a plane, by myself. I was flying to Italy for a two-week vacation. And did I mention I was ALONE?

What was I thinking? Since my divorce, I had only taken one trip, and that was with my daughters to Mexico. Now, I was traveling to Europe all by myself. I was diving right in--no baby steps here.

My "Rome Adventure" was the most glorious experience. I will never forget the things I did and saw there. Returning from a stroll to the Colosseum, I was walking up the Spanish Steps toward my hotel when I decided to stop at the Hard Rock Café. I was sipping a glass of wine, when a man, his wife, and their two beautiful children walked over to me.

I was a bit taken aback by their boldness, but I smiled. Then the man casually said, "You are beautiful." His strong Italian accent confirmed he was a local. I'd heard the reputation of Italian men, but it was obvious that his wife was not threatened by the compliment he gave me. It was said in such a respectful way I wasn't embarrassed. I thought how sad it was that we seldom tell others how we feel, yet this stranger seemed to be able to do so quite naturally.

The next day, as I walked through shops in town, I passed a store where a man stood outside hanging tee-shirts on a display rack. He asked in broken English, "Are you from America?" I replied that I was. Eyes wide, he enthusiastically asked, "Are you a movie star in America?" I smiled and quickly informed him that I was "a grandmother" in America. But, I decided right then and there that I was surely going to enjoy the charming Roman culture.

I must admit that when the time came to pack my belongings and board the plane for home, I was saddened. Leaving Rome meant returning to my small condominium, which was yet to feel like home to me. I was thrilled to get back to my daughters and my grandson but facing the emptiness in my heart was not a welcomed thought.

I still had a few days left before I had to go back to work, so I used the time to journal. Writing was a newly cultivated activity that allowed me to refocus and set goals. I was learning about myself and what I enjoyed. I learned my favorite color is pink and going to a movie by myself is peaceful. I enjoy reading a good book and watching the history channel on TV. I love to paint, and I love hummingbirds and butterflies.

Most importantly, I want to become the second greatest influence in my life's direction, the greatest influence being Jesus, who has been beside me every step of the way. I now know I am not alone or forgotten by those in my life who matter to me. I'm not afraid to try something new and different. I'm not afraid to live alone. Getting to know me has been exciting!

I love to travel. Since the Rome trip, I've been to Hawaii, and to Mexico several times. I've also traveled within the United States. I've peered into an inactive volcano from a helicopter's vantage point, I've driven over the Golden Gate Bridge, ridden on a train and visited eleven vineyards in Napa Valley. I've taken a dinner cruise on the Pacific Ocean and kayaked on the Atlantic Ocean. I've taken a ten-day river cruise down the Mississippi and stopped in four states along the way. And, I've conquered fears with each adventure.

I'm often asked how I was a mother to my children when I didn't learn nurturing behaviors from one single family member. The answer is easy, I gave them what I needed and deserved as a child. I gave them what was never given to me and I later learned to give myself, unconditional love. We all make choices regarding everything we face in life. We can choose to treat others as we were treated or we can choose to treat others the way we want to be treated.

I was gaining self-confidence in my ability to survive on my own, but I continued to struggle with self-worth. More than three years after the divorce, I hadn't started dating because I didn't trust my judgment. My blindness to what was happening in my marriage scared me. I hadn't had the slightest hint of suspicion that Jonathan might be seeing other women. What might I miss in another relationship?

I'd been asked out several times by Franco, a man from my workplace. My answer was always the same "No."

One day, I was at my desk, transcribing a letter when Franco called. He was driving to the office from the airport and would be arriving within the hour. Because he'd been on a business trip for a week, I was catching him up on what had been going on at the office when, out of nowhere, he asked me out to dinner.

I'm not sure why today was any different, but it was, and so was my answer. He said he'd pick me up at six at my condominium. I hung up the phone and felt something I hadn't felt in such a long time...joy!

After work, I drove home to get ready for

my date. As I looked in the mirror while applying my makeup, I noticed I was smiling. I hadn't smiled unprompted in a long time. Franco picked me up right on time and took me to a very nice restaurant.

We talked easily about where we were in our lives and a bit about how we got there. He listened. He asked questions. He seemed genuinely interested in me as a person, which was refreshing. When he drove me back to my condo, he said he'd love to make me dinner the next night. I accepted without reserve.

Over the next few months, Franco and I became inseparable. I saw him at work as well as several evenings each week. I was always so comfortable with him. He was the kindest man I'd ever met. And...he was Italian.

Franco had impeccable manners, and he treated me like I was someone to be cherished. The first night I went to his home for an authentic Italian dinner, he was waiting for me in his driveway as I arrived. He immediately walked over to the car to open the door for me.

Inside his large Mediterranean style home, I was taken aback at how beautifully decorated it was with sculptures and artwork displayed to perfection. He led me into his spacious kitchen, so he could tend to the pasta on the stove.

On the granite island in the center of the massive room sat an arrangement of strawberries with several dipping choices. Next to the strawberries was a freshly poured glass of red wine. I stood at the island, sipping wine and nibbling strawberries as he fussed around the kitchen, putting the final touches on our meal, which was superb. When I left that evening, he walked me to my car and gave me the sweetest, most memorable kiss.

I'd never been treated so kindly before. When we were out, he was attentive and solicitous of my every need. He took me places I'd never been, right in my own city. We drank cappuccino on his deck that overlooked the mountains as the sun rose from its horizon and turned the clouds a beautiful pink.

We walked the snow-covered streets downtown to look at the Christmas lights in the trees that lined the streets. We shopped for decorations for the large tree he put up in his living room, and then we decorated it together as we shared wine and laughter. That was the first time I'd ever decorated a home with anyone other than my two children. The experience was more special than I could have ever imagined it to be.

I was having the time of my life. We talked for hours, something else I wasn't used to. He never seemed to tire of me, and I was interested in everything he said. He was tender and loving. He was handsome and strong, and we were falling in love! I met his family and he met mine.

With the exception of my young grandson, who did NOT want me to date, the rest of my family adored Franco. Dakota actually loved being around Franco, because he was amazing with children. My grandson just didn't want his Nana to have another man in her life. He'd never had to share me with anyone.

I discovered Dakota's conflicting emotions one evening as we were leaving Franco's house after a day of fun. As I pulled out of the driveway, I looked at my grandson in the mirror and asked if he'd had fun. From his car-seat perch, he nodded his head and said, "Yes." But then, in his precious voice and with his limited understanding of romantic relationships, he added, "You don't need Franco as a friend anymore because I'm your friend."

I smiled at the angelic face framed by my rearview mirror and said, "Oh, my darling little Mister Man, you will always be my friend, a very special friend. And so will Franco, because my heart is big enough for both of you." In time, Dakota gave in to Franco's genteel charm and decided that I could have TWO friends.

Unfortunately, as Franco and I spent more and more time together, I began to push him away. I felt so conflicted. I wanted to keep this gorgeous, generous, loving man in my life, in my heart, and in my very soul. But I didn't feel I deserved how wonderfully he treated me.

I was unused to being cherished and loved, doted on and appreciated. To be valued by another person was so unfamiliar that I began to feel anxious. Panicked. I questioned how he could treat me as if he adored me when my mother and my husband didn't. I was unable to accept his love as genuine.

I felt guilty that so much of his energy went toward making sure my needs were met, although he made his caretaking seem so effortless. I could not convince my mind that I deserved such a devoted man. So, I set out to sabotage the relationship, and after a couple of years, I ended it.

I broke his heart and I broke mine. Although I'd grown, and my emotional health had improved in the three years since my divorce, I was not ready for the emotional depth Franco was offering me. I didn't know how to accept the unconditional love he brought into my world.

I was no longer in therapy and my new survival skills, still in their infancy, were being tested. I spiraled downward. I had the most amazing love in my grasp, and I rejected it. I hated myself for hurting Franco, and I disappointed myself for not feeling worthy of him.

I will never forget Franco. I will always love him and I will forever be grateful for the beauty he brought to my life. However, my old demons had returned to remind me just how unlovable and undeserving I was.

I abandoned the healthy coping skills I learned in therapy in favor of what I formerly knew. I turned inward, and I hated what I found there--an ugly, unwanted, unloved child. I felt unworthy and hopeless again. I'd fought so hard to climb out of the depths of self-hatred, only to find myself right back where I came from, cowering in the corner of my mind, wanting to die.

On a snowy, winter day that was dark and gray, just like my mood, I tried to get out of bed but had neither the will nor the inclination to do so. Finally, I walked downstairs to make coffee, hoping that maybe the warm liquid would soften the hard shell that surrounded my heart. As the long day wore on, my mood became darker and heavier.

Coatless, I trudged barefoot through the heavy snow to my condo's detached garage. I stepped inside, closed the door, and got into my car. I started the engine, leaned my head against the headrest, and closed my eyes.

Waiting for the exhaust fumes to transport me to a place where pain and loss didn't exist, my life flashed through my mind. I could hear the engine's hum, but that was the only reminder of the present. I was sucked into the past, feeling the abuse, the neglect, the rejection, the infidelity and the systematic destruction of my soul by those who were supposed to love me.

Fifty-five years passed behind my closed eyelids. I saw it all, and I felt it all, and I wanted out of the pain. My maladaptive interpretation of my former life that told me I was unlovable engulfed my mind and heart, and my spirit descended into despair. My new self was still in its infancy, not grounded enough to fight the inner turmoil or find hope to go on.

As my consciousness began to fade, I envisioned my beautiful daughters, and I began to cry. I made mistakes raising them and I was sure I had damaged them. I desperately wished for another chance to raise them from a healthy perspective. I didn't want to hurt them anymore, and I absolutely didn't want my blackness to spill onto the stark-white purity of my sweet grandson.

The car fumes and the sickening thoughts beckoned me, pulling me deeper into a dark abyss. I asked God to keep my lovely daughters safe. They would have much better lives with my ugliness and unhealthiness removed.

Suddenly, I heard a tiny voice calling, "Nana, come!" I saw my grandson's big round eyes and loving smile. His beautiful face framed in the brightest glow I'd ever seen. His chubby hand was stretched toward me, summoning me as he had so often done. His appearance was as real as if he was right there with me in the garage.

My eyes flew open and I turned, expecting to see him seated next to me in the car. Of course, he wasn't actually there, but his presence felt so real I gasped. Suddenly, I was desperate for fresh air.

My lungs bursting, I flung open the car door,

took four short steps to the garage door and threw it wide. The blast of cold air made me suck in another breath. I felt the frozen ground beneath my bare feet, and the falling snow hitting my face.

As clean air filled my lungs, I was jolted from the past into the present. As before, I had not wanted to die, I only wanted to escape the excruciating pain and the suffocating blackness that engulfed me. I had three people counting on me. I had to live for Shari, RaeLynn, Dakota and for any future grandchildren I might be blessed with. I had to live for me.

God was battling for my life against a dark force that convinced me I had damaged my children, that they needed to be free of me and my woundedness. But God's power was stronger.

He allowed me to see the purity, the innocence, the unconditional love of my beloved grandson. Dakota's sweet voice summoned me back to him and to my daughters. No matter how much pain I felt, I could not leave them.

I would NOT leave them the legacy of pain that I fought so hard to rebuke. I would NOT encumber my grandson with the legacy of his grandmother abandoning him. I would make a grander choice. I would live.

I vowed to God that I would conquer the last of my demons. I had to remember the healing journey is just that, a journey filled with bumps and detours. I would always be faced with life's obstacles and the choices as to how I'd meet those obstacles, but throughout, I would have my precious family. I would also have God.

When a loved one commits suicide, those left behind struggle to make sense of their intentional death. While I can't speak for others, I can speak for what went through my own mind. I didn't believe I was good enough to be around anyone, especially those I loved. I was motivated to hurt myself to keep from hurting those I loved. My belief system needed to change. I needed to immerse myself in self-care so that the tools I'd acquired in therapy could override my old beliefs when faced with a difficult situation.

After my final suicide attempt, I crafted a self-improvement plan for myself. I worked more diligently on strengthening my life skills. I made goals. I made a bucket-list of things I wanted to do or accomplish.

I made friends. I indulged myself. I took a weaponry class and obtained a concealed carry permit. I learned Tae Kwon Do with RaeLynn. I also blew out my knee doing a flying back kick, but we both earned belts along the way.

I'd begun my life transformation by moving into the condo the day I left the home I'd created for my husband and daughters. In time, I realized the condo was a dark reminder of a devastating time in my life. I needed to make a home that did not have pain associated with it.

I came across a cute little house under construction and located the builder, who happened to be the person who built my condo. I put a contract on the house that day. As the new owner, I was able to choose the interior colors of the walls, flooring, and countertops.

I'd gone through this slow, conscientious process many times before for the houses my ex-husband and I lived in together. This time, however, the house was for me and I was excited. My first house as a single woman.

I learned I no longer liked the dark colors I

used to select. I wanted bright, cheery colors. I wanted lots of windows with minimal coverings. I wanted cream-colored furniture rather than dark heavy furnishings and soft pastel paint on the walls rather than dark walnut paneling.

As I decorated my new home and reflected on its contrast from my past homes, I knew the changes weren't due to a shift in designing trends as much as to an internal shift in me. I was no longer in a dark, depressed frame of mind. I was taking control of my life, my behaviors, my decisions, my wants, and my desires--and it was exhilarating!

I sold my condo for a nice profit and the builder made me a great deal on the house because I'd purchased the condo from him. I moved in within a month of signing the contract and immediately bought a hot tub for the patio and a lawnmower.

These decisions may not seem like a big deal to most people, but for me, they were huge. For over 50 years I'd been unable to make even the most fundamental decisions for myself. I was a blatant case of arrested development. But now, I was making my own decisions. I experienced the consequences of making bad decisions and the thrill of making good ones. The triumph and satisfaction that follow good decisions did wonders for my self-esteem.

As I began to "come into my own", as the saying goes, I was occasionally faced with self-doubt and fears. I was well aware of how unsafe the world can be and I proceeded with caution.

I was getting to know myself in a way I'd never been allowed to before, but I still only had the vaguest idea of who I really was at my core. I believed I needed to be perfect.

However, I was learning that making mistakes is vital to mental and emotional growth. I was progressing forward rather than staying stagnant or frozen in fear. I no longer wanted either option in my life. I wanted to develop and blossom in whatever way I could.

I'd been in my new house only a short while when I received a call from the nursing home where my mother resided. I hadn't been back to see her since that visit so long ago when I confronted her regarding the ravages of my childhood. Yet, they had my phone number.

The caller informed me my mother had died of a stroke. She also told me that because I was her closest living relative, I was responsible for her burial and outstanding medical bills. The irony did not escape me that when I visited so many years ago I was told my mother only had a son, not a daughter. Now, I was her closest living relative.

I collected my thoughts in time to let her know I would NOT be paying the medical bills, not even for the last aspirin my mother took, nor would I pay her burial expenses. I told the woman my mother was to be cremated as an indigent at the state's expense. I would collect the cremains as soon as I could catch a flight.

Then, I called my brother. I'd only seen him a couple times since my wedding day. Although we hadn't formed a very close bond after so many years apart, we tried to stay in sporadic communication. When I called him to let him know our mother had died, he made it clear he wanted nothing to do with her or her cremains. But, he added, "I will pick you up at the airport and you can stay with me." I was only at his house for a day, the mortuary called to say I could come the following day.

I had a fitful sleep that first night as so many thoughts, memories and pain flooded my mind and my heart. My mother was gone. I could no longer hold the hope that she'd call me and tell me how sorry she was. That she'd tell me how much she loved me and how much she wished she could have been a good mother to my brother and me. I buried my face in the pillow and sobbed for this great loss--the loss of a mother I never had. My mother's death made my orphan status permanent.

In bold divergence to the blackness of my mood, I wore white slacks and a soft coral blouse with turquoise jewelry. I could barely contain the lump in my throat. I wanted to scream and tear my clothes like they did in biblical times when someone was in remorse or grief.

I wanted to throw something, to run away, to claw at something. I needed to do anything other than act like I was in complete control of myself. My brother, sister-in-law and I walked to the car to begin the long trek to the mortuary without speaking a word. The silence between us continued throughout the journey.

After he parked the car, my brother told me he would not be going inside with me. He wanted nothing to do with our mom, in life or in death. I told him I understood, got out and slowly ascended the steps toward the massive double doors alone.

I introduced myself to the mortuary director and could see his mouth forming words, but I couldn't hear anything he said. Nothing registered. Beads of perspiration formed on my forehead and the palms of my hands were moist.

I started to tremble. I couldn't calm my body, my heart raced, and I felt like I was being pulled down a dark tunnel of despair. "I need to leave," I blurted. "Could you please give me the cremains, so I can be on my way?"

Moments later, I held out my hand to grasp the handles of the bag they offered me. I was shocked at how heavy it was. I'm not sure what I expected, but I'd emptied the ashes from my fireplace enough times to know these ashes were much, much heavier.

I thanked them and left through the double doors I'd entered. My brother walked toward me, and I collapsed in a flood of emotion, sobbing into his shoulder, still clutching the bag. He let me cry for as long as I needed. When I pulled from his embrace, I quietly said, "I've never held my mother before."

The next afternoon, my brother took me to the airport to fly home. I notified the airlines that I would have cremains on board, wrapped the bag in plastic, and put it in my suitcase. When the plane landed, I retrieved my luggage and removed my mother's cremains before I got into Shari's car. On the hour-long drive from the airport to my home, I held the bag containing my mother's ashes on my lap.

Later, alone in my living room, I looked in the outer bag for the first time. Inside the bag was a box, and inside the box was my mother. With her again on my lap, I looked at the ceiling and talked to my dad.

I told him mama was up there somewhere and asked him to go find her and embrace her. I told him that while she made many, many mistakes and had hurt me terribly, I felt she had also been hurt. I told him I had forgiven her and I wanted him to forgive her, too. I cried myself to sleep on the sofa still holding my mother in my arms.

I grieved my mom's death for a while--for what never was and for what never will be. I have full intentions of giving her a Native American burial ritual of some sort and then scattering her cremains in the mountains near where I live. But more than 15 years since her death, I still have her with me. Now that I have her, I just can't seem to let her go.

I eventually moved through that sad time and focused on enjoying my family. Excitement entered my life when RaeLynn told me she met a young man. They fell in love and married a couple years later. I adored him the moment I met him. He was tall, dark and handsome, and he made my precious daughter happy. They moved into a new house and started to build a life together.

Shari moved to a nearby city with Dakota. I later learned the move was, in part, due to her need to separate herself far enough from me to discover she could make it on her own. I was devastated because I thought I'd done something wrong.

Fact is, I'd probably done a lot of somethings wrong, but my human mistakes are not what made her leave. She was a grown woman now. I had been such a powerful influence in her life that she had a personal desire to individuate in order to find herself and to embrace her individuality.

She wanted to find out what was hers and what was mine in terms of thoughts, beliefs, and concepts. More than once, I had to remind myself that this was a natural process that should happen with all children. But I was pleased I had the strength to let her go.

We remained close during her couple of

years in another city. We talked often and saw each other often, and then the day arrived she and Dakota moved back. Both my daughters now live nearby, and we support each other as we always have. We are family and family is important.

And nothing says family better than a new baby. My first granddaughter arrived six years after Dakota, to the very month! RaeLynn, who had at a young age decided she didn't want children, reversed that decision within two years of being married. Her pets and her nephew had been enough for her up to that time.

I think she realized that love doesn't divide, it multiplies. So, she and her husband decided to start a family. And I had another grandchild to hold and dote on.

My first granddaughter was a beautiful baby with a contagious smile and bright green eyes. My heart overflowed with love for her. RaeLynn was a patient and loving mother to her newborn. Watching her care for her daughter made me happy she'd changed her mind about children. Today, she can't even fathom her previous conviction, nor can I.

While I was on the road to recovery, I still found myself falling back into a submissive role with the men I dated. I also found that they took advantage of that submission. Part of the distrust I had was distrust of myself. I wasn't convinced my strength was grounded enough to stop me from losing myself in a relationship.

However, I did risk opening my heart again. Tim and I had been close friends for several years, and during his divorce, we talked off and on. Well, he talked and I listened.

He was hurting over betrayal in his

marriage, and I understood what he was going through. One day, we found we were no longer crying about our dissolved marriages. We were laughing at each other's jokes.

It didn't take me long to recognize his inability to interact on a personal level. He could talk all day long about his life or his interests, which were centered around money or the making of it. But he could not talk to any depth about anything else.

He showed no interest in me as a person, only in what I could give to him. Talking with him on the phone, he'd drone on and on as I silently listened to him. Finally, he'd ask me a question, but before I could complete my answer, I'd hear him snoring on the other end of the line.

Our one-sided conversations would have been a red flag to most people, but I thought I could be the one person who would change him. I still had not learned that you cannot change another person. They must want to change on their own.

We boarded a plane for a trip to Bali. We were both excited for this romantic holiday, but before we left, I told him that I was not happy. I told him that his selfish, it's-all-about-me attitude was reminiscent of my marriage. I didn't feel valued and wasn't sure our relationship was going to work out.

He said he would make more of an effort to show interest in me, so I said I would give our relationship three months. If I did not see significant determination to move in a better direction, it was over for me.

I had spent a lifetime waiting for my turn to be recognized and it never came. I would not linger in another one-sided relationship. I stood by my word and gave him the three months I promised, but when that period came to an end, so did the courtship. I closed that chapter of my life and moved on. This time, I felt stronger, and the break-up didn't shatter me.

I felt sadness over the end of this one-sided connection, but the greater sadness came with my realization that I rarely drew healthy men into my life. The part I played in these scenarios was my struggle to maintain my individuality. Unhealthy behavior attracts unhealthy people.

I decided to do more things that would bring ME joy and build MY self-confidence. My goal was to become more consistent with the changes. Now, I read, I journal, I laugh, I cry, I work, I travel, and I play. I am alone at times, but I am never lonely. I revel in the pleasures of my family, my friends, and my adventures.

One day, while living next door to RaeLynn and her little family, I received a call from her to come outside. My six-year-old granddaughter was standing in the driveway, proudly wearing a little shirt that read: I AM A BIG SISTER. That was how I learned I would be a grandmother for the third time.

I would soon have another baby in my arms, another child to love. I was overjoyed. Before long, we learned we could expect another baby girl!

My grandchildren came into my life and quickly filled the cracks in my heart. They remind me to play and sing and laugh and dance. They make me feel like I'm the only grandmother who ever lived.

Dakota, my first grandchild, is 21-years-old. He has grown into the most extraordinary young man with a heart for helping others. My oldest granddaughter is 15-years-old, a statuesque beauty and an amazing volleyball athlete who has a quick wit. My youngest granddaughter, my last grandbaby is almost nine. She is a darling, blue-eyed charmer, who astounds me with her brilliant mind.

All three of my grandchildren are special, all three are unique, all three are treasured, and all three have me wrapped around their fingers. I value the individual gifts they bring to the family and the awesomeness of their exceptional personalities. Most of all, however, I'm intrigued by what unconditional love can do to make a child's heart soar.

Having never experienced unconditional love as a child, I find it beautiful to see how a person thrives in it. My beloved daughters have proven to be the most incredible women and mothers. They've raised their children with kindness and love. I'm in awe of both of them every day and I'm beginning to realize the part I played in turning the tide of our family legacy.

I hope my grandchildren will read this account of their Nana's journey for one reason. I want them to know the strength it takes to rise up against the incredible odds I faced throughout my life. I want them to know the determination and courage required for me to stand up after being knocked down time and time again.

I want them to know no matter what I faced in life, I prevailed. I want them to know if I had not found that resiliency within myself, they would not exist today. And I want them to know my DNA runs through their mother's bodies and now through theirs, empowering them with the same strength and resiliency.

I found the courage to overcome adversity and I learned to love myself along the way. I stopped the legacy of abuse, alcoholism, spiritual rigidity and secrecy that was handed down to me and could have been passed on to them had I chosen a different path. Instead, I gave them a legacy of unconditional love, strong relationships, truth, integrity, and transparency. I want my daughters and grandchildren to feel the freedom that comes with loving themselves, honoring themselves and forgiving themselves. It frees them to love, honor and forgive others.

I had once wanted my mother and my family to actually look at me and see all the possibilities of me so that I could believe in the possibilities as well. They were not able to do that which left me scarred, but not beaten. I trust my descendants will not only see the possibilities of me, but they'll accept the gift of knowing my fight was ultimately their victory. My struggle to break the chains that tethered me to the belief I was *nothing*, was for their freedom. The freedom to embrace the belief that they are *everything!*

During their formative years, I showed my daughters what an unhealthy woman looks like. In their adult years, I showed them how to walk the long road to healing and how to live in truth. I don't ever want my kindness to be mistaken for weakness. I hope my integrity is recognized as my greatest strength. I pray that's how they remember me.

Shari and I once took a trip to Sedona, Arizona, a most extraordinary city. We arrived back at our hotel after dinner and stepped onto our deck to take in the beauty of the night. Sedona is a place with very few street lights, which allows a breathtaking view of the moon and stars.

I was reminded of my little girl self, who once sat on my daddy's lap while he told me the crescent moon was his toenail. I could see all the stars in Daddy's eyes as he looked at me. He died not long after, but I always kept him close and honored his memory by passing the toenail story on to my daughters and grandchildren.

On this particular night in Sedona, I saw the familiar crescent moon and the stars filling a black canvas, the same ones I'd seen when I sat on my daddy's lap when I was three-years-old. Their beauty caught my breath. I couldn't take my eyes off them.

I wanted to memorize how the moon looked hanging in a sky teeming with billions of stars. Without illuminations of city lights, the moon and stars seemed as if they were close enough to touch. I reached up and felt my daddy looking down on me. And I had to smile at how I had come full circle.

You may wonder how I could share this graphic story with so many strangers without shame and embarrassment. In past times, I couldn't tell my story. I was unable to reveal it with those I knew, much less those I didn't know.

I was extremely protective of my past. I wasn't sure whom I could trust to hold it with the gentleness I needed. I was very ashamed of my life. I was ashamed of me. I didn't want anyone to know that I could be so unlovable, so damaged, so appalling.

Through my therapy and even through the writing of this book I can say what happened to me in my past isn't MY shame. It never was. The shame belongs to those who hurt me. I can now hold my head up high. I am a survivor, I am a warrior.

God doesn't promise us that bad things won't happen, only that He'll be there when they do. I believe my life is a testimony to that promise. My innocence was defiled, and my childhood stolen, but my latter years are blessed beyond measure. I reached for Him as a forgotten child, and He has not once let go of my hand. If what I had to go through made me who I am today, I have no regrets.

Writing this book has been bittersweet. In order to put my story on paper, I had to go all the way back to my earliest memories and remember my feelings at the time. To say it was excruciating is an understatement. Reliving my orphanage experience proved to be impossible to express on paper. It continues to be the most unspeakable event in my life. Conveying the impact such a tiny soul (Dakota) had in saving my life is also something that words will never be able to adequately articulate.

In fact, as I was drawing near the conclusion of the book, I had a most disturbing nightmare in which I was in a car my mother was driving. Suddenly, she hurled the car over the edge of a cliff in an attempt to kill both of us. I screamed so loud the sound of it startled me from my sleep.

I sat up in bed and had to admit to myself that she, in fact, did try to murder both of us, over and over again. Putting my pain on paper was difficult, but it forced me to own the feelings, and the exercise was healing for me. The past is mine, the memories are mine, and the pain is mine, and the *healing* is also mine.

This book spans over 70 years. My life has

been a rocky journey. Oftentimes, I fell off the path I was created to travel. Loved ones tore my soul apart and left me with scars so deep they'll never disappear. But those scars knit together, forming a new fabric of my soul. They made me stronger than I would have been otherwise.

My God never deserted me, even though I thought He had at times. I know He was right beside me, and His heart was breaking right along with mine. The night I called out to Jesus in the orphanage was the night my heart and spirit found their purpose.

I continue to suffer from post-traumatic stress disorder or PTSD. I probably always will. My body still interprets an abrupt noise, a loud voice or sudden movements as potential threats. Crowds make me nervous because I can't see around everyone; I can't see clearly what they are doing, and therefore, the situation becomes too unpredictable for my comfort.

If I see a parent pushing a child in a stroller, I worry that the sun is too bright for their eyes or too hot for their skin. If I hear a child cry, I search them out to see if the child is being hurt. More often than not, I approach the parent and make a comment about their precious offspring.

That's my way of defusing the moment, just in case the parent is becoming frustrated and that frustration might lead them to hurt their child. My internal view remains that parents will harm their children rather than protect them. I have learned to adjust my thinking today, but it doesn't come automatically to me.

~~*Shari*~~

The prefrontal cortex is the part of our brain that sits behind our forehead (shown below in the front of the head). It is the last part of our brain to develop and, in fact, isn't done growing and maturing until we are approximately 25-years-old. That region of the brain is responsible for executive functions such as cause/effect thinking, logical reasoning, and high- level, complex problem-solving.

How often do we say to children, "Didn't you think about the consequences of your decision?" or "Why do I have to keep repeating myself about this every day?" The answer lies in the fact that their prefrontal lobe is not fully developed.

As I mentioned earlier, we cannot access this part of our brain when we're in our limbic brain (shown below in the back of the head), which is when we're fearful and trying to survive.

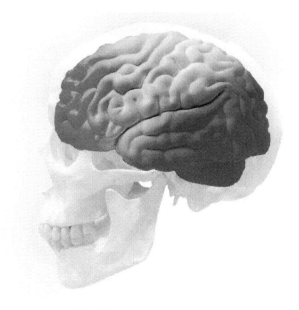

Printed with permission of Beyond Blue Media

My mom had lived so long in her limbic brain, scared and fighting for her survival, that it took years for her to learn how to regulate her fear and enter her prefrontal lobe.

We also transition to our limbic brains when we're angry because, beneath anger, we can usually find our familiar friend--fear. Remember, the survival brain is interested in one thing, our survival. To help us survive, the limbic brain institutes one of the six major reactions that live in this part of our brain--fight, flight, freeze, faint, fornicate or feed.

Even though my mom was growing and becoming healthier, she retreated to her limbic brain each time she attempted suicide. She was desperate, alone, afraid and not able to think clearly enough to access one of her newly developed coping skills. Although the limbic brain is concerned with survival, the reactions that live there can be self-destructive. She chose "flight" by attempting to take her own life. She wasn't thinking through what this really meant, that if she were dead, she wouldn't be with her children and grandchildren.

She couldn't see past the immediate moment, and at that moment, she simply wanted to leave the pain. She has since learned how to identify when she is entering her limbic brain. She's learned what physical cues are present when she gets triggered (Refer to the Trigger Cycles illustrated in earlier pages 284-287).

She's learned that when her heart races and she tenses, she must take deep, long inhales. When she does this, she calms her central nervous system and can access her prefrontal lobe. There, she can THINK through her decisions and choose a tool to help her cope.

Located on either side of the brain are two important systems that often do not get enough credit for the enormous function they perform. One is called the amygdala. This part of the brain holds our emotions--fear, anger, joy, overwhelm, peace. The other system is called the hippocampus. It provides a timeline to those emotions.

When we watch children on a rollercoaster squeal with delight, we think back to the happy feeling we had (amygdala) when we rode a roller coaster at the age of eight (hippocampus). The good feeling we had back then can be conjured up and we can almost feel the exact sensations again. If we get a phone call from our frantic teenage child who's just gotten into a fender bender, we remember. We know what it feels like to be a new driver, to get in that first accident, and to fear the wrath of a parent (amygdala). We remember the feeling we had in our past and can pull it up in the here-and-now (hippocampus).

When a person has experienced extreme trauma, the hippocampus sometimes gets confused about the timeline of events and tricks the brain into thinking the trauma is currently happening to them. I have a friend who grew up in a gang-infested neighborhood. As a child, he often heard gunfire outside his home at night. When this happened, his mother instructed him to drop to the floor and hide under his bed to be safe.

As an adult man, I knew him to be successful, calm and fearless. One summer, he took his children to Disneyland for a week. They stayed in a hotel right across from the theme park.

After they returned to their hotel room that first evening and began to get ready for bed, he heard gunshots and literally jumped on top of his children. Before they could ask what was happening, he rolled them under the bed to protect them from the bullets.

However, what they heard wasn't gunfire. It was a firework show coming from Disneyland. He and his terrified children lay under the beds for several minutes before he realized he was not a young boy back in his childhood home. Rather, he was an adult having a "trauma response."

What clinicians have known for a long time is that trauma work is about making sure the hippocampus (the timeline) matches up with the amygdala (the emotions). When a client has PTSD (post-traumatic stress disorder) he/she often believes that what occurred in his/her past is happening to them today. The work of a good therapist is to help clients understand that what they are experiencing as current trauma, *actually* happened in the past and today they are safe.

When we're stressed, our bodies produce a chemical call cortisol. Having some cortisol floating around our bodies can be good. It propels us to get things done, to drive safely, to study for that huge final, to memorize our lines for the play. Or to build up the nerve to ask someone we are attracted to on a date.

However, when we experience large amounts of stress over prolonged periods of time, cortisol can take its toll on our bodies. It can create belly fat, health problems, and sleep disturbances. How people respond to stress varies greatly.

Some people who've experienced consistent, prolonged and extreme forms of stress can function rather well. Others may struggle and might have periods of time in their lives where managing the past or present stresses become difficult, while others develop posttraumatic stress disorder in response to what they've experienced or witnessed.

The National Institute of Mental Health says the following about PTSD: "PTSD is a disorder that develops in some people who have experienced a shocking, scary, or dangerous event. It is natural to feel afraid during and after a traumatic situation. Fear triggers many split-second changes in the body to help defend against danger or to avoid it. This "fight-or-flight" response is a typical reaction meant to protect a person from harm. Nearly everyone will experience a range of reactions after trauma, yet most people recover from initial symptoms naturally. Those who continue to experience problems may be diagnosed with PTSD.

People who have PTSD may feel stressed or frightened even when they are not in danger" (National Institute of Mental Health, 2016).

Feeling she is in danger, even when she isn't, can be a common occurrence for my mom. In the past, hearing a baby cry in a restaurant would reduce her to a fearful, distraught mess. She'd immediately freeze, with a look of terror on her face. Her breathing would become shallow and her eyes wide.

To her, a baby crying baby meant the child was being abused. She could not listen to logic and would frantically scan the restaurant, searching for the innocent little victim. After years of work, mom is now able to practice mindfulness techniques and self-talk that helps her calm her PTSD responses.

When she hears a baby crying, she still becomes wide-eyed and panicked. But she recognizes what's happening and takes a deep breath, moving from her limbic brain to her frontal lobe. She tells herself several reasons for the crying are possible, such as hunger, boredom, a wet diaper or sleepiness. She also tells herself that the baby is not "her." She is an adult now, capable of obtaining help if she needs it. When she spots the baby, she calmly watches, not only to make sure the child is being treated properly but to enjoy the cuteness that comes with little ones. She adores babies.

Mom has learned how to ground herself in the present moment, rather than allowing her fear to transport her to her past. She's learned to recognize her triggers and to change her thoughts from "all babies are abused" to "I was abused, but that doesn't mean every baby is." Responding rather than reacting comes from a place of emotional regulation, which Mom has developed through practice. In doing so, she has owned her own story, discovered the power of staying in the present and found peace in formerly stressful situations.

~~*Jann*~~

I learned very early that no one was going to just give me what I needed. As a result, I have a tendency to not rely on others. Thankfully, as I get older, that once-needed survival mechanism is not as strong in me. I've learned to ask for help. I've also learned my loved ones are happy to help me.

That sad little girl with the burns, bruises and hollow eyes is now a beautiful part of me. She was once broken, alone and loathed--even by me. Today, she is the part of me who enjoys life and loves to play. I gently take her little hand and I tell her to be well, to be loved, to be honored and to be cherished. I tell her being loved, honored and cherished begins with me.

Life made me wary of the world, but I thank God I retained the ability to see its beauty. I am no longer that shell of a girl who cannot think on her own. I am no longer that desperate girl who sacrificed herself because she didn't believe she was worthy of love.

I have fought hard to reclaim my worth from

the ashes of pain and abuse, but the fight was worth it. My abusers no longer determine my value. Back then, I couldn't run from the abuse, but I now know I can escape uncomfortable situations.

I no longer allow myself to be so intimidated I become invisible again. I hope to always have a new life chapter to write. For now, I'm happy to have found peace. My belief system has changed. I now have a voice. I own my own narrative and I have purpose. I am ME and that's enough!

~~*Shari*~~

Writing this book has been difficult. I knew much of my mother's story yet reading it in detail broke my heart. Thinking of her as a scared, abandoned child who endured excruciating pain from her mother fills me with anguish. Envisioning my sweet mom alone and afraid all those years in the orphanage where the last remnants of her childhood were taken from her is almost more pain than I can bare.

When I think of her dreaming up a treasure chest that she looked at every night to survive extreme neglect, I weep out of anger and grief. That deprivation and heartless treatment should not have been my mom's story. It should not be anyone's story. And yet, her sad story is one I've encountered in different variations throughout my career.

"Why do bad things happen to precious children?" is a question many ask. We live in a world of good AND evil, as well as free choice. God granted us the freedom to choose. Some selfishly choose greed, manipulation, control, hatred, and destruction, which result in horrendous consequences.

For me, the more important question is, "What will you do with the pain in your life?" The easy path to follow is the one we were taught by example, the one that validates the lies and negative beliefs we have about ourselves.

That path is familiar and doesn't force us out of our comfort zones. Unfamiliar paths are frightening, especially if they demand that we face our demons. The paths that challenge the lies we believe about ourselves are rough and rocky. But in the end, they force us to decide every day to become better rather than bitter.

I could not have asked for a more compassionate, kind-hearted, loving mother. We are mother/daughter, but we are more than that. We are best friends and soulmates. Because we are so close, I often struggle with "survivors guilt". I experience a sense of sadness and regret that she experienced such pain, while my life has been free of such tragedy.

I am in awe of my mother's strength and resiliency. I have more gratitude than words can ever convey that she decided as a young child, in the depths of her despair, that she would change the course of her life. In doing so, she changed my life and my sister's life, our children's lives, and one day, their children's lives.

The legacy of my mom's life that had been passed down for generations included addiction, darkness, and hatred. With her decision to take a different path, she shifted the trajectory of her family's lineage and broke the chains that had kept those before her in bondage. She stared evil in the face and realized her only hope was to look to heaven and ask for help. Her answer came back loud and clear, "I will show you which way."

Epilogue

~~Dakota~~

So, you see, my life could have gone a completely different direction. I could have become an alcoholic or a strung-out drug addict, who let anger and fear rule my life. After all, that was where my family was headed, had my Nana not decided to live her life in a different way.

I grew up hearing about how clients my mom worked with struggled with addiction and were so stuck in their pain they couldn't see a way out. They couldn't find a different path. Even as a youngster, I realized we all make choices, and I wondered why they didn't choose another way.

My mom and grandma talked a lot about "legacy" when I was a child. At the time, I didn't understand what that word meant. As an adult, I've come to realize how important the decisions my grandma made were for my mom and aunt, for myself and my cousins, and our future families.

For generations, my grandmother's family lived in darkness, which they passed down to her. But she decided she wouldn't follow their example. Instead of hatred and bitterness, she showered my mom and aunt with love.

In turn, my mom was able to give me all the love I could ever possibly need. She showed me what it meant to be a man of God, and through her daily actions as a mother, I was able to "see" Jesus. I have no doubt that I will raise my children with the same love, gentleness, and compassion.

I love my mom and nana with all my heart. We have a bond that's rare for a son, mother, and grandmother. At the age of 21, I can honestly say I really enjoy hanging out with both of them. I love to travel with them and laugh with them.

When I'm struggling, I reach out to both of them. We understand each other, and we're real and honest with each other. I go to bed each night, knowing I am loved immensely.

My mom tells me a story of when I was about four-years-old and playing with my Legos, while she and my grandma visited. They were talking about my great-grandpa. My nana said, "I wish Dakota could have met my daddy."

Without looking up from my toys, I apparently said, "I did meet him in heaven before I got here."

My mom tells me they'd never spoken of him in my presence before. I hope that's true. I hope I did meet him. I picture him saying, "Take care of Jann-a-Baby, and let her know how much I love her."

I hope I have done that for her as much as she has for me. I hope he watched and applauded as his daughter broke the chains that kept the generations before her tied to despair. I hope he saw her make a different life for my mother, myself, my aunt, my cousins and all the children who will follow.

Jann-a-baby 3-years-old

Jann's dad

Jann's painting of her "Daddy's Toenail"

Acknowledgements

We want to thank RaeLynn for her beautiful design of the book's cover and my two granddaughters, whose silhouettes represent the internal struggle between the inner child and adult self.

We are eternally grateful to Janet, Darcy, Kris, Robin, Andrea, Cathy, Damond, Thad, Chris, Mary, Jim, Matt, Dave and my son for their support in providing an invaluable critique of our book and correlating presentation. We are indebted to Becky Lyles, our editor who helped us sound much smarter than we really are.

Finally, we'd like to say a special thank you to Neda whose kindness and safety allowed for the courage to face the past and eventually heal.

References

Eliot, George (Mary Anne Evans) n.d.

Brown, Brene, Ph.D. 2007 *I Thought It Was Just Me (but it isn't)* New York, New York: Penguin Group

Citation (Def. 2). (n.d.). In *Merriam Webster Online,* Retrieved June 1, 2018, from http://www.merriam-webster.com/dictionary/citation. Webster Dictionary

Citation (Def.1). (n.d.) In *National Institute of Mental Health*, Retrieved March 17, 2018, from https://www.nimh.nih.gov/health/topics/post-traumatic-stress-disorder-ptsd/index.shtml

About the Authors

Jann is retired and enjoying her life to the fullest. She thrives in her roles as mother and grandmother. Sharing her journey through this book and speaking engagements with Shari have brought her internal peace and hope for others.

Shari is a licensed clinical social worker and has had a 28-year career as an adolescent therapist and clinical director at several residential facilities. She is a consultant for various treatment programs across the nation and is an adjunct professor. She feels blessed to live near her mother and her son.

Shari and Jann enjoy speaking at universities, treatment facilities, retreats and community events. For more information about their talks or coaching, visit www.sharisimmons.com. Their podcast, www.whichwaypodcast.com can be found on Mental Health News Radio Network.

66936347R00219

Made in the USA
Columbia, SC
23 July 2019